Dad tried to hide from his children the fact that he didn't have a conventional job. There were various fabrications, the most common being his role as the powerful head of a local construction company. In fact, every day when he left for "work," at the oddly late hour of 10 or 11 A.M., he would tell us about some new project he was developing: a skyscraper one month, a three-story beach house or a suite of offices the next month. I remember how he used to bounce me on his knee and answer all of my silly questions about the construction trade.

I was fascinated with creativity—more specifically, building things from scratch. I was quite impressionable and for the most part believed just about anything Dad would tell me. For the longest time it never occurred to me to ask my father why he always wore a suit when he was going off to a construction site. I think back on it now and laugh at the notion of Dad ten stories up, checking out I-beams in his sharkskin suit, Merino wool turtleneck, and Italian leather shoes. He couldn't possibly have looked more out of place.

THIS FAMILY OF MINE
the *New York Times* bestselling memoir from
VICTORIA GOTTI

**This title is also available from
Simon & Schuster Audio and as an eBook**

VICTORIA GOTTI

THIS

Family

OF *Mine*

WHAT IT WAS LIKE

Growing Up Gotti

POCKET STAR BOOKS

New York   London   Toronto   Sydney

Pocket Star Books
A Division of Simon & Schuster, Inc.
1230 Avenue of the Americas
New York, NY 10020

First Pocket Star Books paperback edition January 2011

POCKET STAR BOOKS and colophon are registered trademarks of Simon & Schuster, Inc.

For information about special discounts for bulk purchases, please contact Simon & Schuster Special Sales at 1-866-506-1949 or business@simonandschuster.com.

The Simon & Schuster Speakers Bureau can bring authors to your live event. For more information or to book an event contact the Simon & Schuster Speakers Bureau at 1-866-248-3049 or visit our website at www.simonspeakers.com.

All photos courtesy of author's personal collection.

Cover design by John Vairo Jr.
Jacket photograph © Erin Patrice O'Brien/Corbis
Photograph of John Gotti © AP/Richard Drew
Picture frame © Stephen Shepherd/Photonica/Getty Images

Manufactured in the United States of America

10 9 8 7 6 5 4 3 2 1

ISBN: 978-1-4391-5451-9
ISBN: 978-1-4391-6322-1 (ebook)

As always I dedicate this book to my family:
For better or worse—in good times and in bad,
I will always love you all.

To my three sons, Carmine, John, and Frank—
you can't imagine the love I feel for you.

PROLOGUE

The gates separating St. John's Cemetery in Middle Village, Queens, from the living, breathing outside world are appropriately impressive—a baroque expanse of wrought-iron swirls seems to cascade from heaven itself, serving as an unmistakable line between life and the afterlife. Within these forty acres rest some of the most famous and infamous denizens of New York society, a wildly eclectic group that includes the controversial artist Robert Mapplethorpe, the bodybuilder Charles Atlas, numerous politicians, and Mafia dons Joseph Colombo, Carlo Gambino, and Vito Genovese. Death plays no favorites, makes no distinction. In the end, despite our differences, we are all the same. And now this was to be the final resting place of my father, John Gotti.

More than one hundred cars snaked along the roads of the cemetery, in neat and orderly fashion. Mercedes, Cadillacs, and a small fleet of Lincoln Town Cars—all black, all filled to capacity—followed closely behind an overstuffed flower car; at the very front of the line was a glistening black hearse.

The funeral procession meandered down the winding, grassy road, until the hearse reached its destination. Then, like a row of dominoes, car after car followed suit.

PROLOGUE

As we pulled up to the chapel, a small old man with hollow eyes and a white beard emerged from the caretaker's cottage and scurried across a narrow path. He fumbled for a set of keys in his pocket before unlocking the mammoth stained-glass doors.

One by one, mourners emerged from their cars and filed somberly into the chapel. I was accompanied by my three sons—Carmine, John, and Frank—my sister, Angel, and my niece Victoria, Angel's daughter. I rode in one of ten family cars. As usual, Angel and I were on the same wavelength, with similar thoughts racing through our minds. When the car stopped, neither of us moved for the door—whether through fear or dread, it was almost as if we were paralyzed, both having been raised by the same man and following the same traditions for years. Neither of us could bear the thought of saying good-bye to Daddy. Meanwhile, everyone was waiting outside the car for us to join them before moving inside. Sickeningly, but predictably, a swarm of paparazzi had assembled not more than fifty feet across the road, buzzing in anticipation of their money shot. We'd been in the public eye long enough to know the rules of the game—there was no way we were going to do anything that would attract greater attention from the photographers.

The chapel was lit with flickering white votive candles and ancient Tiffany-style lamps above providing meager illumination, which added to the funereal ambience. Gray and musty, the space felt less like a chapel than an antiquated living room. In the back of the chapel, the floors were covered with worn green carpet, the walls bore old-fashioned floral-print wallpaper. Dark wood antique furniture was scattered around the room: a sofa here, a chair there, with flimsy beige slipcovers protecting most pieces.

As gospel music issued from overhead speakers, the mourners continued to file in; the immediate family members took their seats first in a row of narrow pews at the front of the chapel, followed by relatives, friends, and acquaintances. I sat to the right of the first row, sandwiched between my mother and sister. Dad's casket, made of mahogany and trimmed in gold leaf, was a mere three feet in front of us, and being so close to him—knowing that his body was inside that wooden box, and would soon be buried forever—was almost more than I could bear. I felt faint. It had been more than thirteen years since I had been able to hug my father or even touch him; for thirteen years, six months, and four days, he had been imprisoned at a super-max federal correctional facility in Marion, Illinois. Our visits with him only allowed for conversation, laughter, or tears, our bodies always separated by a wall of Plexiglas. Now here he was, so close, but still in a prison, still beyond my reach. I don't know which was worse for Dad (or for me), jail or death.

Tears soon came freely as a flood of anguish, sadness, and regret washed over me. I had not told him nearly enough times just how much I loved and needed him, and just how important he was to me. As I rocked back and forth, sobbing, my mother leaned over and put her arm around my shoulder.

"It'll be all right, baby," she said.

I nodded, held her hand. Hers was a warm and maternal gesture, but I knew in my heart that nothing would be all right ever again. The backbone of our family was gone—and the prospect of my father's absence both saddened and terrified us. The fear in Mom's eyes was unmistakable, just as it had been the night before, when I'd found her pacing the floor of her master bedroom at 3 A.M.

"I can't imagine my life without him," she had whispered.

Her anxiety was understandable and shared by each of us. My dad's strong sense of tradition and the importance he placed on family had produced an extraordinarily tight clan. We had gathered at least once a week, for Sunday dinners of pasta and delicious stuffed meats, a tradition in our family stretching back for more than three decades. It was Dad's favorite day of the week, when we all came together in one house to laugh and swap stories over a family meal. It was heaven on earth for my father: a few hours when he wasn't troubled by business or legal matters, when his children and grandchildren surrounded him, eating and smiling, for hours on end. These were his favorite moments. So important were these gatherings to my father that even after he went to prison, he made sure we continued the tradition. It was one of his last wishes before he was sent away. For the most part, responsibility for hosting Sunday dinner would fall on my shoulders, and I happily accepted the job.

"No matter what happens," Dad would always say during our conversations on a visit, or on the telephone while he was at Marion, "you have to honor this tradition."

It's strange how something as simple as a Sunday dinner weighed on my mind at that moment. Dad was gone, and with him perhaps some piece of the obligation (or at least the urgency) to continue our Sunday tradition. I knew we would never again come together as a complete family, that the tradition had come to an end. It just exacerbated the grief I felt. Without Dad to pull us together, I knew there was a chance that the Gottis would quickly splinter.

"Don't get too caught up in your own lives to remember the importance of being together," he'd said shortly before passing, in the last letter I'd received from him.

I gazed at the casket, memories of decades of Gotti family tradition filling my head and my heart.

We'll try, Dad.

ONCE FAMILY AND close friends were seated, an additional crowd of mourners was granted access and permitted to stand in the back of the chapel. The room was filled to capacity, and yet hundreds of mourners, some whom I knew very well, others not at all, were left outside.

The chapel fell silent as the priest bowed his head and began to speak.

"Our Father, who art in heaven . . ."

His voice resonated in the chapel, and yet his words barely registered, I was so lost in thought. Outside, a thunderstorm had moved in. With the shift in weather came flashes of lightning, crackling thunder, and then rain, pounding against the chapel windows. Although the room was full of people, I suddenly felt alone. In the throes of grief, I wanted to scream. I wanted the ceremony to stop. But I hadn't the strength even for that. After two days of crying, I could barely muster the energy to speak.

"Thy kingdom come, thy will be done . . ."

As the priest continued, mourners from the back of the room were invited to approach my father one last time. As they passed by, each person gently placed a single long-stemmed red rose they had been given on top of the casket.

PROLOGUE

It was a solemn, unifying ritual, bonding mourners from a broad spectrum of social classes. Many of these men and women had attended my father's wake and had a story to tell. The elderly, homeless lady from Ozone Park, Queens, who between sobs had told me of Dad's generosity, how he had regularly given her money for over twenty years. The sanitation worker who claimed Dad had helped put his only son through college. The housewife from Rockaway Boulevard who credited Dad with saving her daughter's life after a grim diagnosis of leukemia; he had arranged for a pioneering oncologist from Boston to oversee the young girl's care. Then there was the affluent, elderly man—a former CEO of a major corporation—who tearfully divulged an unpaid (and unpayable) debt to my father. Dad apparently had helped the man face and eventually overcome a "troublesome and dangerous" gambling addiction. The Ivy League kid, a nineteen-year-old freshman, with his parents in tow, who credited Dad with saving his life after an ill-advised and dangerous boyhood prank had nearly sent him away to prison. The young man's parents, a middle-aged couple from Italy who had emigrated a decade earlier in search of a better life for their only son, choked back tears as they told the story of how my father had arranged for a top-flight defense attorney to represent their son—although not until Dad had "scared the kid straight."

Even a well-known local newscaster was indebted to Dad because he had saved her father's life after the poor guy had fallen in too deep with a couple of made men from Brooklyn. The mobsters had been enticed by the man's investment strategy, which turned out to be little more than a badly planned get-rich-quick scheme. When the venture inevitably failed, the Brooklyn investors demanded much more than their money back.

And so it went, story after story. I'd heard them for years, and I heard even more and then some at Dad's wake and throughout the day—tales of benevolence that belied the tabloid image of John Gotti.

"Give us this day, our daily bread . . ."

The New York papers circulated the rumors that the diocese had refused to accept my father's body and host a Catholic mass for him. The tabloids claimed that the "Gotti family had been turned down." There was absolutely no truth to this—we never requested that Dad be buried with a full Catholic mass.

Nevertheless, my mother was enraged by the controversy. She carried vivid memories of the diocese embracing Dad only a few years earlier, characterizing him as a pillar of the community after he'd agreed to fund a much-needed face-lift for a neighborhood church in Queens. Mom later labeled the Catholic Church "a house of hypocrites": "When John Gotti's money or help was needed—and welcomed—he was a wonderful man. But in death, he couldn't offer the Church much, and the moment the negative controversy surfaced, they turned their backs to suit the politically correct standards that were expected of them."

So when the subject came up, Mom was adamant: there would be no request for a Catholic burial mass for Dad. Let that speak for itself.

"On earth, as it is in heaven . . ."

The crowd at the back of the room inched forward; each mourner made the sign of the cross, laid down a rose, and paid his or her final respects. As the pile of flowers mounted on the casket, one man caught my attention. Perhaps it was his wool trench coat worn in June, or maybe it was the air of unease about him. He seemed nervous—holding his coat closed, his eyes darting around the room—while making his way to the coffin. What was most noticeable was that he didn't have a rose.

Security noticed as well, and moved in closer—one tall, burly guy to the right of the trench coat, another to the left. In the blink of an eye, the interloper was hoisted up and carried out the door. I was later told he was a reporter—the trench coat had been used, not very effectively, to hide a video camera. Of course, he wasn't the only reporter posing as a mourner; nearly two dozen members of the press would be physically removed from the chapel before the service ended. That there were mourners not supposed to be in attendance was of great concern to some of the bereaved men present. These men were the "higher-ups" in the mob, and the FBI went out of their way trying to spot them in the crowd. These mobsters were forbidden by law enforcement to attend the funeral, and the unwanted publicity played an even bigger factor.

"Lead us not into temptation . . ."

Immediate family members were funneled through a side door, led by nearly a dozen security guards whose primary function was not to protect us from enemies but to keep the press at bay. We filed into the waiting limousines amid flashing bulbs and harsh inquiries. One reporter stared right into my eyes and asked, with a hint of a smile, "Victoria, how are you holding up?" He aimed a microphone in my direction, nodding conspiratorially.

"Come on, what was it really like . . . growing up Gotti?"

CHAPTER ONE

"Papa Was a Rolling Stone"

Winter 1952

The door blew open with driving force; shards of wood like shrapnel sprayed the cold, cramped Brooklyn railroad flat. To a twelve-year-old, the U.S. Marshal's arrival came in the form of an unfathomable explosion that would haunt his dreams into adulthood. Two local police officers and one marshal from the housing department had been dispatched to evict a poor and hungry family of thirteen—despite the fact that Christmas was less than one week away.

My father lay huddled with his six brothers, all forced to survive in one room, on two mattresses, in the musty three-room apartment. It was in the dead of winter and none of the Gotti children—seven boys and four girls, ages five to sixteen—had clothing suitable for protection against the elements. Dad would later recall that evening as being not only unbearably cold but accompanied by a dark, empty sky.

The Gotti children were accustomed to sharing tight quarters. If it seemed unnatural, even cruel, it was nonetheless preferable to sleeping on a cold bare floor "or being homeless," as my father used to say. The family bounced around in those years, from a poverty-stricken section of the South Bronx to a modest apartment in Sheepshead Bay, Brooklyn. My grandfather, John Senior, made some money in an all-night card game and moved the family into a middle-class neighborhood; however, it wasn't long before his luck (and money) ran out. Within a few months the Gotti clan ended up in more humble surroundings, a shabby apartment in Downtown Brooklyn. "Times were hard," my father said. "And they were about to get a lot harder."

The eviction in 1952 was swift and heartless. Dressed only in worn flimsy garments, the Gotti children and their mother, Fannie, stood shivering in front of the dilapidated apartment complex that only a few minutes earlier had been their home. John Senior was out that night, off on one of his business trips. Monthly rent on the apartment was a paltry sum, but even that proved more than my grandfather could manage.

Philomena "Fannie" DeCarlo Gotti was a hardworking housewife who often took on odd jobs outside the home— doing the neighbors' laundry, cleaning apartments, bagging groceries at a local market to help make ends meet. But lately there never seemed to be enough money. The family was barely able to keep food on the table and heat in the apartment. Conversely, my grandfather, John Joseph Gotti, was a perpetual adolescent, forever in search of excitement and fun. An avid gambler, drinker, and womanizer, he rarely held a steady job; whenever he got the "itch," as Grandma called it, he would take off for parts unknown, typically accompanied by some barmaid he'd only recently met.

There were times when Grandpa hit the road on one of his so-called "business trips" and didn't return for months.

For a while he had a job as a camera grip for a major film studio and even traveled to Hollywood on one occasion. This failed to result in any sort of legitimate career, but it did produce a handful of entertaining tales. My grandfather was fond of embellishment, and so he would tell anyone within earshot of his work-related war stories, like the time he met Jane Russell.

During the filming of *Gentlemen Prefer Blondes*, Grandpa swore the gorgeous actress was attracted to him (forget for a moment the professional chasm that separated the lowly tech and the leading lady), and that she looked for excuses to talk to him. According to his story, she even winked at him on occasion.

Then there was the time he met Tony Curtis at the studio commissary. Grandpa insisted the two had become fast friends.

"That guy is a class act," Grandpa had often said. Then he would smile and laugh. "Very personable, too."

So instantaneous was their bond that Grandpa and Tony Curtis went out together that very night and took the town by storm. They drank themselves blind, eventually winding up in a seedy motel with a "couple of real lookers." Or so Grandpa claimed, anyway.

The odd brush with greatness apparently was far more important to my grandfather than the mundane responsibilities of family life. It seemed not to matter that he had a large family to feed, or that there was never enough money to pay the rent or heating bill. And every so often, the Gotti family was kicked to the curb.

This naturally produced a degree of cynicism in my father, who years later would erupt any time he read a cliché-ridden newspaper article or book that described Grandpa as a hardworking Italian immigrant.

"These fuckin' bums that write books—they're worse than us," he would rail. "Lies. All lies! My father was born in New Jersey. He's never been to Italy in his whole fuckin' life. He never worked a day in his life. He was a rolling stone. He never provided for his family. He never did nothin'. He never earned nothin'. And we never had nothin'."

DAD RECALLED HIS mother's reaction while standing at the curb on the night of the eviction, in the freezing cold, wearing a tattered sweater over a worn and faded house-dress. She was only in her mid-thirties, but looked closer to fifty. The years, overloading her with work and anxiety and neglect, had not been kind to her. Grandma was a "cold woman," Dad often said, hardened by years of sacrifice and disappointment. Mostly, Dad blamed his father for this. A man was supposed to take care of his family: put a roof over their heads, food in their bellies, and keep them warm in proper winter clothing. But, rather than struggle to fulfill his responsibilities and obligations, Grandpa chose instead to run—usually to the nearest bar to drown himself in his failure as a husband and father.

On this evening my father saw that she was understandably upset. Although Grandma rarely showed weakness in front of her children, the tears streamed down her cheeks. She stared at the old apartment building, then out at the street, and then back to the apartment building. Her eyes, my father noticed, were empty and sad, and the expression on her face frightened him.

The Gotti clan stood shivering outside for nearly an hour that night, a mid-winter drizzle chilling them to the bone. "An hour," Dad said. "But it felt like an eternity."

Exhausted and fearing for the welfare of her children, Grandma finally took action, marching the entire, rain-soaked clan nearly a mile through the streets of Brooklyn to the House of the Good Shepherd, a church-sponsored residence for "wayward girls" (the facility catered to young, single women who had unplanned pregnancies). It must have been painful for Grandma to beg—she was a proud woman, after all—but that is what she did. For the sake of her children, she asked for mercy, and Sister Mary Margaret, dressed head-to-toe in black, responded with kindness, showing Grandma and the Gotti children to the building's attic.

In reality, it wasn't really an attic at all; it was a four-room apartment, a conversion made in the early 1940s to accommodate housing needs for the staff. Although the apartment had only an efficiency kitchenette, it was better than nothing, and Grandma saw its potential. The living room was really more of an alcove, adjacent to the kitchenette; it would likely serve as a fourth bedroom for the oldest male children. The two other rooms would be shared by Grandma and the remaining children, including my father, at least until Grandpa could find his way to the family's new home. No one knew when that would be, but at that point, one of the three bedrooms would then be used as a master, resulting in eleven children sharing two small rooms. Tight quarters, to be sure, but, as Dad explained, "It was definitely better than the alternative."

The days that followed would prove nearly as bleak. At

the age of twelve, Dad was forced to hit the streets and find work, as were the other Gotti children. Everyone was expected to pull their own weight, especially the boys.

Dad combed the neighborhood looking for employment. Options, he quickly learned, were limited. A corner service station on Fulton Street had recently dismissed two mechanics in an effort to cut costs. A local deli already had two full-time day workers and three part-time night staffers. The manager at the A&P supermarket offered little encouragement, telling Dad he was too young for anything but carrying bags for customers. My father gave that one a moment's consideration before spotting a crowd of eager boys fighting over customers in the parking lot. Realizing that his pay would consist only of tips, and that the store already seemed overstaffed, he walked away.

Not enough customers, not enough hours, not enough money.

SIX WEEKS LATER, my grandfather ambled down the street to the House of the Good Shepherd, having easily tracked the family down through a network of friends and acquaintances. Along the way, he'd been told of the eviction and the dire circumstances faced by those whom he had abandoned. If his father felt guilt or remorse, Dad said, it wasn't readily apparent. Accountability was not high on Grandpa's list of virtues. He preferred to play the victim, forever damning the world and cursing God for having dealt him a raw hand. And so he rationalized his behavior and his vices—the alcohol, gambling, loose women, and the nasty temper as well.

Grandpa turned up at the attic apartment late one night, itching for an argument with my grandmother. At first he rang the bell and waited patiently, but there was no answer. After three tries, he began pounding the door like an impulsive child—pounding and kicking with such force that Sister Mary Margaret nearly called the police. Realizing who the belligerent man was, she told him, "Please, sir. Use the top bell."

MEANWHILE, OBLIVIOUS TO the commotion three stories below, my grandmother and her brood slept peacefully. Of all the Gotti children, only two were awake. Dad was restless and couldn't sleep, and one of his younger brothers, I believe Ritchie, was wide awake because he had to go to the bathroom. Since there were seven boys in a single room, and only two beds for them to share, the Gotti sons took turns. One night someone was lucky to get a semi-comfortable cot, and the next one was handed an old army blanket and relegated to sleeping on the floor. That particular night, my father was lucky to have been assigned a cot.

Or so he thought.

Since the attic apartment was a considerable distance from the main plumbing, a bathroom had never been installed. What had begun as a generous offer of temporary shelter for my grandmother and her children had evolved into a more permanent arrangement. In exchange for room and board, my grandmother was expected to clean and maintain the House of the Good Shepherd. This meant washing and waxing the massive wood floors every night, as well as cleaning the mess hall after dinner. And there were

7

additional duties: monthly window cleaning, repairing and sewing (such as pillows, blankets, and quilts), and any other household repairs that had been neglected. Given that my grandmother already had a full-time job at a local butcher shop, this wasn't the most ideal arrangement, and it surely took its toll on her health and temperament. But it was the best that Grandma could manage at the time; until she had saved enough money to rent another apartment, or until her husband returned (hopefully with a few dollars in his pocket), it would have to do.

The bathroom was actually one floor below the attic apartment, and since heat was scarce throughout the old building, the hallway was usually frigid. Not surprisingly, the Gotti children dreaded those nights when they had to navigate a cold and unwieldy trip to the bathroom. Dad would slide out from under his blanket and weave his way through a minefield of sleeping bodies, all the while shivering uncontrollably. If he was unlucky enough to step on someone's hand or foot, the ensuing yelping and fighting would provoke an angry appearance from my grandmother—something none of the kids wanted.

While Dad continued to toss and turn, his brother Ritchie fought the urge to pee as long as he could—and when the pressure turned to pain, he jumped from the bed and stumbled toward the door. As luck would have it, the door wouldn't open. Uncle Ritchie desperately jiggled the handle from side to side, pushing in the door, ever so slightly, and then pulling back.

Push . . . pull. Push . . . pull.

Still nothing.

With Ritchie's bladder on the verge of giving out, he

frantically sought another option. He looked around the room for a container, anything he could use to relieve himself. But a quick scan turned up nothing. He was ready to explode. Dad watched his brother make a mad dash for the bedroom window rather than soil himself or his cot. He ripped it open, and peed into the cold night air. How could he possibly know Grandpa was standing beneath the window?

My grandfather was a terror; his ill temper had the shortest of fuses. Beatings were the norm; even at twelve, Dad couldn't escape them. Sometimes the violence was so severe that my father would miss school for days; the blackened eyes, swollen lips, and bruises too painful and shameful to be shown in public. The poverty and abuse, both mental and physical, that my father experienced as a child helped shape his outlook as much as anything else.

When my grandfather finally made it inside and upstairs to the attic apartment, he headed for the back bedroom—straight for the person responsible for his unexpected shower. Of course, my father was scared speechless. He hopped back into bed and pulled the old army blanket up over his head, trying hard to stop trembling. My grandfather pushed in the old wooden door and stormed into the room, stepping over bodies, poking each kid with the tip of an umbrella. The first to jump, he figured, was the one already awake, and thus the most likely culprit. But Uncle Ritchie lay still as a rock—while Dad, still unable to sleep, tossed and turned. He jumped when Grandpa poked him. So naturally, he got the blame.

The beating Dad endured that night was worse than any he'd ever received before. His face was so badly bruised that my grandmother pulled him out of school for several days. As a boy, Dad and his siblings did their best to avoid pissing off their father; what none of them had counted on was the possibility of pissing *on* their father.

THE FOLLOWING WEEK, my father managed to get a job delivering laundry. He worked after school and all day Saturday for fifty cents an hour, plus tips. He used an old push-cart with rusty wheels to haul the large packages around Downtown Brooklyn, about a mile or so from the Gotti household. At the end of the week he handed his pay over to my grandmother, keeping only $1.50 for himself. The fact that Dad was forced to turn over most of his wages didn't bother him in the least; mature beyond his years, he felt proud of being able to help support his family.

Unfortunately, his happiness was short-lived. Three months later, in the spring of 1952, my grandfather got restless and left home again. This time my grandmother fell apart. To my father's eyes, the change was remarkable. Fannie became depressed and withdrawn. Nothing seemed to matter anymore.

The days that followed were dark times for the entire family. And for a twelve-year-old, Dad shouldered an unusually heavy burden. It wasn't just the beatings that had stripped him of his innocence; it was the constant verbal abuse dished out by my grandfather. As my father once said to me, "How many times can a kid hear that he's a piece of shit before he begins to believe it? How many times can a kid hear that he'll never amount to nothing, because he is nothing?"

According to Dad, there were two strict rules necessary for survival in the Gotti household (at least whenever my grandfather was in residence): "Keep your mouth shut—and run like hell." Usually he received advance warning before an actual event took place. Simply listening to my grandfather's rants provided insight as to what was likely to happen next. Still, there was no way to know for certain when the proverbial shit would hit the fan.

Perhaps the most cataclysmic event took place in the middle of the night in mid-February 1952. Sister Mary Margaret roused the Gotti children from a comfortable sleep and gathered the family in a downstairs parlor. Dad knew that something was terribly wrong. Where was their mother? Even Sister Mary Margaret's offer of hot chocolate and cookies couldn't mask the dread and fear that hung in the air.

The children, who lived in a state of perpetual hunger, ate voraciously, anyway. When they were finished, Sister Mary Margaret calmly issued the bad news. Their mother had fallen "ill," euphemistically referred to back then as "exhaustion." Today, of course, the condition is more commonly referred to as depression. In its most severe form, it results in a complete emotional collapse. The years of trauma had finally exacted their toll, all the bickering and fighting, the sickness that permeated every aspect of her marriage to my grandfather. It had become too much for Fannie to bear, and when my grandfather took off the last time, she withdrew into herself, to the only place, perhaps, where she felt safe.

Grandma, Sister Mary Margaret explained to Dad and his brothers and sisters, had been admitted to a local hospital and placed in the "hardship ward." Because there were no relatives willing to accept financial and custodial responsibility, the Gotti family was effectively splintered. The children were separated and sent to various places, some more toxic than others. Most of the kids went to live with old neighbors who had become friends; a few weren't as fortunate. My father and his older brother, Pete, for example, drew the shortest straws and were dropped off at the Brooklyn Home for Boys, not knowing when—or if—their mother would ever come back for them.

CHAPTER TWO

"Hey There, Lonely Girl, Lonely Girl"

The officer stared down at the gangly, dark-haired girl in front of him. She couldn't have been more than eight or nine years old. And yet, here she was, out on her own, well after midnight, walking through Central Park.

"Are you okay?" the policeman asked.

She had enormous brown eyes, olive skin, and dark hair in a shoulder-length bob that would surely be adorable if cleaned up. Her tattered black pea coat was nearly two sizes too small; her face was smudged with traces of dirt.

He pulled out his walkie-talkie and radioed headquarters.

"I have a possible runaway in Central Park."

By now, the girl was crying—tears spilled down her face, streaking her dirty cheeks. The officer smiled politely and noticed the girl's shoulders rising and falling. Beneath her flimsy coat she was shaking uncontrollably; whether from fear or cold, he couldn't say for sure.

It took a McDonald's cheeseburger, a package of Twinkies, and a half bottle of Coke to gain the kid's confidence. She told the officer her name was Victoria Lorraine

DiGiorgio, and she lived mostly in a home—Sacred Heart Academy for Girls—and on rare occasions stayed at her mother's apartment on the Upper West Side of Manhattan. She'd only seen her father a few times and didn't remember exactly where he lived.

It was two weeks before the Christmas holiday, and Sacred Heart had closed for winter recess. Most of the girls had gone home to spend the holidays with their families—everyone, that is, except young Victoria, my mother. Mom told me she'd learned two days earlier that her mother would not be picking her up for the customary winter break.

"I'm sorry," said the officer. Mom said he was a kind man. And she could tell these types of stories never failed to tug at his heart—a kid alone in the park at Christmastime.

My mother just shrugged. "No surprise. I hardly see her at all these days."

But earlier that day, the thought of spending another Christmas without family so saddened her that she decided to take matters into her own hands.

In the school admissions office Mom had found her file. There was a white index card with the words "Emergency Contacts" written at the top. Underneath there were two addresses, one for her mother and one for her father. His name was John DiGiorgio; he was twenty-seven years old and he lived in Queens.

Mom told the officer how she'd managed to take two buses to her father's house in Long Island City. When she arrived at the two-family brownstone, she'd pressed her face to the smoky glass, rang the bell, and stepped back. Despite the smudged windowpane above the front door, she could see her reflection. Her hair was a bit messy from the forceful winds and light snow; her school uniform, a green plaid vest and matching skirt, was wrinkled from the long bus ride. She brushed her hair with her fingers and smoothed the creases of her worn jumper—the last thing she wanted was to make a poor impression on her father. And yet, she thought, she still looked like a pathetic waif.

She told the officer she was most curious about his appearance. She wondered what traits they would share, what features had come from this man she'd never met. Her chin? Her mouth? The shape of her ears?

When a chubby woman in a white uniform answered the door, my mother froze. She stood in the doorway for nearly a minute before whispering.

"I need to see my father."

The woman wasn't receptive; at best, she was incredulous, opening the door only an inch or two, just enough to wave a hand at my mother, as if she were nothing more than an annoying bug. The woman scolded her, too, saying something about calling the police if she didn't leave immediately. Then she slammed the door.

Mom walked forlornly to the street and looked up at the second-floor window. It was then that she saw him. He was handsome, with a full head of ink-black hair and cold brown eyes—as cold as the dark side of the moon. He was standing with both hands on his hips, staring down at her with a blank expression on his face. And then he did . . . nothing.

Nothing.

He just stood there, staring down at my mother. A few moments passed. Their eyes locked again. And then he turned away from the window and disappeared, receding like a wave.

Mom told the officer that the search had been something she needed to do, something that made her realize her place in the world. Her father wanted her even less than her mother had wanted her, if that was even possible. Now, Victoria realized, she could simply disappear from the planet, just slip off into the unknown. Would anyone even notice?

She decided to run away. She'd gotten as far as Central Park, but when evening turned to night and the wintry winds turned frigid and forceful, she became scared; perhaps, she reasoned, running away wasn't such a good idea after all, and she gave the officer her mother's address.

When the officer and Victoria arrived at the Upper West Side address there was no one home. He stopped by the superintendent's office and picked up a spare key for 4J, a two-bedroom apartment on the west side of the building. It was sparsely decorated: a sofa, two club chairs, an armoire, a television, and a small wooden dining table with four chairs.

Rather than leave the child unattended, the officer sat down on the sofa and waited. Mom later told me he could have left her with a neighbor—after all, his shift had ended nearly an hour earlier—but something still tugged at his heart.

The officer saw to it that Mom got cleaned up and ready for bed. Her room was surprisingly sterile and lacking in décor—not only didn't it look like a child's room, it barely looked lived in at all. No wonder the child was so sad.

It was nearly 3 A.M. when the officer was awakened by the rattling of keys at the front door. Seconds later a woman appeared in the apartment. She was tall, brunette, and nicely dressed. She was also inebriated; she lurched clumsily into the living room. As the officer reached over and turned on a table lamp, their eyes met. The officer smiled.

"Good evening, ma'am," he said, removing his cap.

The woman said nothing, but merely fell back into one of the chairs and sighed.

TO SAY THAT my mother was an unwanted child would be an understatement. My grandfather was not yet eighteen years old when he met my grandmother. He was a garage mechanic in Queens; she was a hostess at a restaurant in Manhattan. Faye Petrowski was on her way home one morning after working the night shift at a twenty-four-hour diner. She was very attractive, with long, dark curls, big brown eyes, and high cheekbones. She was petite and thin, and when she walked down Euclid Avenue in Brooklyn, more than a few heads would turn.

Among the men smitten with Faye was John DiGiorgio, a handsome Italian from a hardworking, well-to-do family from Astoria, Queens. The DiGiorgios were right off the boat, having traveled to Ellis Island from Cascina, Italy, in the early 1900s. John's father had been a fiercely ambitious man who rose from laborer to magnate, building one of the most successful construction companies in Queens. His mother was a traditional Italian housewife who spoke very little English.

The couple had big plans for their oldest son, and those plans did not include his marrying a non-Italian from the poor side of town. Yet, despite his parents' protests, John continued to chase after Faye. He couldn't help himself, really—he was hopelessly in love. And so they began dating.

They would sneak around the Queens neighborhood in an effort to hide their budding romance. They were madly in love, in that intoxicating, overwhelming way that only adolescents can know. John couldn't keep his hands off her. But Faye was raised a good girl and was saving her virginity for when she got married.

One night, when they were alone at an older friend's apartment, kissing led to petting and petting led to . . . well, more. My grandfather "was wild with passion," he'd later tell those who would listen.

That night, things got out of control. They ended up naked and wrapped in each other's arms. John lost his mind in the moment and begged Faye for sex; she refused. The rendezvous ended with him ejaculating all over her thigh.

For both of them, a brutal lesson in biology and procreation would soon follow. Six weeks later, Faye found out she was pregnant. "How could that be?" she wondered aloud in the doctor's office. "We didn't even have sex."

The physician shrugged. He'd seen it all, heard it all. No point in giving a lecture now. That time had passed. Faye was distraught. There was no way she could adequately explain this to her family. Surely they would never believe she was pregnant—and yet still a virgin! Instead, they would respond with anger and bitterness and resentment, and in the end, they would do what most Catholic families did in these types of situations: send her away to a home for *wayward girls*. She had some decisions to make. She loved John—and he definitely loved her—but his parents were "old school" and they expected their oldest son to marry an Italian girl . . . no exceptions! He told Faye that there was no way they would be happy about the pregnancy—no way they would give their blessing for marriage. In Faye's eyes, John's failure to stand up to his parents, and to accept responsibility for his actions, was nothing less than a fatal flaw. It was, in the end, a deal breaker.

My grandfather was devastated by Faye's reaction. Finally, in a desperate attempt to regain her affections (and respect), he proposed. "Let's elope," he said. "We can be happy."

This was not exactly what Faye had in mind. My grandmother was proud. She refused to run away from anything; there was no way she would allow herself to be tied to a man who lacked courage. And so she bid young John DiGiorgio farewell.

In the end, Faye decided to have the baby, a dark-haired girl who was the spitting image of her handsome father. But much time would pass before John laid eyes on his firstborn child; by that time he was married and expecting another child with his wife, Della, a short, blond Italian girl who had recently moved with her family from Italy to Astoria, Queens. It was a marriage happily endorsed by his parents.

MY MOTHER HAS always had mixed feelings about the topic of her conception. It was difficult for her to talk to me about her earlier years, as she was embarrassed and ashamed, just as she is conflicted about the odd and volatile nature of her parents' relationship. Eventually, they did have sex. Indeed, the on-again, off-again romance carried on well into his marriage, even resulting in a second pregnancy—this time a son. But my grandfather was married. My grandmother found out she was pregnant approximately one month after she and my grandfather had a terrible fight, one so bad it left dents in the walls and broken dishes, and a vow by both parties "never to see each other again." As a result, Faye stubbornly waited months to tell him about the second pregnancy. His initial response was, "Are you sure it's mine?" This infuriated my grandmother so much that she scheduled an abortion the next day. She was nearly six months' pregnant.

As for my mother? Faye was an old-fashioned woman who had neither the desire nor the inclination to raise a child alone, so she enrolled her only child in Sacred Heart Academy shortly before her fourth birthday. From that day on, Victoria was on her own, a little girl without a home, without parents . . . without family. She was rootless, an inescapable fact that both saddened and defined her for many years to come.

CHAPTER THREE

"Ooh, Child,
Things Are Gonna Get Easier"

My father's stay at the boys' home was strictly regimented. All of the children were forced to adhere to a daily routine of chores and exercise in exchange for room, board, and food. Three square meals a day consisted of rice cereal with sour milk in the morning, a bologna sandwich for lunch, and a small portion of chicken and rice at night. Wake-up time was 6 A.M. Chores began at 6:30. Classes began at 8:30 and ended at 2:00 in the afternoon, with more chores to follow. By dinnertime, my father was exhausted and famished.

He had clashed with other boys at the home, as well as with the priest who ran the place. Fights and confrontations broke out on a daily basis with little or no reason at all. Most of the boys were simply angry young men, feeling rejected and depressed, each taking his frustrations out on the others. Dad claimed he was exposed to things at the home that made even his toxic home life, with his abusive father and bickering parents, seem tame by comparison. To pass away the time, Dad played sports with some of the other kids. The home put together a football team and played skirmish games every Saturday. But because there were no other teams to compete against, Dad grew bored. When the parish priest approached him and asked him to box, Dad looked at him funny. "You want me to fight?"

The priest laughed. "Not the kind of fighting you and the other boys have been doing in here—I want to help you get rid of the frustration and anger you're carrying around. Give you a chance to pound your fists and not get into trouble."

Dad jumped at the chance and in time came to enjoy boxing very much. He got up early every morning and trained for two hours. Every Saturday, the home hosted an amateur boxing event and soon Dad held one of the highest records. John Joseph Gotti had finally found something he really enjoyed doing—and was really good at. But even his newfound affinity for boxing did little to mask the dismal surroundings that were now his home.

It was a time Dad did not recall with fondness. He would never discuss the darker aspects of life at the home in any greater detail, preferring to say only that the worst part was not knowing whether he would ever be reunited with his family. As it happened, Dad's stay lasted only six months. Grandma was released from the hospital and when she arrived to take him home, he couldn't help but notice how much weight she'd put on. The moment the release papers had been signed and they were heading toward the subway to the House of the Good Shepherd, Grandma announced that she was pregnant—again. She was nearly six months along, her rounded belly irrefutable proof that another Gotti heir was on its way. Dad had mixed feelings about the pregnancy. Part of him was happy because the pregnancy meant Grandpa wouldn't raise his hand to Grandma, at least for the next three months, but he also knew that the last thing the family needed was yet another mouth to feed.

Dad was happy to return home, but apprehensive about seeing his father. The family slipped easily back into the old routine in the apartment at the House of the Good Shepherd. Dad joined the local gym, a free, church-run program for poor kids. Every day after school, he'd head down to the gym and spar for hours with some of the local boys. He found a trainer who believed in him and decided he wanted to be a professional boxer. Dad's father used to box amateurishly, when he was a teen—but as with everything else Grandpa had started in life, he never got far. But young John showed much promise—a ferocious temper and a hard right hook—each time he was in the ring. Dad told me years later that the engine that drove him was the pent-up anger he harbored against his father. He told me that each time he hit the punching bag or an opponent, he would pretend it was his own father. And Dad was a good boxer, too. His trainer believed that he could make him an impressive contender. It was the first dream my father believed was possible.

A few short months after the family was reunited, it was time for another Gotti baby to join the household. Dad recalled the night his mother went into labor. Curiosity pulled him into the bedroom where the birth would take place, but he did not go beyond the threshold. His older twin sisters, Rosy and Lucy, hurried around the room, carrying pots of boiling water and clean rags. Private physicians were far too expensive; even the local clinic, which treated patients on a first-come, first-served basis, required at least some meager donation.

23

My grandmother had given birth so many times that my grandfather saw no harm in teaching his oldest daughters the rudimentary mechanics of delivering babies. He believed it was a perfectly natural act on the woman's part, and that "nature would take its course in the end." Besides, this was the early 1950s, a period when home births were still considered an acceptable alternative to hospitalization. My grandfather would have reasoned that peasants once bore children in barns or cabins, without the benefit of running water or electricity; surely my grandmother would have no problems in her own comfortable bed.

This wasn't the twins' first experience with childbirth. Together, just a few years earlier, then barely teenagers themselves, they had successfully delivered another male Gotti. So they were familiar with the process.

My grandmother's labor intensified; she began screaming out in pain. Between labored breaths, she shouted, "Something's wrong." My father stared helplessly as he watched his sister Lucy race from the bedroom to the kitchen with an armful of bloody towels. She dumped them into a laundry hamper next to the linen cabinet, grabbed a pile of clean sheets, and quickly returned to Grandma's side.

"You need to call Doc Hansen on Dean Street," she said to Dad. "Tell him to come right away." Then she shut the bedroom door behind her. My father dialed quickly and told the doctor there was an emergency at the Gotti home.

"Please come right away!" he begged.

Only a few minutes later and before the doctor arrived, Rosy came out of the bedroom carrying what Dad assumed was nothing more than another bundle of bloody towels. In actuality, she held in her hands the eighteenth Gotti child, stillborn. Rosy was crying. The baby had suffered from a condition commonly known as spina bifida and was severely deformed. He was born with his spine protruding through his back; his left foot and three fingers of his right hand were missing.

THIS TRAGEDY IN the Gotti household only served to intensify my father's anger. He wondered why his mother couldn't go to a hospital to give birth like most of the other mothers he knew. He cursed the poor and miserable lifestyle they were forced to endure—he cursed his father's inability to properly provide for his family. Most of all, he cursed his father's selfish ways. For the most part, Dad took out his frustrations in the gym and on the streets. As he grew into a formidable teenager, he'd go down to the local bar or pool hall, looking for trouble. In Brooklyn at that time, the toughest young guys ran in packs or gangs, in part to avoid vulnerability but also because mayhem was more fun when perpetrated with your buddies. Dad found he was more suited to life on the street than life in the high school classroom. So, after the horrible events that night at home, and with his mother being cared for by his sisters, Dad went out. Not yet seventeen years old, he ventured into a lounge on the corner of Fulton Street in Brooklyn. It was a rowdy gathering place for the mostly male working class.

My father made a phone call to one of his friends—a kid they called "Fats"—and gave him some instructions.

"Round up the boys and meet me at the lounge."

My father found it hard to get the thought of his suffering mother out of his head. But a few beers and the company of his pals helped ease the sting, and before long they were hatching plans to get their hands on some easy and much-needed money.

On the other side of town lived a man named Tommy "Botts" Marino, a bookie with a well-deserved reputation for draining residents of their weekly paychecks and cheating them out of their winnings. Marino was a man with few admirers, although this seemed to have little impact on his business. Since most customers were habitual gamblers and fearful of retribution, they complied with whatever terms Marino set. Marino ran his enterprise with ruthlessness and arrogance. It wasn't unusual for him to administer, or at least order, beatings severe enough that the victim ended up in the hospital; arson was a favorite tactic as well, and on more than one occasion a debtor found his house burned to the ground. The day before Grandma went into labor, one of Dad's friends told him that "Willy the drunk" was hit by a car and taken to a nearby hospital. Willy was one of the neighborhood fixtures and Dad really liked him. Willy started drinking after his wife died, and when he lost his house to the bank and ended up homeless, he became the town drunk. Still, he was harmless and Dad felt sorry for him. Often, some of the other neighborhood kids would tease and taunt Willy, and Dad would come to his rescue. Just before Willy got hit by the car, onlookers saw Marino shoving him to the street—into oncoming traffic.

On that night my father needed to channel his anger somewhere and his thoughts turned to Botts Marino. He decided it was time to take the bookie down a notch, maybe give him a taste of the grief he had heaped upon his own people for so many years.

The story has since become the stuff of legend. My father waited until Marino made his regular neighborhood rounds, which he did without fail virtually every night. My father and a few of his friends sat patiently near the corner of Fulton Street. As Marino approached, they pounced, pummeling him to the ground and beating him to a bloody pulp.

"Not enough damage to kill the guy," my father recalled. "But enough to let him know that if he continued to bother these good people, he would pay a price. A hefty price."

It was with that single act—an act of brazen machismo, born primarily of anger and frustration—that young John Gotti earned the respect and attention of the neighborhood folk. "Crazy Horse," they called him—and did so with admiration.

Even at such a young age, my dad attracted people whose problems seemed insurmountable. They would soon come to him with one gripe or another, seeking assistance or compensation. Dad always cheered on the underdog, and any chance he could, he would help someone less fortunate than him. Some problems were more easily rectified than others, and my father was shrewd enough to know when to act on his own and when to seek the counsel of the more worldly and respected elder men who ruled the social club on Fulton Street.

CHAPTER FOUR

"Knights in White Satin"

I t was 1956—the year the New York Yankees defeated the Brooklyn Dodgers for the World Series title. Elvis Presley's "Heartbreak Hotel" claimed the number one spot on the *Billboard* charts, and the top-grossing movie at the time was *Giant,* starring Liz Taylor, Rock Hudson, and the latest Hollywood heartthrob, a brooding kid named James Dean. Young women everywhere swooned at the mere mention of his name, while young men imitated him and his *Rebel Without a Cause* demeanor. And nowhere was this truer than in Brooklyn.

Gang lore has always been painted with a romantic brush, the violence and death overshadowed by the power of brotherhood and the allure of wealth. There was a reason *West Side Story* was such a blockbuster, and it had less to do with choreography and catchy tunes than with the public's fascination with gangs. Teens, in particular, were vulnerable in those days, when membership in a turf-minded gang was the ultimate status symbol. The black leather jacket, slicked-back hair, and tough-guy attitude could be seen in almost any teenage Brooklyn male back then. It was *the* look—especially among the toughest gang members.

At the age of sixteen, my father dropped out of school. Later on he would say that quitting school was one of the great regrets of his life. His decision was provoked by an accident that left him crippled and hospitalized for months. There was much speculation surrounding what really happened during this incident. It was widely reported that Dad and a few neighborhood kids were offered twenty dollars to steal a cement mixer from a construction site. And allegedly, things did not go quite as planned. The cement mixer tipped over and fell on my father's toes, crushing them in the process. And the so-called swagger so often used to describe my father's gait was attributed to a limp caused by the accident.

Not true.

The real story, as told to me by Dad and Grandma, is much less dramatic than the embellished neighborhood gossip.

Dad and a few of his friends were offered "a few bucks" to move some furniture for a neighbor. While crossing the street carrying an antique chair, my father was hit by a moving cement truck, crushing his leg and four toes. He was forced to drop out of school—and his boxing career was finished.

But drifting from one menial job to another didn't encourage my father, either. The only positions available to "wops" (as the Italians were unapologetically known) were degrading jobs, like cleaning toilets at the local movie house. When my father was fortunate enough to land something respectable, like pumping gas at a local gas station, my grandfather often sabotaged his efforts. It wasn't unusual for Grandpa to come along and cause a ruckus because he needed money to gamble. The incidents were humiliating for Dad, and bad for business, so my father would lose his job. Even before the accident, when Dad was fortunate to make a few dollars boxing, Grandpa was always ringside, waiting for the payout. That's probably why Dad told me years later that he believed education was the most important thing in a person's life. "Something no one can ever take away from you."

By the time he was seventeen, Dad had grown resentful of those fortunate to grow up privileged, or anyone who had enjoyed a childhood more pleasant than his own.

"Kids like me, we didn't dream of becoming doctors, lawyers, or accountants," he would say, sometimes with more than a trace of bitterness. "Those professions were for the rich kids—the kids with respectable fathers and mothers." Being poor had taught my father that surviving was much more important than dreaming. He would never walk away from his own obligations. He would do whatever it took to survive.

Dad often noted that his own father deserved credit for teaching him one thing, and one thing only: fear. As a boy, Dad feared hunger and poverty and loneliness. More than anything, though, he feared the beatings he absorbed at the hands of his father. He learned early on to defend himself against those who were bigger, stronger, and more powerful. He learned to use his fists as a weapon, because they were the only tools at his disposal. Later, his role models were those who were similarly disenchanted with society and its usual rules of decorum: the local hoods who hung around the Brooklyn street corners. My father learned that running errands for these men made him quick money and gave him an advanced education in street smarts. He grew up believing that these men—who wore expensive suits, flashed shiny diamond pinkie rings and attracted all the pretty girls, not to mention neighborhood respect—were worthy of his admiration. And so he emulated them.

My father, along with his brothers Peter and Gene, Angelo Ruggiero, and a few other teens, formed the Fulton-Rockaway Boys, a street gang in Brooklyn. Angelo was known as "Fat Ange" since he was pudgy as a teenager; he would become a lifelong friend. In the many books that have been written about my father and his cohorts, Angelo is nicknamed "Quack-Quack," an allusion to the fact that Angelo supposedly couldn't keep his mouth shut. He is typically depicted as an inveterate gossip, forever chatting recklessly about everything from mob-related activities to the personal lives of those around him.

This was a myth, or most of it, anyway. While Angelo did love to chat and gossip, he earned the nickname Quack-Quack for a thoroughly prosaic reason: he literally walked like a duck. His toes pointed out to the side with each awkward step, giving him a distinct waddle in his stride. It was a gait he'd developed as a growing adolescent, and it had become even more pronounced over time as his waistline expanded.

Angelo and my father were inseparable as the years passed, to the point where they rarely did anything—professional or personal—without the other. They worked, hung out at the social clubs, had dinner, drank, played, and fought together.

Another member of Dad's gang was Wilfred "Willie Boy" Johnson, a Native American, who went on to become a prominent amateur boxer. He and Dad met in the gym, after an amateur boxing match.

It came as no surprise to any of these young men that Dad rose rapidly to leadership in the club.

With active participation in any gang came the very real risk of spending time behind bars; indeed, incarceration was considered nothing less than a rite of passage. In 1957, at age seventeen, my father was arrested for the first time. He was charged with unlawful entry in the wake of a turf war with another neighborhood gang. The charges were later dismissed, but Dad would be arrested four more times—for crimes such as petty larceny, aggravated assault, and possession of bookmaking records—while he was still a member of the Fulton-Rockaway gang. The arrests didn't amount to much, if any, time in jail and were seen more as a way of establishing credibility among the gang than anything else.

The social club on Fulton Street became my father's second home. Even before he was eighteen he was for all practical purposes an emancipated minor. The situation at home never improved; in fact, it worsened. My grandfather and grandmother were constantly at each other's throats—and when they weren't beating up on each other, they would direct that violence toward their kids. Grandpa had all but abandoned any hope of securing a decent job, and the financial burden of supporting the household fell solely on the older Gotti boys. Although each week my father would turn over most of his earnings, he looked for any excuse to avoid going home at night. Dad realized early on that his money did more good when given to people really in need, like an elderly woman who lived above the Fulton Street Social Club. "If the family dog gets kicked in the belly every time he comes home from a walk," my father explained, "sooner or later he'll stop coming home."

My father grew to despise his home life and its abusive, volatile environment. Often he would crash at the Smiths', a neighboring African-American family with a son who had befriended my father. The Smiths lived next door to the House of the Good Shepherd. Mammy Mae Smith had six boys of her own to feed, yet she always welcomed Dad and his siblings at her table. John was her favorite Gotti boy she would tell him he was as handsome as Clark Gable. She would also tell my dad that he was special. She told him he had "admirable leadership" qualities that would no doubt benefit him when he was older. She even went so far as to suggest that he might someday become a man of great importance. Never had anyone paid my father such a compliment; he was accustomed to hearing insults and criticism, so Mammy's words were soothing to his soul.

Mammy Mae was a woman Dad truly loved and respected. She had his trust, and not many people fell into that category. Dad often spoke of her, never failing to describe her as "special." She provided my father with whatever minimal self-esteem he had in those days.

When Dad needed a warm place to sleep, he knew he could count on Mammy Mae, who would always leave the back door open so he could let himself in. Typically this would happen after one of my grandfather's alcohol-fueled rages, which were easily heard throughout the neighborhood.

Most nights, though, Dad would stay at the Fulton Street Social Club, crashing on a sofa in the back room. It was a moderately sized storefront with a small alcove in the back that was used as an office. The Fatico brothers, Danny and Carmine, were kind enough to let my father stay there, so long as he agreed to keep an eye on things after hours should anyone uninvited come snooping around—like one of the local cops.

Like my father, the Fatico brothers were young and impressionable men; they were also "tough guys, cool," and thus admired around the downtrodden neighborhood. It was the ambience, though, of the Fulton Street Social Club that my father found irresistible. The camaraderie and the air of respect that surrounded the men who hung out there impressed the young John Gotti enormously. It provided an escape from his miserable, depressing, impoverished life. It was a home and these men became his only family.

He'd made up his mind to be just like them.

DANNY AND CARMINE Fatico belonged to a crew that answered to the head of the Mangano Family, the legendary mobster Albert Anastasia. Carmine, the elder of the two brothers, was a capo. Anastasia was brutally killed in October 1957 by two gunmen as he sat in a barber's chair at the Park Sheraton in Midtown Manhattan. The assassins were never identified. Until his brazen daytime murder, Anastasia was my father's mentor. After the infamous barbershop hit, Anastasia's underboss, Carlo Gambino, was elected leader and the family name was changed from Mangano to Gambino.

Normally, underage boys lucky enough to be granted permission to hang around the club were assigned various mundane duties: cleaning up at night, making coffee and espresso during the day, and running various errands. If you succeeded in reaching the level where you were trusted with errands outside the club, it usually meant you had impressed one of the elders in some meaningful way; they saw you not only as "trustworthy" but as a "potential earner" for the crew. And so you were taken under their wing and groomed for the business, instructed in their methods, and infused with street smarts. From their earliest introduction, the Fatico brothers were apparently quite taken and impressed by John Gotti.

"Your dad was a remarkable man, even at sixteen," they once told me as a teenager at a Fatico family gathering. "We saw qualities—leadership qualities—that grown men learned and possessed only after years of living and working on the streets."

Dad would say that these mature qualities were less God-given than they were acquired—born out of his quest for a better life, a life far different from his dark and dreary childhood.

Physically, my father was of average height and weight. But he was much stronger than he appeared. For one thing, his often calm exterior masked a ferocious temper, a genetic gift from my grandfather. Most men were exposed to his outbursts only once; after that, they did their best to avoid provoking him.

Years later, my father would often rationalize his "bad temper" by placing blame on his horrible childhood and the constant need to protect himself. But this ferocious side complemented his street persona. The Fatico brothers, for example, viewed my father's temper as an asset, especially when it came time to collect payment from a client.

Danny, the younger and more fashion-conscious of the two Faticos, was particularly fond of young John, treating him like a son. He frequently sent my father out on "collection runs," using baby steps as an initial approach: collecting outstanding balances from less threatening individuals such as the local baker, butcher, or gas station owner. These funds were collected to ensure "protection"—a small amount each month to discourage other ruffians or gang members from attempting to shake down the shop owners, or, even worse, damage or destroy their belongings or storefronts. Protection money also ensured an audience with the neighborhood leader should they ever need to express a gripe or require assistance in reconciling a dispute. When it came to the more serious stuff—situations that required more than muscle and intimidation—Fatico usually sent one of his older and more experienced men. He didn't want my father to get mixed up in anything petty or stupid. When the time was right, Fatico would have more important assignments for my father.

This slow indoctrination, though, eventually led to my father becoming restless. Running numbers and making the same mundane pickups week after week began to bore him. He itched for more action—a way to make more money. At the same time, his home situation had become almost impossible to endure. My grandfather continued to gamble, drink, and frivolously spend whatever little money he'd earn from odd jobs. The standard of living in the Gotti household continued to decline, just as the frequency and intensity of the beatings absorbed by my father escalated. But there was a subtle change in the family dynamic: now that my father was no longer a skinny little kid, it took much more effort on the part of my grandfather to actually cause him real harm.

It became easier, though no less vile, for Grandpa to hurt Dad with words. The sting of my grandfather hurling epithets through a boozy haze and my father stoically absorbing the blows had a lasting impact, leaving invisible bruises that never quite healed.

It became common practice for my grandfather to begin his rant the moment he came home for dinner. On one such occasion, he returned home after an all-night card game and demanded that my grandmother keep the house quiet so he could get some sleep. He let her know he expected a "hot and hearty" dinner when he woke up. Usually, there was never much food in the house, and the kids had been forced to live on rice, vegetable soup, and greens. My grandmother had all but exhausted her line of credit at the local butcher shop, the same shop where she had once been employed. Even though she was a proud woman, she was not above begging her former boss for scraps—some edible cut of meat one of the employees would probably throw out—if it would help feed her family, or, even more important, if it would allow her to throw together some sort of meal that my grandfather wouldn't reject as inedible.

That night Grandma got lucky. She returned home with a good-sized steak, which should have been enough to satisfy my grandfather and feed some of her hungry brood. But my grandmother was afraid to trim even an ounce off Grandpa's steak. So, while he dined on the entire juicy cut of meat, the rest of the family divided up a leftover shepherd's pie and a loaf of stale bread. As my grandfather devoured his succulent steak, his hungry children watched and salivated. This did not sit well with my father.

Dad waited until his younger siblings—Billy, Gene,

Marie, Ritchie, Patricia, and Vincent—finished their meals and left the table. He waited until the last one filtered out of the room and the kitchen door closed behind them. Then he slammed his fist down on the old butcher block table so hard that one of the legs nearly gave way, and my grandfather's plate fell into his lap. By now my father was on his feet and my grandfather was wiping food off of his pants. Horrified by this sudden development, and the mayhem it was likely to precipitate, my grandmother stood cowering in a corner.

Years of abuse had taken its toll. The anger Dad had swallowed so many times, through so many years, now crept to the surface and fueled a pride and courage he hadn't known he possessed.

"There was no fear," he later recalled. "Only pure and raw defiance."

Words Dad normally uttered only under his breath, in the moments *after* a beating, suddenly poured out of his mouth.

"You're a selfish prick!" he shouted. "Can't you see those kids are hungry?" He remembered yelling those words along with many others, and the great relief it brought to finally say the things he had kept inside for so long.

My grandmother stood frozen, beyond shocked. Grandpa dropped the remains of his dinner, sending the chipped plate crashing to the floor and shattering into a million pieces. Father and son squared off.

The initial blow struck my father in the head; it barely caused him to wobble. He was prepared to strike back, ready and able to drive the old man into the ground. And he wanted to. Nothing would have felt better, at least in the short term.

But he didn't.

For better or worse, my father had been raised to respect his parents, to believe that there was almost no greater sin than to hit one's father. It was the ultimate form of disrespect, and my father just couldn't bring himself to sink to that level. Giving his own father some of the same foul-mouthed lip was one thing; hitting his own father was quite another. Instead, he let Grandpa strike him again— hard—in the face. Once, twice, three times. The last blow nearly caused him to go down. He staggered toward the kitchen door. By now my grandmother was crying, trying hard to hold back her loud sobs. She was moving about the tiny kitchen, jockeying for position in the middle of the room, trying to find some way to get between her husband and her son.

Years later, Dad told me he was so tempted to hit his father that night. At the same time, he knew once he raised his hands up to his father, there was "no turning back."

The beatings continued with mostly the younger Gotti kids. One night my father came home to the sound of his thirteen-year-old sister, Patricia, screaming in terror. Dad raced inside the house and into the kitchen, where he found his father eating dinner, and Patricia beaten, bruised, and locked in a small kitchen pantry. My grandfather, in a fit of rage, had knocked her around and then imprisoned her for good measure. He'd caught her speaking to a neighborhood boy a few hours earlier and was determined to teach her a lesson.

My father sprang into action, first freeing Patricia from the pantry and making sure she was not in any immediate danger. Then he turned to face his father.

"Why don't you beat up on someone your own size!" he shouted.

My grandfather didn't show an ounce of fear or concern, and went on eating his dinner. When he was done, he grabbed a coat and hat from the closet, ready to go out for the evening. Except my father blocked his way. Again, young John told his father that he was a "selfish prick." My grandfather hit him—causing an impressive gash just over Dad's left eye. But unlike all the times before, Dad didn't just stand there and take the beating. Years of constant rage and humiliation prompted my father to finally swing back, forcefully and purposely. My grandfather was stunned. He wobbled, then fell to the floor. Dad stepped over his father's limp body on his way out the door. Over his shoulder, he yelled to his mother, "How can you stand there and let him beat your kids?"

CHAPTER FIVE

"The Duke of Earl"

The withering heat of summer had come early to the city in 1958, with temperatures soaring well into the nineties by mid-June. The asphalt patches used to repair the potholes of winter had already begun to wear, dissolving into a messy goo that stuck to the soles of my mother Victoria's new spectator pumps. She had bought the expensive shoes as a gift to herself, to celebrate a new job as a telephone operator.

She'd waited three months to get an interview with the utility company, and now, finally, she had a decent job with decent pay. For some time she'd been living hand to mouth; after paying for the room she rented at Aunt Bessie's boardinghouse in Astoria, Queens, there was barely enough money to put food on the table. The boardinghouse wasn't exactly the Ritz, but it was the best she could do at the time. Her circumstances, however, were about to change. The new job would allow my mother to move out of the boardinghouse and get her own apartment.

What an improvement it would be. No more nights trapped in a tiny bedroom on Euclid Avenue, and Aunt Bessie always breathing down her neck and sticking her nose where it didn't belong. Mom wanted nothing more than to get out of the boardinghouse, to put some distance between herself and the old bitch.

The ill-tempered old woman wasn't her real aunt; that was a moniker she favored, as if it would somehow make her a more appealing and thoughtful person. My mother dutifully complied. Victoria Lorraine DiGiorgio was not yet seventeen years old, and was generally content to take the path of least resistance, whatever was necessary to find peace in her life. This was her second stay at the boardinghouse; the first was several months earlier, shortly after she had dropped out of school. After several weeks of bouncing between her friends' apartments, Mom searched the classifieds but came up empty. On the advice of a girlfriend, a boardinghouse alumna, and with nowhere else to turn, Mom turned up on the doorstep of Aunt Bessie's dilapidated, two-family Brooklyn home.

"It was one of the worst places I ever lived," she would later say.

The old woman made it clear from day one that room and board came with a price. In addition to monthly rent, Victoria was required to perform chores around the building. She didn't really mind; it helped the hours pass and provided some structure to the day. Not too long after my mother first moved in, she met a personable young man named Willy, an ambitious Irish immigrant, with "black Irish looks and a bright, perfectly white smile." Willy worked with his father in a steel factory not far from Aunt Bessie's place. To Victoria's eyes, he seemed like a man with potential. After only a few months of dating, he proposed, promising my mother "an easier, less complicated life, one where you'll never have to worry about paying the bills." This was not a small carrot to be dangled in front of my mother; it was precisely what she wanted to hear. My mother was young and searching for someone—anyone—with the capacity for love and the ability to protect her.

My mother has always had mixed feelings about her early childhood. It is difficult for her to talk to me about those early years, and the odd and volatile nature of my grandparents' relationship. Being raised in a home. Being called a "bastard" and finding out she almost had a brother seems to have taken quite a toll on her. My mother still cries when discussing this part of her family's history.

In those days, it was scandalous to have a child out of wedlock and keep it—scandalous behavior that was barely a notch above running whiskey. Regardless, my grandmother was a woman who had neither the desire nor the inclination to raise a child alone, so she enrolled my mother in Sacred Heart Academy shortly before her fourth birthday. From that day on, my mother was a child on her own, a little girl without a home, without parents—without family. She was rootless, an inescapable fact that both saddened and defined her for many years to come. But the loneliness is what bothered my mother the most. At Sacred Heart Academy, the nuns were cold and distant. They served as strict disciplinarians rather than warm chaperones or compassionate protectors. Mom never knew how it felt to be loved and wanted by anyone—except Uncle Tony and Aunt Dolly. Uncle Tony was Grandpa's younger brother. Younger, but certainly more mature and responsible. When Grandpa abandoned my mother, Uncle Tony stepped in for a while and tried hard to play father. He was only eighteen years old. But he was engaged to be married. His fiancée, Dolly, also adored Mom. The couple often visited on the weekends and treated Mom like their own daughter. Sadly, when Aunt Dolly and Uncle Tony announced they wanted to adopt Mom, all hell broke loose! Out of jealousy, spite, or his own guilt, my grandfather absolutely forbid it. He didn't have the guts to take responsibility and raise Mom on his own. But he refused to allow another man to do so, either—especially his own brother. Perhaps it was the fact that my mother would serve as a constant reminder of his earlier fuck-up. I call it plain selfishness.

When Mom met Willy as a teenager, he seemed to be everything she was looking for in a man. He promised stability, a family, and a home. She fell hard for his charm, and it wasn't long before the two young lovers eloped to City Hall. But after they were married, Mom realized she had made a big mistake.

Willy and his father both lost their jobs in the following weeks when the factory hit on hard times and shut down; soon bills were going unpaid and creditors were knocking at the door. More important, Victoria came to the sad realization that she wasn't in love with Willy; maybe she'd never been in love with him to begin with.

"There's nothing worse," she would tell me years later, "than waking up beside someone and realizing you don't love them."

Mom left Willy and moved back into the boardinghouse just a few months after getting married. Aunt Bessie wasn't thrilled to see her, despite the fact that Mom's old room was still vacant and Bessie really needed the money. So the old woman taunted my mother and rubbed her nose in her mistake at every opportunity. Bessie also let Victoria know that she was on house probation, and the next time she left, she wouldn't be allowed back.

Eager to become self-reliant, Mom took on as much work as she could possibly handle. In addition to her job at the utility company, she found an ad for a waitress at a local bar. Soon, she figured, she'd have enough money socked away, and then she could say good-bye to Aunt Bessie forever.

THE COCKTAIL WAITRESS job wasn't anything impressive, but it was enough to bring in some extra needed cash. Victoria held the ad in her hand and double-checked the address. It was just across the street from Aunt Bessie's and thankfully the appointment wasn't until a half hour later, just enough time to stop at home and freshen up.

My mother walked the six blocks from the subway stop to the boardinghouse, passing the usual familiar faces along the way: Timmy the butcher, who always made sure he saved some bologna ends for her; Mrs. Phyllis, the neighborhood seamstress, forever scrutinizing the young woman's outfit for any loose threads; and Teddy the baker, who was unfailingly kind, and on this day offered her a cold glass of iced tea, which she gratefully accepted. Across the avenue, a fire hydrant had been opened, allowing a bunch of neighborhood kids to frolic in the steady, forceful stream of cold water. Mom couldn't resist kicking off her shoes and letting the cool water splash on her legs.

No one minded, least of all the teenage boys hanging out in the street. Victoria was petite, brunette, graceful. The gangly little neighborhood girl had matured into a beautiful young woman, with deep, brown Italian eyes. Small wonder that on that sticky afternoon in Brooklyn, she attracted the attention of every male on Third Avenue.

One of those men was an unwanted admirer—a middle-aged pickup artist who figured all he needed in his bag of tricks was an ability to whistle and hurl juvenile "compliments." The man grew angry when the young lady ignored his catcalls, and he soon began spewing obscenities. As Mom rounded the corner near the boardinghouse, she thought it wise not to go straight home. The last thing she needed was some wacko knowing where she lived and returning at some point looking for trouble.

The man was behind her, obviously following. She looked up and down the avenue; the closest place to seek refuge was the pub where she was due for an interview in just a few minutes. Victoria slipped her high heels back on and darted inside the bar. There was a jukebox in the corner playing a teen favorite, "The Duke of Earl." In the rear of the bar, a pack of young men chatted while shooting pool. One man, in particular, took notice right away. He was handsome, Mom recalled, "in a movie-star way," and well-dressed, in a navy suit and matching navy-and-cream tie.

Within a few minutes the young man had taken a seat at the bar and begun nursing a Scotch and water. Mom eyed him carefully, surreptitiously, not wanting to stare. She ordered a Coke and waited at the bar. Eventually, though, she slid her Coke down the bar and hopped on the bar stool next to him. Believe it or not, Victoria was the aggressor; John Gotti was the shy boy.

"Excuse me," she began. "Do you mind if I sit here for a few minutes?"

Dad looked her up and down. He was not accustomed to young women taking the lead in these situations, and so he viewed her with a degree of apprehension. At the same time, there was no denying that he found her extremely attractive.

He also noticed she was watching the door intently.

"Expecting a jealous boyfriend?" he joked.

"No."

"Husband?"

Mom laughed and shook her head.

"No, just a pest—or a pervert. I'm not sure what he is."

She pointed to the back of the bar; the man in question had followed her inside and was watching her carefully.

My father nodded. He gestured to a pair of his buddies, who quickly appeared by his side. Dad gave instructions to approach the man and let him know, in no uncertain terms, that the lovely young brunette at the bar was unavailable. If the man had a problem with that, he was to let my father know, and the two of them would settle matters the old-fashioned way.

Of course, it turned out to be no problem at all. The man might have been smitten, or even perverted, but he wasn't stupid. In those days, in that part of Brooklyn, it was already widely known that John Gotti was not to be provoked. As the leader of a neighborhood gang, he wielded considerable power. If you crossed him, you'd pay for it.

And so the man nodded subtly, respectfully, and quietly walked out of the bar. That's when Victoria told John she

47

was there about a job. He seemed surprised, but he smiled to be polite.

"You're too pretty to work at a bar," he replied.

My mother nodded. "I need the extra money. I don't really have a choice."

Dad called the bartender over, leaned across the counter, and whispered a few words in the man's ear. The bartender eyed my mother approvingly and smiled.

"Welcome to my bar," he said. "You start this weekend."

Victoria got the job, just like that.

The two continued talking. The conversation flowed easily, free of the awkward, empty moments that typify most initial encounters. After several hours—and several shots of Scotch for Dad, and a few Brandy Alexanders for Mom— they finally left the bar. It was nearly closing time. Victoria couldn't believe she'd allowed herself to stay out so late on a work night, but she couldn't help herself.

"There was just something about John Gotti that drew people to him, like a moth to a flame," Mom later explained. "He was that charismatic, that charming. I knew before we left the bar that night that he was the man I was going to marry. He was, as the song said that day, 'The Duke of Earl,' as far as I was concerned."

MY FATHER WALKED the beautiful girl home that night. He couldn't believe they shared such a similar bleak upbringing and background. Six months later they moved in together. Though this was a scandalous arrangement in 1959, neither Mom nor Dad had family that they felt they needed to answer to; they were on their own. Their first apartment was a small studio in Downtown Brooklyn. The ensuing two years would prove challenging, but the love they felt for each other managed to hold them together. Money was still scarce.

Even though he was bringing in more greenbacks than he had in the past, there never seemed to be enough at the end of the month to meet the bills filling up in the mailbox. Strong-willed and passionate, Mom and Dad had endured more than their share of disagreements and separations, some more volatile than others. The fights sometimes resulted in one of them leaving for days at a time. One such incident sent my mother into an emotional tailspin because, as fate would have it, she found out she was pregnant shortly after she left Dad.

Mom weighed her options. Years later, she would tell me, "It was all I thought about day and night; I couldn't focus, couldn't function. Your father and the pregnancy were all that was on my mind." She considered different scenarios. As she would also later tell me, "I knew in my heart I still loved him and wanted this baby. But the circumstances and the timing couldn't have been worse."

MY MOTHER ARRIVED at the East Flatbush Women's Center with tears in her eyes. She thought about her own mother—young, alone, and pregnant—and how badly that situation had turned out. As much as she detested the idea of getting an abortion, Mom was terrified of having the baby. But she realized she couldn't go through with it, she couldn't stamp out the life growing within her. She thought of the younger brother who had been aborted, and became nearly sick to her stomach at the notion of repeating "such a horrible and heinous act."

"And so I didn't walk from the clinic," Mom said. "I ran."

With nowhere else to turn, she reluctantly went back to the boardinghouse. Aunt Bessie was waiting at her usual perch, leaning out on the windowsill on the second story.

"Hah!" the old woman chortled. "He went and kicked you out, huh?" She shook her head disdainfully. "Your Mr. Wonderful."

Mom ignored her nasty comments and calmly requested a room to rent. Preferably, she said, the same room she had occupied in the past.

Bessie hacked and wheezed, and continued her mean, drunken rant. My mother let it wash over her. She thought for a moment about running away. But where would she go? She knew her husband, Willy, still loved her and would take her back in a heartbeat. They were not officially divorced, and not even the fact that she was carrying another man's child would have mattered to him. But she was in love with my father, and no doubt believed—or at least hoped—that he would come looking for her. Mom would never admit it, but I believe that's the real reason she went back to Aunt Bessie's: it was the only known address my father had for her; this way, at least, he could find her.

My mother went up to her room and unpacked her things. She didn't have much, just a few frayed nightgowns, two or three suits for work, T-shirts and jeans, and her most treasured possession: a photograph of her and my father at the Copacabana in Manhattan. They often went there during the time they lived together. The night the picture was taken they were with Marie and Angelo Ruggiero, and the foursome look as though they had not a care in the world.

LUCKILY, MOM'S STAY at the boardinghouse was short this time around. One night, while she was visiting my aunt Marie and uncle Angelo at their Brooklyn apartment, my father showed up. To my mother, my father appeared weary and defeated. She'd never seen him look so vulnerable. "As long as I live," she said, "I will never forget that look on his face."

Dad's tired eyes were glassy; Mom suspected he'd been drinking. At first she was surprised to see him there, but she quickly surmised that Angelo must have alerted him that my mother was expected to drop by that evening. Dad shuffled into the apartment, and all my mother could think was *Thank God I look good.* She'd been careful to do her makeup and put on a dress, just in case Dad stopped by.

Dad stood inside the doorway of the apartment for a few awkward moments, with no one saying a word. Angelo and Marie weren't sure whether they should stay or leave. The apartment was tiny, so leaving meant, quite literally, leaving the building. There was nowhere to seek privacy, so Angelo and Marie stayed. They hoped to encourage Mom and Dad to end their silly separation.

It was my father who broke the uncomfortable silence.

"What is it that you want? What is it that you want me to do?" he asked.

My mother paused before answering. Her voice catching with emotion, she responded, "I want this." She gestured to the apartment. "I want a house with a white picket fence, children playing in the front yard, and maybe a dog."

By now she was getting tears in her eyes.

"And I want us to get married, like Angelo and Marie."

Dad was surprised. Finally, he began to speak.

"I don't know if I can give you some of those things. But one thing I do know is this: I'm no good without you. I feel like half of a man and I don't want to live this way."

Before the two even got close enough to embrace, Mom announced she was pregnant and Dad nearly hit the floor. Suddenly, the sadness and apprehension drained from his face, replaced by a look of pure joy. It was, my mother would fondly recall, as if he had won the lottery.

THE HOUSE WITH the white picket fence, the dog, and even the marriage came a bit later.

There were, after all, obstacles in their path.

"We still had one very big problem," Mom explained. "I was already married—to a man I didn't love."

Getting the marriage annulled was no small task. Dad used his contacts to secure the services of a lawyer who handled the annulment. It proceeded quietly and reasonably, in large part because Willy, to his great credit, chose not to contest my mother's request. He was a gentleman, unsuited to do battle with the likes of John Gotti; moreover, he loved my mother too much to stand in her way. Victoria loved another man, and carried that man's child. What was Willy to do but grant her wish and get on with his life?

CHAPTER SIX

"Going to the Chapel"

The wedding wasn't your typically lavish, over-the-top mob affair. At the time, my father remained on poor terms with my grandparents; and my mother was still estranged from her parents. So the ceremony was small and intimate, attended only by a few close friends and family members.

My father's relationship with Angelo Ruggiero had evolved into such a strong bond that they practically considered themselves to be brothers. Because of the close friendship between my father and Uncle Angelo, my mother and his wife, Marie, quickly became pals. In the fall of 1962, with Angelo and Marie present as witnesses, my mother and father finally tied the knot.

The two had already been living together for a few years, and my sister, Angel, was born in 1960. This was a nearly unforgivable sin back in those days. To my parents, though, it wasn't such a big deal. After all, the couple had been together, and living on their own, since they were sixteen years old. So in many ways they considered the ceremony to be a mere formality.

The previous years had centered on more practical

concerns, like finding a proper place to live and successfully staving off eviction.

Poverty was also certainly an issue: Dad spun through a revolving door of employment and unemployment, while Mom tried to put away a few dollars from her savings. Because Dad was so old-fashioned—especially when it came to women working—Mom quit her job with the phone company. Somehow they managed to save enough money to get a little place of their own, and that's when they had their second wedding. It was a no-fuss, no-frills civil ceremony on November 14.

The Fatico brothers wanted to host the wedding party. But pride kept my father from accepting their generous offer; he was adamant about paying for everything, despite the fact that he hadn't a penny to his name. Years later Dad claimed that he had gotten lucky at another all-night card game the night before the wedding and managed to win over a thousand dollars—enough not only to cover the cost of the wedding, but to pay rent for the next few months.

Uncle Angelo made all the arrangements. The tables were to be draped in winter-white cloth linens and set with porcelain plates and sterling silverware, with a centerpiece of white daisies, and a bottle of Cutty Sark whiskey to be placed at every table. But when Angelo arrived two hours before the party, he discovered not Cutty, but some cheap alternative on the tables. My mother vividly remembers Angelo's reaction when he discovered this transgression and confronted the club's owner. At first the owner refused to change it. It meant less money in his pocket if he had.

"Your uncle grabbed the poor guy by the throat and threatened him," Mom said. "He said, 'There better be bottles of Cutty on every table or there's gonna be a problem—a *big* problem, if you know what I mean!' "

Needless to say, within a few minutes, the rotgut had been removed, and Cutty Sark was being unloaded by the case.

The ceremony and reception took place at a rented hall in Brooklyn—a private two-room lounge owned by a neighborhood guy. Dad would tell me years later that the entire event was a break-even proposition, with wedding gifts basically covering the cost of the ceremony. Whatever was left over—and there wasn't much—was stashed away for a rainy day. Clearly, this was not like something out of *The Godfather*, with the bride and groom enjoying an elaborate spectacle and walking away with enough cash to buy a mansion and put all of their future children through college. There was, instead, a simple gathering of family and friends.

That was enough for Mom and Dad.

IN THE WEEKS that followed, my father did his best to find steady work. The Gotti financial situation was bleak, and with a second baby on the way, about to get even bleaker.

My mother busied herself most days trying to master the skills of a traditional housewife. This was not a small task for her, since she'd had little training for the job. Having been raised at a school for girls and not by her own mother, Mom had not learned even the basics of cooking, cleaning, and sewing. She took her new role seriously, even going so far as to register at the local library and take out several instructional books for the budding homemaker. They were guides, mainly—cookbooks, sewing manuals, and the like. Try as she might, though, Mom's culinary skills were frustratingly slow to develop.

"She couldn't boil water," Dad often joked. "Even soft-boiled eggs came out wrong."

Frustration, combined with the hormonal swings of pregnancy, often drove Mom to tears. The crying jags came without warning, and at all hours of the day and night. There wasn't much my father could do, and the helplessness tore at his pride, as well as his heart.

One night, while Dad was out at the social club, playing cards and messing around with the guys, a man came around with a cardboard box—inside was the cutest little dog Dad had ever seen. The man was trying to find it a good home. Dad, who had quite the soft spot considering his well-earned reputation for toughness, took one look at the puppy and fell in love; he decided immediately to take the dog home.

Dad was sure that the dog would do wonders for my mother's emotional state. He also thought, quite correctly, that this adorable, tiny puppy would distract Mom in times of depression. How could you look at the little guy and not smile?

Dad was correct—to a point. Mom had always wanted a poodle while growing up. "The kind that the rich and fancy ladies paraded up and down the wealthy blocks of Manhattan," she'd say. Also, poodles were the "it" dog of Brooklyn in those days.

So Dad put a big red bow around the dog's collar and took him home to Mom. He handed her the box proudly and explained that the little pup wriggling inside was actually a baby poodle, rather than a mutt. Mom eyed the dog curiously.

"Why doesn't he look like a poodle?"

Dad hesitated.

"Ummm, he will," Dad stammered. "Give him some time, until his hair grows out, or his fur. He just needs one of those fancy haircuts and a few curlers in his hair. We'll take him downtown in a few weeks, when the weather gets warmer, and the groomer will fix him up. Trust me, he'll look just like the poodle he is."

Mom believed him; she fell for the story and for the little puppy with the red bow, whom she named "Bitsey." After a month of the adorable little monster chewing his way through the apartment. Mom took him downtown to a pet salon. She walked in proudly, and holding the scraggly little mutt tightly under her arm, she marched right up to one of the groomers and asked for a "poodle cut."

The groomer summoned the shop's owner. The two men stared at the dog for a moment, then retreated together to the rear of the salon to talk. Within a few minutes they reappeared, and soon my mother was engaged in a heated discussion with the owner about the type of haircut that was appropriate for this particular animal, which, according to the salon owner, was obviously no poodle. "It's a mutt," he informed Mom.

She did not take this news well.

"I almost died!" she said. "I wanted to kill your father— the sooner the better. I left the salon so embarrassed; I never wanted to show my face in that part of town again."

Within a few days, cooler heads prevailed, and Mom came to the realization that perhaps it was the thought that mattered: Dad had merely been trying to cheer her up. She forgave him.

As for the dog, he turned out to be a terror. The mutt lasted in the apartment for just a few more weeks before his incessant barking and growling caught the attention of the landlady, who politely reminded my mother that the lease contained very specific wording on the subject of pets: they were not permitted. In the end, Mom found a new home for the dog—she gave it to my grandfather. Mom spent much time trying to get Dad and Grandpa to make amends. A slow process, since Dad was still too resentful of his father.

For thirteen years, the dog was a loyal and beloved companion to Grandpa. Bitsey went everywhere with him, from the neighborhood social club to the local bar, to the neighborhood OTB parlor. The two were practically inseparable; where you saw one, the other was usually right behind. Sadly, Bitsey disappeared during one of Grandpa's all-night drinking binges. Typically Gramps brought Bitsey inside the bar on these sojourns, and had him sit up on a stool, obediently, right next to him. But on this night Bitsey was gone. Someone had deliberately cut his leash and made off with the dog.

This devastated my grandfather; to this day, I honestly believe he loved that dog more than he loved all of his kids put together. It's hard to explain or rationalize, but there was something about his relationship with the dog that brought out the best in the old man. And when Bitsey was gone, he fell into mourning, walking around in stunned silence, searching for his "best friend." He would rail at no one in particular, vowing to get the person responsible for Bitsey's disappearance. But nothing came of his threats or his efforts to find the dog.

As for my mother, at least her mood was temporarily

lightened by my father's good intentions. But reality soon intruded. The young couple fell behind on the rent; the afternoon mail brought bills and threats to turn off their utilities. The phone was the first to go; they could live without that, of course, but how would they manage without heat? My father fretted endlessly—it seemed there was no difference between his bleak and depressing childhood and the life he'd made on his own. He just couldn't seem to dig them out of the hole, and it made him feel like a failure.

Things were about to get even worse.

Just weeks before my mother was due to give birth, the landlady served them with eviction papers. As an added touch of cruelty, she pasted the two-page summons on the apartment door for everyone in the building to see. My father walked around in utter despair that day, desperately searching for some solution. His wife and unborn child were about to be thrown into the street. It was as if he was reliving his own childhood, with one significant exception: this time, he had to shoulder the responsibility—and the blame—himself. It nearly drove him mad.

He turned to Danny Fatico and begged for work. He told Fatico about the rent that was due and the upcoming baby's birth. He told Fatico he was desperate and willing to do anything to make some money. Fatico offered to pay the rent—but Dad refused. He was too proud.

At my father's insistence, Danny helped my father land a "job." The duties were simple; not exactly legal, but simple. He was to hijack a load of goods, ladies' dresses, from a truck delivery at JFK Airport. The heist was rudimentary, according to Fatico, and involved very little risk. He introduced my father to the other members of the "team." Each person had an assignment, culminating with the dresses being dropped off with a local fence. Once payment for the intercepted shipment was secured, everyone would be compensated for their efforts.

The heist went off without a hitch. My father was paid enough money to pay the back rent and two months forward. There was also enough left over to buy a secondhand crib for his new baby. To my father, it seemed almost too good to be true. Easy money for easy work.

Or so it seemed—until two detectives showed up at the door a few days later. They had questions. He had no answers. They slapped him in handcuffs, placed him under arrest, and ushered him out of his apartment, leaving his very pregnant wife behind.

CHAPTER SEVEN

"Born to Be Wild"

Although less imposing in stature than my father, and certainly lacking my dad's inherent toughness, Uncle Angelo became a formidable mobster, largely due to his partnership with Dad. Over time the pair recruited a powerful crew, including such loyal members as my father's two brothers, Pete and Gene, and "Willie Boy" Johnson. Friends since their early teens when they ruled the Fulton-Rockaway Boys, this group boasted an uncommon closeness, and over time wielded considerable clout. They made their bones with petty crimes: stealing cars, running numbers, and hijacking trucks filled with cigarettes, liquor, and ladies' garments. This enabled my father and his crew to become what the elders in the Gambino Family called "good and impressionable earners," resulting in progressively favorable recognition. After Dad's arrest for hijacking the truck full of dresses, he was sentenced to only a few months in the county jail.

It was during this period that my father met a powerful mobster who would have a profound impact on his life: Aniello Dellacroce. Everyone—from underlings to close associates and friends—referred to him as "Neil" or "Mr. O'Neill."

He was a brash, foul-mouthed, and brazen man who had his own headquarters at the Ravenite Social Club on Mulberry Street in Manhattan's Little Italy. It was a two-story brick building, nearly windowless on the ground floor. Privacy, in Dellacroce's world, was paramount, as my father would come to learn.

For years Dellacroce had heard about John Gotti's exploits; he knew of the young man's reputation for being a good earner. Years later Dellacroce would acknowledge "keeping a close eye on Johnny Boy" as a means of recruiting him into Dellacroce's crew. He saw something special in my father, "an innate leadership quality." He also recognized a dark side to John Gotti—a wild and unbridled temper that couldn't be tamed and would later serve as an asset to the up-and-coming mobster. He figured Dad would rise quickly in the ranks and urged other elders to keep tabs on the kid from Fulton and Rockaway.

Now, with Dellacroce's help, my dad was bringing in enough dough to rent a better, two-bedroom apartment. The task of finding a suitable place was assigned to my mother. Mom looked through the classified ads and found something she deemed appropriate, something in the right neighborhood geographically and economically.

"It was ideal when I read about it in the newspaper," Mom later explained with a chuckle. "So I took it—sight unseen. But I should have known something was amiss when the man on the phone agreed to personally move us in! That's right—after I spoke with him, he offered to send a truck to pick up our furniture the very next day. When I walked into that apartment, having arrived with everything we owned . . . well, I don't know what I expected—but the dungeon behind that old wooden door was definitely *not* it!

"When your father came home later that night, he was speechless—utterly speechless. Still, he was willing to make the best of it; there was nothing else we could do. We had no money left."

Dad continued to work and hustle, with inconsistent results. Once, for example, someone provided him with inside information about a shipment of television sets bound for Kennedy Airport. They were color television sets, no less, and for Dad this was a potentially huge score. Color TVs were a rare commodity. So, of course, my father was more than interested in the possibility of intercepting this shipment.

He gathered his crew together and went over the heist. They planned everything perfectly, right down to the last detail. It went off without a hitch—or so they thought. One of the television sets even came home with Dad. My mother, exhausted from trying to transform the dungeon into a castle, couldn't have been happier with the gift. Watching television was one of my mother's small pleasures, so when Dad walked in with a brand-new color TV to replace their old black-and-white one, she was ecstatic.

"It was as if we'd won the lottery," Mom recalled. "I became addicted to it after only one week."

As with any addiction, though, there was always the potential for withdrawal.

Alas, the cops apparently had gotten wind of the heist and were well on their way to cracking the case by the time Mom got through the first episode of *I Love Lucy*. Dad, whose intuition and connections led him to believe that law enforcement officials might soon be knocking on their door, insisted Mom get rid of the new toy.

"I cried for days, as if the world was going to end," Mom said. "It wasn't so much that I was home alone and pregnant; but, having gotten the new color TV, I gave the old one to the landlady downstairs!"

Mom had traded the old black-and-white television for a nearly new radio. When Dad took back the color television, Mom came to rely on the small radio as a means of entertainment while home alone. Three days after Dad took away the TV, the radio broke. Apparently it was used, a rebuilt radio. The landlady pulled a scam on Mom. When Mom showed up on her doorstep, the landlady wouldn't open the door. In fact, she turned up the volume on the television to drown out Mom's voice. Mom left the radio in front of the landlady's apartment door with a note taped to it that said, "Here is the piece of junk you used to con me out of my television. Either give me back my TV or I'll send my husband down to speak to your husband."

The two women got into a heated argument. The landlady refused to give the television back. Now she had the broken radio and the black-and-white television—and Mom was furious! The women yelled until the landlady's husband came home from work. He was not a stupid man. He'd heard all about John Gotti and didn't want any trouble. So he insisted his wife give the TV back to Mom. The landlord's wife did so reluctantly. But, to be spiteful, she left the television on the ledge of the second-floor landing—knowing full well Mom, being very pregnant at the time, couldn't carry it up two stories. Mom tried—when she got to the top of the third floor, huffing and puffing and utterly exhausted, she finally realized that she couldn't carry it up another floor. But rather than let the landlady win, Mom kicked the old TV with all her might and watched it bounce down the ten or eleven steps. She left it at the foot of the second landing and yelled down to the landlady, "Try and watch the TV now!" When Dad came home later that night, he found the broken television wedged between the second and third floor of the apartment building. It took him five minutes to climb around it in order to get to our apartment on the sixth floor.

Since few things upset my father more than seeing my mom distraught, Dad decided to go out and find her a color television the old-fashioned way: by paying for it.

Well, sort of.

He entered an all-night poker game, hoping his luck would change and he'd make some money. He did—nearly five hundred dollars. But instead of using it to buy fancy suits, or as a down payment on a new car, or even a security deposit for a nicer apartment to rent, he went out and bought Mom the biggest, most expensive color television he could find.

Dellacroce, who'd been at the poker match, had been duly impressed with Dad's success, which seemed fueled by equal parts luck and guts. Thus, Dellacroce often made unannounced visits to the Fulton Street Social Club. He wasn't thrilled with the location or the way it was so run-down. After a few of these visits, the club's headquarters was moved to a more discreet area in Ozone Park, Queens. The new club was a two-story building with a first-floor storefront; it was called the Bergin Hunt and Fish Club, and was located near Kennedy Airport, in a small, close-knit neighborhood of Italian immigrants. The locals paid frequent visits to the social club; some were merely being cordial, while others understood the benefit of offering their respect to the new sheriff in town. If one had a gripe about something going on in the neighborhood, results were much more likely to be achieved by working through the social club than by going to the cops.

It wasn't long before the generous and eager-to-please John Gotti assumed the role of a modern-day Robin Hood in Ozone Park. When the law failed them, the locals often turned to Johnny Boy; if traditional justice was not forthcoming, then street justice would suffice. Ironically, the NYPD's 106th Precinct headquarters was just a few blocks away, but was of little assistance to the Italian immigrants, who were near the bottom rung of the social ladder, and absorbed nearly as much racism and hostility as the few African Americans who resided in the overwhelmingly white community.

My father became a staunch advocate for the folks who lived near the new social club. If a man had a meddlesome neighbor, Dad stepped in and brokered the peace. If a few neighborhood punks had graffitied a storefront, Dad forced them to scrub it clean. And if a house was robbed or vandalized, Dad hunted down whoever was responsible and forced them to make restitution. Dad was no fool, and understood early on the importance of currying favor with the community. Just as he needed respect from the elders in his world to achieve his goals, he also needed support from the rank-and-file—the men and women who would do business in his neighborhood.

Word of the new social club quickly spread. People came from up to ten miles away to meet their newly anointed street boss. Most of the people who dropped in were hoping for an audience with my father; if so inclined, he might be able to help them with some problem in their lives, whether personal or financial. No dispute was too small or too large; the boss had free reign to intervene. Often, as a sign of his gratitude, Dad also bought cases of groceries and expensive cuts of meats and distributed these goods to all the neighbors in Ozone Park. Aside from being generous and considerate, Dad also did his fair share of campaigning, which would help him later on as he rose up even higher in the life.

There were perks to the position, of course. At holiday time, men from the neighborhood would express their gratitude to my father by dropping by with homemade pies and other delicacies that their wives, girlfriends, or mothers had baked. In exchange for their support, my father would throw a party every July 4, with enough free food, amusement park rides, soda, cotton candy, and entertainment for thousands of people; neighbors would invite family and friends from as far away as Staten Island and Manhattan. This event grew larger with each passing year, and featured one of the most impressive displays of fireworks in the metropolitan area, no small accomplishment given the challenge of securing the proper permits. Somehow, though, this never presented a problem for my father, perhaps because so many of the local cops chose to look the other way. As a general rule, they were more than willing to turn a blind eye to activities at the social club, especially where my father was concerned.

The July 4 bash was the talk of the town, from Brooklyn to the Bronx, and from Staten Island to Central Park. The turnout of revelers and spectators, whose numbers often included FBI agents in unmarked cars, taking notes and snapping photos, was astounding.

At one such celebration in the late 1970s, the fireworks display went awry. A man stationed on a nearby rooftop had accidentally dropped a lit cigarette into a box of explosives, setting the roof on fire. Flames spread quickly to a neighboring building.

Thankfully, the fire department responded swiftly and doused the fire in short order. The show ended prematurely with ambulances and cop cars flooding the area. After the fire department deemed the rooftop safe again, the police ordered the crowd of party revelers to vacate the premises. Many of the local residents grew angry and began yelling at the cops. There were no serious injuries, but my father was enraged. He ordered all his men from the social club to clear the streets and get all the people out of harm's way. The neighbors were understandably disappointed that their spectacular block party was brought to a premature end. Something had to be done with all the leftover food, so hundreds of families went home that night with fresh meats, salads, and supplies to fill up their cupboards.

The people of Ozone Park lined the streets that night and cheered my father as a hero. It was a watershed event for John Gotti, in many ways the beginning of his rise to prominence in popular culture, and the first indication that he was destined to become a formidable figure in the brutal, often unforgiving world of the Mafia.

CHAPTER EIGHT

"Havin' My Baby"

I t was the unpredictable and inciteful 1960s, and protest demonstrations cropped up everywhere. President John F. Kennedy had the unenviable task of leading the United States out of the Cuban Missile Crisis and would soon become embroiled in the abomination known as the Vietnam War. Elvis Presley still owned the pop charts. Meanwhile, on the lips of every neighborhood guy from Flatbush Avenue to Dean Street was the name of my father, John Gotti, who had just pulled off the biggest heist of his life. And it didn't take place in any bank, airport, or betting parlor, either. According to my father, the biggest "score" he ever made took place inside a hospital.

Inside, the corridors were empty and dark, and for a city hospital, they were surprisingly quiet. As Dad made his way down the hall, he spotted the nurses' station up ahead and came to an abrupt halt. He waited in the shadows until the nurses were busy and distracted. When the coast was clear he made a beeline for the elevator doors.

My father was headed back to the maternity ward. He'd been there just hours before, basking in the glory common to new fathers. But when the hospital's bursar dropped by

Mom's room with the bill, the glory had subsided and Dad broke out in a cold sweat. He was just twenty-two years old, and far too proud to admit he had no money or means to pay the tab. The memory of that tragic day when his own mother had given birth to a stillborn Gotti boy haunted his dreams; there was no way he would allow his wife to give birth at home—or anywhere other than a proper hospital. Whether he could pay the bill was beside the point; some things were not negotiable. So when Mom asked if the bill could be paid in installments and was told "no," my father had to come up with a plan.

DAD MADE HIS way to Mom's bed and stood there for a moment, watching her as she slept peacefully. Mom was surely exhausted. Years later, when told the story of this night and of my birth, Mom said she was so "out of it" that when hospital officials came around with my birth certificate, asking my name, Mom thought they needed her name and answered, "Victoria." My name was supposed to be Kimberly. Instead, I was named after my mother completely by accident.

Dad did not want to disturb her slumber, but time was of the essence. He had to move quickly—and quietly. He pulled the blankets off Mom's feet and tickled her big toe. She was startled at first, and tried to speak. Dad put a finger to his lips. He whispered for her to get dressed and then made his way to the nursery.

I was born at the perpetually understaffed Methodist Hospital in Brooklyn. Dad waltzed into the unguarded nursery, scooped me up like a football, and took off down the corridor. He made his way back to Mom's room and handed her their new daughter in a tightly wrapped bundle. Then he took her arm and gently led her out of the room and out the front door of the hospital.

Outside, an early winter storm was raging; blasts of arctic air cut through my mother's robe, chilling her to the bone. Uncle Angelo stood at the ready and helped my mother down the front steps. Dad, clutching me in his arms, followed closely behind. It would be a long and difficult trek home that night—thirteen blocks through slush and snow and freezing rain.

Mom and Dad were kids themselves when they were married. They were in their late teens when my sister, Angel, was born. I don't think it made much difference she was a girl, as the first child is always exciting. When I came along, baby number two, I'm sure Dad was disappointed. All he ever wanted was a son, an heir. This was common among Italian families—daughters were loved; sons were coveted. Moreover, male heirs signified greater virility and strength in the father. So, the more a man was prone to machismo, the more likely it was that he would wish for male progeny to pass along the family name and solidify his own legacy.

I suppose Dad was less than ecstatic when the doctor came into the labor and delivery waiting room and announced that his wife had delivered a baby girl—again! But his mood quickly lightened. He began telling me the story of my birth (and subsequent "kidnapping") when I was old enough to speak, never leaving one detail out. The story never veered; it was always the same: "When the doctor came out and announced I had another daughter, a part of me was disappointed—I will admit. But the moment I laid eyes on you, I fell instantly in love! You had the thickest patch of jet-black hair, the biggest hazel-green eyes, the cutest button nose, and the deepest cleft chin—my chin! You were a miniature Elizabeth Taylor. I couldn't wait to prance you up and down Prospect Park."

As he would tell this tale, Mom would nod in affirmation, adding that I was the spitting image of Dad. Not just in appearance, but in personality as well.

When we arrived at the railroad flat on Eighth Street, Dad placed me in a lopsided cradle and stood, staring and smiling, for the better part of a half hour. Years later, he would insist that we bonded instantly and forever during that walk through the snow.

"It was," he would say, "the most lucrative and memorable heist of my life."

CHAPTER NINE

"The Cat's in the Cradle"

wo years later, my father's wish came true: my mother gave birth again, this time to a boy. To the surprise of absolutely no one, the heir apparent was named after his father.

John Angelo Gotti was born on February 14, 1964, a date with no small amount of symbolism. My mother and father, of course, would stress the romantic notion that Junior's birth on Valentine's Day reflected their undying love. Others—historians and humorists (or humorous historians)—might point to the irony of John Gotti Jr., son of the most influential mobster in modern times, being born on February 14. It was the date of the St. Valentine's Day Massacre—when mobster Al Capone sanctioned the execution-style murders of several rival mobsters in a warehouse in Chicago.

My brother's arrival was a celebrated event both in the Gotti household and in the streets, where my father was, by this time, climbing the ladder of leadership, at least among his crew. The birth meant my father now had an heir, someone to follow in his footsteps—someone he could groom to take his place in the dark and dangerous underworld. It also gave him bragging rights, for as much as Dad strained to reassure his daughters that he would have been perfectly content to live in a household of women, there was never any doubt that my father longed for a son.

My mother, on the other hand, did nothing to hide her joy at the presence of John Junior. Mom was a self-described "boy mommy," a result, she said, of her own miserable upbringing. She truly believed that had she been born a male instead of a female, everything would have been different. Rather than pushing her aside, her parents would have wanted her and loved her, and maybe even stayed together as a family. This belief remained with my mother for years and undeniably impacted the way she raised my sister and me.

As a child, John was as ordinary as the next boy; at times rambunctious and hyperactive, at other times polite and well-behaved. He was showered with love and affection, treated special in a way that is unique to the firstborn male in Italian families. But it never went to his head. He was, for the most part, really grounded. From an early age, John was always the most popular boy in his grade; other children would gravitate toward him, vying for his attention and friendship. Even the older boys in the neighborhood wanted to hang out with John and his crowd.

It goes without saying that this made it quite difficult for me to have any male friends; once they were introduced to my brother, they chose his company over mine. This became something of a hindrance to me in my early teenage years, when I became interested in boys; my brother would never allow any friend of his to get close to his big sister. Angel was four years older than John, so her boyfriends were not threatened by her little brother, or even interested in him at all.

I learned that my brother would do two things to ensure that any boy who took an interest in me would disappear from my little life: one, he would befriend the boy, which permitted him access to my brother's popular group of neighborhood pals; two, he'd threaten the boy, telling the poor kid he couldn't have it both ways. If he wanted to be part of John's posse, then he would have to stay away from his sister. Those were the rules, and they were not negotiable. Not surprisingly, most boys chose John over me.

I'd often complain about this to my mother, sometimes to the point of crying. But John was her life, her obvious favorite, and he could do no wrong in her eyes. She'd try to appease me by saying something like, "It's probably for your own good, anyway."

It was during these teenage years that I'd come to resent my brother's obvious control over my life. Overnight, it seemed, we'd gone from being best pals and playmates to competitive siblings. And, for better or worse, it was also then that I began to see signs of my father's domineering personality surface in my brother.

Mom later gave birth to two more sons, Frankie and Peter, much to my father's delight. Having three sons made him proud as a peacock. Having two daughters also made him proud. He doted on each of us in his own special way, often playing up the special traits we possessed and doing his best to bring out the best in each of us. My sister Angel's special trait was her always easygoing personality. No matter what the circumstances, Angel was always happy. She could cheer you up during the most trying and difficult times. Dad called her affectionate names like "Sunshine" and "Miss Personality." Angel and I always got along as sisters. I rarely remember anything bigger than a spat between us. Of course, we fought over typical "sister issues" like borrowing a pair of shoes or a favorite sweater. But we always stayed close. Angel was just as tough as she was sweet, especially when it came to protecting my siblings or me. If anyone dared to push us around, she was always there to shield us. When it came to me, my father was most proud of how smart I was. In John, it was his leadership ability . . . in Frankie, his obvious dedication and love of sports . . . and later with Peter, his sensitivity.

Frankie was born October 15, 1967. Dad, of course, was thrilled to welcome his second son into the world. Frankie Boy, as we called him, was a sweet, kind, and giving child. He was exceptionally independent, as most middle children tend to be. He always managed to satisfy himself and rarely cried as an infant. Mom always remarked on "what a quiet and unselfish" baby he was. As a toddler, Frankie remained self-sufficient. He played well with other kids and Mom rarely had cause to go up to school or scold him. He had a few close buddies he'd often invite for sleepovers.

Even though he was a popular kid at school, he was extremely shy whenever he was around girls. Being "husky" always gave Frankie a complex. His fears and embarrassment stemmed from a bunch of ignorant and cruel kids who made fun of him, typical schoolyard bullying. It was the only hang-up my little brother had. Still, he was far from obese and he was handsome as hell. He had a head full of dark, thick curls; my siblings and I called him "Curly-Q." As beautiful as his hair was, he hated it. Any chance he'd get, he would beg Mom to take him to the barber for yet another haircut.

John and Frankie Boy were close in age and got along well. John would always take Frankie along on outings with his friends or to local neighborhood sporting events. Frankie loved sports, especially football, above all else in life. He was so determined to lose weight at a young age because he'd feared he would not be allowed to play sports when he got older.

By the early seventies my parents had a houseful of kids and were, by their standards, living "the American dream," though it had taken many difficult years to get to this point. They both always placed great importance on their children and our well-being. This was comforting to me and my siblings. Despite the fact that we were still considered lower class, and living in an apartment in Brooklyn, we had what money simply could not buy—a close-knit family.

From the time we were able to walk and talk, my parents taught each of us to look out for one another. "Blood is thicker than water" was instilled in each of us. As a result, we learned to set aside the usual issues accompanied with sibling rivalry, like jealousy and resentment, and strived to stand by each other—especially when Dad went away to jail.

CHAPTER TEN

"Leaving on a Jet Plane"

I have fond memories of growing up in Downtown Brooklyn. Although it was a predominantly Italian neighborhood, there was also a small Jewish community whose members ambitiously, and smartly, bought up numerous brownstones that would one day become some of the most prized real estate in the city. While the Italians generally stuck together, there were divisions even among this community.

The most obvious line separated them into two groups: those who were "legal" and those who weren't. Members of the latter camp were pejoratively referred to as "wops," and in many sections of New York, they occupied the lowest rung of the social ladder. "Wops" were resented and despised, and they routinely held the lowliest and most menial of jobs. In truth, these illegal Italian immigrants were paid so poorly that it was nearly impossible for them to support their families. To make ends meet, many of these men would take second jobs, often moonlighting for the local mobsters. To these men, this was not a question of ethics or morals; it was merely a question of survival. Hard physical labor during the day was followed by some type of criminal activity at night. The nighttime work often paid better than the daylight work. Most of these men did not think about the consequences of their actions; they did what they could to feed their families.

South Brooklyn—namely, the Prospect section of the neighborhood, running up and down Fifth Avenue—was filled with illegal Italians. Surprisingly enough, my family wasn't one of them. I'd found this out years later while researching the Gotti family tree. It seems my great-grandparents had taken the voyage from Italy to America on a ship from Naples. The couple settled in Little Italy with intentions of saving money and getting a place a bit farther from the bustle of the city. Eventually they chose the Mount Vernon section of the Bronx—and for practical purposes ended up in Downtown Brooklyn.

South Brooklyn was lined with stores catering to their Italian constituency. The aroma wafting from these vendors filled the air; food was never far from an Italian's mind. Fresh bread, pizza, and pastries were all around us. An assortment of cured meats and aged cheeses hung in the windows. Money was scarce for us, and we couldn't buy nearly as much as we wanted, but sometimes it was enough simply to walk down the street and take in the aroma.

Social clubs, too, were popular and prevalent. Men with crisp suits and shiny pinkie rings hung out there all day. On nice days they'd play cards outside all day and well into the night. You could hear them telling jokes; you could watch them conduct business. These were the men—not the cops or lawyers or shopkeepers—who garnered the most respect. And everyone who passed by had the good sense to acknowledge their place in the neighborhood hierarchy.

Some of these clubs were bars. Being a curious child, I often wondered why these bars would be open so early in the morning. As I got older, I began to understand that these clubs were hang-outs, not legitimate places of business.

Often, we'd find my father sitting outside one of the clubs, talking to these men. After a quick hello, Dad would send us on our way. From the earliest age, my father kept his worlds separate. Work was kept in one place, family in another. In his opinion, those two worlds were not to intersect. But the fact of the matter is this: Brooklyn—especially Downtown Brooklyn—was considered Mafia territory. If you were Italian and lived there, it was presumed that you were in "the life," as it was known. Even now, some thirty years later, when people hear Brooklyn, a great many of them immediately think Mafia.

My siblings and I rarely went inside these social clubs or bars. On one occassion, I remember my father taking us to the New York Aquarium. It was the end of summer—Dad wanted to spend some extra time with us before school started again in September. Earlier that week, he'd taken my sister and me shopping for school clothes. Because we were poor, it was really the only time we ever got new clothes. I remember Dad clumsily navigating his way around the girls' section in Macy's department store. Usually, Mom did all of our shopping—but Dad got lucky the night before and won four hundred dollars on a horse race. He couldn't wait to take us on a shopping spree. Normally, because we were poor, we weren't the best-dressed kids at school—but we weren't the worst, either. The embarrassment Dad once faced, the mean and ugly names the other classmates called him and his siblings because they were shabbily dressed, remained fresh in his memory. As a result, he was more conscious of the way his own kids dressed. Mostly, because we had so little money, Mom made most of our clothes by hand. She used discounted bolts of fabric and an old sewing machine. On our way to the aquarium that day, John and I were dressed in matching red, white, and blue shorts that Mom had made for us earlier in the week. We all piled into the backseat of Dad's dark brown Cadillac, and along the way he had to make a stop at one of the bars on Knickerbocker. My brother John and I waited in the car, and when Dad came out a few minutes later we complained that we had to use the bathroom. Reluctantly, Dad took us inside the dimly lit bar. Everything seemed so dark—the walls, floors, tables, and chairs. There were a few men in the back playing a game of cards and when they saw me and my brother, they immediately began smiling and scooping up tens and twenties, and handing them over to us. Dad was livid. No kid of his would ever be allowed to accept money, not even from a few made guys and wannabes who were just trying to show off in front of my dad.

"Say hello and be polite," he quietly instructed us. "But give them back their money."

Then he turned and cordially thanked the older men, adding, "It's not necessary." I went to the bathroom, a dirty, closet-sized space with toilet paper all over the floor. I washed my hands three times before leaving. My brother used the men's room and then begged Dad for a Coke. Dad gave in.

And that's when the trouble began.

There was a young platinum blonde behind the bar, a

cocktail waitress. She was wearing hot-pink shorts, a small white T-shirt, panty hose, and stiletto heels. My brother took it all in without saying a word—until we got home that evening, when Mom asked about the aquarium, and whether we had fun. My brother was more interested in telling her about the "lady named Bunny who kept flirting with Daddy." And predictably, a major fight ensued. I remember them screaming at each other, Mom telling Dad to "get out."

My siblings and I cowered in the back bedroom for nearly an hour, sensing things were about to get uglier.

I remember Dad made his way to the hallway, near the front door of our railroad flat, as if he was tired of arguing and was leaving to let Mom cool off. The next thing I knew, Mom had heaved a large fork from the kitchen to where Dad was standing ten feet away. Incredibly, the fork ripped into Dad's right shoulder.

We were all stunned. There was blood everywhere. Mainly, though, I remember the look of complete shock on my father's face. I don't know whether it was the pain or the sight of his own blood that bothered him most, or the fact that his wife had done this to him. But it was clear that he was stunned. Quickly, though, he removed the fork. Then he ripped off his shirt, revealing an impressive gash. This naturally provoked shrieks of terror from my sister, Angel, and me.

"Daddy's hurt!" my sister screamed. "Oh, God, Mommy killed Daddy!"

Even my mother was floored. She stood frozen at the kitchen sink, not knowing what to do. My father, standing in the hallway outside my bedroom, instinctively reached for something to cover the cut and stop the bleeding.

Imagine my shock when I realized he had grabbed the new plaid dress he'd bought me just days ago. I was so proud and excited that I'd had it laid out on my dresser, next to my new marble notebooks, and a new pair of black-and-white saddle shoes. Of course, I was afraid Dad was hurt, but I couldn't help crying over my new favorite dress after we'd learned Dad was fine. It was the first day of school, and I had nothing else to wear. Being poor will teach you things like that.

The drama escalated when Uncle Angelo arrived. He came thundering up the stairs of the apartment building. He and Aunt Marie lived two floors down and word spread quickly that there was a dispute going on in our apartment. The entire flat was like a battlefield, complete with wounded combatants and terrified onlookers.

The moment Uncle Angelo saw Dad holding the dress over his shoulder—blood-soaked and still dripping down his back—he, too, started screaming. "What the hell did you do to him?" he shouted at my mother. "Why? Why? Why?"

Uncle Angelo gave my mother a final dirty look and rushed my father out of the apartment and to the hospital. My siblings and I sat shivering from the shock, unable to speak or move. Mom, of course, quickly became remorseful. I know she didn't mean to hurt my father, but her anger got the better of her. Exhausted and teary-eyed, she quietly sent us off to bed, feebly trying to assure us that "Daddy will be all right." She told us he'd be home in an hour or so and that by morning, all of this would be just a bad memory.

I don't think any of us actually slept that night. My sister and I shared the room just past the front door of the apartment. All night we waited for Dad's return. We wanted him clean and free of blood. We wanted everything to be back to normal.

It was light out by the time he finally came home. Bandages were easily visible through his white T-shirt, and we later learned that a dozen stitches were required to close the wound. Dad didn't say much when he walked through the door; he gave us each a little pat on the head, smiled, and then retreated to his bedroom to sleep. And, no, he never brought the blood-soaked dress back. My sister, Angel, teased me for days over this.

There were too many episodes and blowups between Mom and Dad to count. And not all of them ended badly or in bloodshed. Some were so funny that I laugh out loud just thinking about them. Like the time Dad came walking in at 6 A.M. after an all-night card game. He was drunk and stumbled into bed, and passed out a minute or two later. Mom couldn't argue with him if she tried. Dad waited till noon before leaving the house again. Mom usually left around 11 A.M. to run errands each day, so Dad did the best he could to avoid a run-in with her. Mom was so angry when she returned later that day and learned that Dad had already left. To get back at him, she called a local moving company and arranged for Dad's things to be delivered to the social club. Around 9 P.M., the movers knocked on the door and told one of the guys hanging around that there was a delivery for John Gotti. Everyone in the club, including Dad, was perplexed. Dad went from being surprised to stunned as the men unloaded a tall, wooden armoire filled with all of his clothes and left it on the sidewalk in front of the club.

Then there was the time Mom and Aunt Marie decided to spy on Dad and Uncle Angelo. The men were inside the club, playing cards. Mom and Aunt Marie were hiding behind a parked car across the street. After waiting for nearly an hour, the two women grew frustrated. They had hoped to see something telling, like perhaps some strange girls talking to their husbands. But that night, nothing went on but the usual, boring card game. So for spite, Aunt Marie picked up a brick and hurled it at the club's front window. Within seconds the men inside hit the floor! They assumed they were under attack from a rival crew. Mom and Aunt Marie hightailed it down the avenue and back up to the apartment. Dad never found out that it was Mom and Aunt Marie.

One of the funniest episodes occurred while Mom was learning how to drive. Dad was very old-fashioned and he didn't believe women should drive. Mom signed up at a local driving school without my father knowing. Unfortunately for her, the instructor was always drunk—so she didn't get much help from him. This was evident when Mom and Aunt Marie decided to steal Uncle Angelo's car. He had come home just before midnight and it was obvious Angelo had a lot to drink. After he'd passed out on the bed, the two women swiped his keys and went joyriding around Brooklyn. But Mom was an inept motorist and managed to sideswipe another car—twice. When Mom and Aunt Marie returned home, they were careful to park the car in the exact same spot. The next morning, Uncle Angelo was cursing and screaming outside the apartment building. But because he was so drunk the night before, he assumed *he'd* gotten into an accident. Little did Mom or Aunt Marie know that he'd actually borrowed the car from Uncle Pete, Dad's older brother. For the next twenty-five years, Uncle Angelo and Uncle Pete argued over that car. Both men never knew it was Mom and Aunt Marie who were actually responsible.

I'd like to say that Mom and Dad somehow found a way to express their love while keeping their disputes to a minimum. But that was simply not the case. I witnessed many fights as a child, some more vigorous than others. Most of the disagreements arose from my mother's dissatisfaction with the late hours my father kept, or the places he frequented, or the people he was with (these three things were all linked, of course). As an adult, I can now say that I understand what my mother must have felt—life was very hard for her. At the time, however, I was more sympathetic to Dad; most of us were. We could not understand why Mom was always yelling, or why she seemed to instigate the fighting. To our young and naïve eyes, Dad seemed to be the victim, and Mom the abuser. How were we to know that her anger was justified?

After each fight or argument, my siblings and I would always have the same talk: "If Mom and Daddy get a divorce, who would you want to live with?" The very thought of it—that our family could be ripped apart—used to make me cry. It was usually my sister, Angel, who orchestrated this conversation, as she was not only the oldest child in the family, but a realist as well.

During my early childhood in Brooklyn, life consisted of Dad trying to hustle a dollar and Mom doing her best around the house to stretch whatever income they had. The fighting continued, of course, ebbing and flowing throughout the years. In good economic times, they fought less; when money was particularly tight, the bickering escalated. In time, my siblings and I grew accustomed to the roller-coaster ride. When you are young and impressionable, and your favorite television shows are *The Brady Bunch* and *Little House on the Prairie*, you expect your own family life to mirror those of the people you see on TV. I really wanted a perfect family—whatever that was. I wanted a mother in the kitchen, smiling and baking apple pies, and a father who worked nine to five and never went away to jail.

Even when Mom would reach the point of exasperation and take off on one of her "excursions," as we called her time away from Dad when we got older, we were less fearful and traumatized. Experience had taught us that eventually—probably in just a matter of days—she would cool off and return. Sometimes, if one of Mom's absences stretched out over a week or two, I would turn to Dad for reassurance. He would always smile and announce rhetorically, "Can a man *ever* really lose his family?"

There was such wisdom in those words, and he delivered them with such authority. It wasn't until I was much older that I came to learn the source of that sentiment. It wasn't something my father had dreamed up. Oh, no. Nothing like that.

They were spoken by Michael Corleone in *The Godfather*.

CHAPTER ELEVEN

"I'll Always Love My Mama"

To some extent, most women of my mother's era discovered that when they married a man, they also married his career. For some women, of course, this was not a problem. But when your husband's career involves a significant amount of illegal activity, things can get a little more complicated.

Contrary to most published accounts, my mother was not fond of this thing called *La Cosa Nostra*. She would tell us years later that she always lived in fear that one day there would be a knock at the door, and she would have to greet one of my father's close friends or associates and try to make him feel comfortable as he delivered the crushing news that her husband had been arrested or, worse, killed.

"When I met your father, I was a young, impressionable, and naïve girl. Like anyone else who met him, I fell enormously and immediately in love with his looks and his personality."

Considering her background, this response was understandable. A young girl from Brooklyn was programmed practically from birth to find a man who was like a father figure: strong, handsome, and proud; a man who would care for her and provide for her. And yet, Mom was not shy about voicing her displeasure with Dad's business and lifestyle, and indeed most of their disagreements in some way were sparked by her disapproval. But back then, the number one priority was feeding her kids and paying the bills.

Oddly enough, as she would discover, there was money in her family—she just didn't have access to it.

Mom and Dad had been together for nearly two years when her biological father, my grandfather, began coming around.

My father by this time was already nurturing a reputation on the streets. He was tough and capable—a man on the rise in the mob ranks. He could make things happen, go away, or be settled with just a few words during an appointment. My grandfather, whom I never really knew, wanted to be a part of my mother's life; he also wanted to spend time with his grandchildren. But with all of this came, by necessity, a relationship with my father. That would prove to be a challenge. When Mom realized Dad was "Mr. Right," she'd brought him around to meet her family. My grandfather was not pleased with her choice in men and let Mom know it. He told her in so many words not to bring "this punk from Brooklyn" to his house ever again. Except, of course, when my grandfather needed John Gotti.

I never trusted my mother's father, especially since his wife had such obvious distaste for my mother. This was evident in the few get-togethers we did have over the years. With my "grandparents" came two aunts, Mary-Beth and "Little Della," and one uncle, John. The two aunts were attractive blondes. Uncle John was also blond and very tall. He was so tall, I always thought of the Jolly Green Giant each time I saw him—in other words, he was frightening to me as a child. Both women would openly flirt with my father, a display of affection that disturbed both my sister and me. We found their behavior appalling, even though we were kids and we couldn't quite articulate our feelings. We also wondered why Mom seemed so oblivious to it. I couldn't figure out if Mom was just so happy to feel wanted by the family she never knew that she was willing to overlook the inappropriate advances of her half-sisters, or whether she just didn't notice.

One night my grandfather invited us to his home, a palatial spread in Port Chester, New York. He was the owner of one of the top contracting firms in New York and was doing quite well for himself. I remember the long drive from Brooklyn, and the feeling of excitement the moment we pulled off the exit to their neighborhood. It was a different world from where we lived, that's for sure. I was utterly amazed by the sight of their property: a three-acre spread with a sprawling two-story home.

As we walked to the front door, Mom wore an expression of pride, an expression that seemed to say, *This is my lineage, this is where I really come from.*

My father's face said something else completely. Actually, it said nothing at all. Dad would never let anyone feel as though they were superior to him, so he put on his best poker face.

Inside, my grandfather greeted my father with a martini, as two or three staff members dressed in white scurried about the mansion, taking coats and preparing dinner. For me, it was surreal—I thought only movie stars, or characters in movies, lived this way. I'd never seen anything like it. The foyer was vast, with glistening black granite floors. There was a long hallway to an even larger space, the family room, we were told. There was a pair of leather couches—one red, one black—a bearskin rug, a baby grand piano, and floor-to-ceiling windows; a sliding-glass door opened to a brick patio, and an in-ground swimming pool. I had never seen an in-ground pool before. We had a plastic twelve-inch tub in our backyard. The "pool" (if you could call it that) only served to cool us off in the hot summer heat. Years later we had many a laugh remembering that pool—as Angel, having quite a vivid imagination, managed to convince most of the neighbors' kids that the plastic tub was in fact a built-in pool. She'd told everyone the pool only looked "small and shallow." But once you got in you were under nearly four feet of water. The neighbors' kids would step into the pool and not see or feel any difference. "You have to sit and stay put," Angel would say. "And then you'll see the difference." She was so convincing, the other kids believed it was a built-in pool. My sister had that way about her—she was so kind and generous and sincere that you couldn't help but believe everything she said. That day at my grandparents' house, when Angel saw the pool, she leaned into me and whispered, "Wow, imagine what the kids from Brooklyn would say if they saw this pool?"

WE WERE SO excited! Naturally we were eager to go for a swim. It was nearly ninety degrees outside and the sun was still out. But no one extended the invitation (and my father wasn't about to ask). Clearly, the intention was for us to look, but not touch.

When we finally sat down for dinner, my grandfather was cordial; my step-grandmother was not. After all, she hardly knew us. We felt like the outcasts she considered us to be. And her daughters were equally dismissive and condescending. They were flirtatious toward Dad and treated Mom with an apparent act of phoniness. My siblings and I were one step short of invisible.

After a few hours, while the adults were busying themselves with cocktails and chatter in the billiards room (I couldn't believe the rooms actually had names), I was bored beyond belief. One of the staff took me by the hand and showed me my aunt's closet, which was filled with old toys—mostly beautiful Barbie dolls. For me—a poor kid from Brooklyn—it was like a trip to FAO Schwartz. The woman took down a bunch of dolls and some costumes and told me I could play on the kitchen floor while she worked. I was as happy as could be—until my aunt Della, who was a good ten years older than I was, entered the room and saw me. She was with a few of her girlfriends, and they stopped right in front of me and stared in disbelief.

She started screaming like I'd hit her in the face. She called for her mother and then, like a child, began scooping up the dolls. She collected them quickly and put everything back in the closet. Then she turned to the housekeeper and screamed, "How dare you let *her* touch *my* dolls!" I will never forget the way she embarrassed me that day.

Aunt Della acted as if I'd been carrying some sort of infectious disease—as if some of my shabbiness and poverty might wear off on the dolls and perhaps she might be infected with something when she touched them. Everyone in the house heard her yelling and came running into the kitchen, deepening my humiliation. I remember my mother just glaring at Della, her half-sister.

My father wasn't nearly as proper or restrained. He took my grandfather into the billiards room and let him have it. Apparently, just minutes before my aunt's tirade, my grandfather had done a bit of showing off himself. In front of one of his neighbors, whom he'd invited for drinks, he got a little drunk and stupidly passed a comment—something along the lines of "All I know, Johnny Boy, is this: you better treat my daughter well or there will be consequences." It was as if Mom had brought Dad home to meet her parents for the first time. Grandpa was trying hard to play the role of concerned father. It was a little too late for that as far as Dad was concerned. My grandfather had had his chance years ago to be gracious and concerned—and he blew it.

My grandfather had delivered this line while showing off a rifle from his collection. For added effect, he'd pointed the rifle in Dad's direction, aiming the tip straight at his heart.

When Dad grabbed Grandpa, he made sure Grandpa's neighbor and friend was privy to what was about to happen. Then he shouted, "First of all, if your daughter ever yells at my daughter again, I'll hand you your tongue on one of your fancy silver platters. Secondly, if you ever call me Johnny Boy again, it *will* be the last time. My name is Johnny—not Johnny Boy. And lastly, the next time you aim a gun at me, you'd better make sure you kill me, because I *will* kill you!"

My grandfather was both stunned and terrified. Our visit ended shortly thereafter, and we drove home listening to Mom and Dad bickering about what went wrong.

"We shouldn't have come—period!" Dad shouted. "Even after all these years, they haven't changed one bit. These people never wanted you when you were younger— what would make you think they'd want you now?"

This last remark deeply wounded my mother, and she began to cry. Predictably, the tears had a calming effect on Dad. Even at his angriest, he had trouble dealing with Mom's tears. And so, in a much softer tone, he said, "Don't you know what this invite was all about? Your father has a problem with one of the unions—something about a job he put in a bid for." He paused, letting the words sink in. "He used you," Dad continued. "He used both of us. He went through you to get to me, in the hope that I could somehow help him win the bid."

Hearing this made my stomach turn, but it didn't come as a surprise. I never knew that side of the family, never remembered them coming around on holidays or birthdays. They were never included at family functions, like baptisms and graduations, and I grew up without any sense of their place in our lives.

ODDLY ENOUGH, NOT more than a few weeks later my mother received an unexpected call from her mother. After apologizing profusely for being absent for so many years, saying, "I just couldn't locate you, my dear daughter," Grandma announced that she was coming to visit.

Mom naturally had mixed emotions about this impending encounter. She wept openly; whether they were tears of joy, sadness, surprise, or anger, I haven't any idea. But whatever she might have felt, it was not enough to prevent her from accepting Grandma's overture, and they agreed to meet the following week.

Grandma had told Mom that she was still living in Manhattan—above a bar, appropriately enough, since Grandma loved her booze. This made Mom laugh, but it did nothing to quell her anxiety. She was a nervous wreck over the next several days, constantly cleaning and straightening and preparing. She made sure the furniture was dusted, the windows cleaned, the rugs vacuumed. Even Mom's appearance was different: she got all dressed up, in an effort to impress her mother.

When my grandmother finally arrived, she presented each of her grandchildren with a small plastic toy. There was no logic to the choice of gifts—it seemed as though she had just grabbed a handful. I really don't think she even knew how many grandchildren she actually had. Dinner was one of Mom's finest: roast beef, rosemary potatoes, homemade cornbread, and a salad. Dad stayed home and joined us, despite the fact that it was Wednesday, the night he ordinarily played cards with the boys at the neighborhood social club.

There was little talk during dinner, mostly just a lot of nervous fidgeting, accompanied by the sound of silverware clanking against plates. No one knew what to say. I'd never met this woman before, and so I tried to reconcile the photos Mom had shown us—photos of a much younger woman with long blond hair and big expressive eyes—with the much older, more haggard woman now seated at our dinner table. The years of hard living had taken their toll. The distended belly, the jaundiced skin, the capillaries snaking across her nose—all were visible signs of a serious addiction to alcohol.

As was always the custom in our house when adult guests came to visit, children were expected to make themselves scarce after dinner. Mom would politely say something like, "Okay, guys, it's time to do your homework."

Of course, my sister and I quickly did our homework and changed into our nightgowns. Our room was in the basement, so we snuck upstairs and listened to the "adult" conversation coming from the kitchen. Even though we were young, we understood what was going on. Grandma was in trouble. She needed help, just like Grandpa did. This time it had nothing to do with any union. Grandma needed money—lots of it. Ten thousand dollars, to be precise.

Ten grand was, in those days, an enormous amount of money—certainly much more than the Gottis had lying around at their disposal.

Still, Dad could never say no to anyone. Somehow he managed to raise the money; Mom guessed he'd borrowed it. When my mother questioned him as to why he gave my grandmother the money when it was clear that she had no intentions of paying it back, Dad just smiled.

"So be it. It wouldn't be the first time I've been stiffed."

To this day, Mom doesn't know whether he did it to impress my grandmother, or because he sincerely wanted to help her. I think Dad kind of liked Grandma—he'd always tell us that he got a kick out of her, and that he'd thought of her as "a real broad." He meant it affectionately. Also, Dad believed what was done to my mother as a child was more her father's fault than her mother's. Dad believed if my grandfather had bigger balls, he would have stood up to his parents and married my grandmother instead of running like a louse. I believe Dad felt sorry for Faye and wanted to help her.

I also believe it was more about pride than anything else. My father's inability to turn down anyone—particularly a relative, even one of questionable character—combined with an insatiable need to look like a big shot at times left him holding the proverbial bag. Grandmother had told Dad she needed the money for unpaid bills, but it was no secret that she also liked to gamble. Even as a kid, I was willing to bet the ten grand was to pay off a gambling debt.

My mother was crushed by the way this entire affair unfolded. She had foolishly, perhaps romantically, believed that my grandmother's intentions were good. My mom had fantasized about this reunion for years, dreamt of the day she would reconcile with her mother, and they would laugh and cry and hug. All would be forgiven.

Instead, she came away even angrier and more disillusioned than she had been in the past. My grandmother, just like my grandfather, reached out for one reason only: because she needed a favor. When Dad was young and wild, both grandparents disapproved of him. However, years later, when they needed his help, Dad was a wonderful guy. They knew he was in the mob, and that he had access to whatever they might need, favors or financing. In my grandparents' eyes, this was neither a liability nor a cause for concern; rather, my father's deepening foothold in a life of crime presented them with an opportunity. He was connected. He could help them.

I was just a little girl, but I could see all of this taking shape before my eyes, and I found it sad. Mainly, I just felt for my mother. Once again, both of her parents had let her down and broken her heart, and as young as I was it crushed me.

Mom was so hurt that she walked around in a fog for weeks. She'd been used by her mother and father. I can't imagine how she must have felt.

In the end, my father helped them both. He had honorable reasons for his behavior.

"It only makes the two of them look like bigger pieces of shit," Dad explained to me at the time. "After all they've done to your mother, we are *still* willing to help them out. It only makes her stronger and them weaker. It shows what kind of people they really are."

Dad was a complicated man, and sometimes it was difficult to comprehend the reasons for his behavior. Certainly he was compelled to perform acts of generosity. But he also craved power, and one of the ways to gain power over someone is to perform favors on their behalf. This was a big one for my father, and he knew that my grandparents would forever be in his debt—exactly where Dad wanted them.

CHAPTER TWELVE

"Bad, Bad Leroy Brown"

I was seven years old when I realized that my father was not like other dads. We were still living in Brooklyn, and unfortunately our financial situation hadn't changed much. Dad repeatedly tried in vain to find a legitimate business opportunity; not so much because he had any ethical problem with being in the Mafia, but simply because he wanted to please his wife and provide his children with a sense of security. Anyone in the life knows that at any moment he could be whisked off to prison and separated from his family for a very long period of time; it comes with the territory.

Dad considered a few business opportunities that friends had brought to him. But let's face it: there weren't a lot of well-paying, respectable employment opportunities for a poor man from Dean Street. In addition to lacking a formal education, Dad had no particular skill or trade. He'd never been taught how to paint or lay carpet or pour concrete. These were the jobs usually reserved for wops . . . grease balls . . . oil monkeys.

Dad tried to hide from his children the fact that he didn't have a conventional job. There were various fabrications, the most common being his role as the powerful head of a local construction company. In fact, every day when he left for "work," at the oddly late hour of 10 or 11 A.M., he would tell us about some new project he was developing: a skyscraper one month, a three-story beach house or a suite of offices the next month. I remember how he used to bounce me on his knee and answer all of my silly questions about the construction trade.

I was fascinated with creativity—more specifically, building things from scratch. I was quite impressionable and for the most part believed just about anything Dad would tell me. For the longest time it never occurred to me to ask my father why he always wore a suit when he was going off to a construction site. I think back on it now and laugh at the notion of Dad ten stories up, checking out I-beams in his sharkskin suit, Merino wool turtleneck, and Italian leather shoes. He couldn't possibly have looked more out of place.

IT CAME AS no surprise that my father was considered the Pied Piper of the neighborhood. Every morning when Dad left for "work," most of the neighborhood kids would gather around the front yard and wait for him to emerge. Sure, it had something to do with the fact that Dad always treated the kids to ice cream, but after a few months of chocolate cones and Italian ices, it was apparent that they were even more impressed with Dad and his obvious charm than they were with his generosity. He'd walk out of the house, chat with the kids as if he were one of their peers, tell jokes, even roughhouse with the boys a little bit. He was incredibly charismatic. I don't really know of anyone who met him and came away unimpressed by his charm. It became a standing joke in our family that Dad was such a charming gentleman that even law enforcement officers swooned in his presence. And as with any joke, it contained a grain of truth. On more than one occasion, detectives were sent to the home to question Dad. Rather than take the house by storm, as they often did when dealing with prominent Mafia figures, law enforcement officials always treated my father with great respect and consideration, often waiting outside until Dad was ready to chat. I used to think it was because my father was so tough—I thought even the cops feared him. But as the years passed and I became more aware of things, I realized that their behavior had less to do with fear than respect, maybe even admiration.

Women, too, were captivated. My father, in general, mesmerized every female who crossed his path. Sure, he had movie-star looks, but anyone who met him understood that it was his old-fashioned charm and sex appeal that was most attractive.

Even the librarian at the Brooklyn Public Library fell under his spell. The moment Dad walked into the library— a mammoth building near Prospect Park on Flatbush Avenue—she nearly lost her breath. Dad would take me there weekly, until I was able to cross the street myself and began sneaking out to the library whenever I could. It was then, around the age of eight, that I decided my passion in life was to become a writer. The smell of the library, of the old leather-bound books, enlivened me. Even the feel of those old books made me so happy. I couldn't wait to grow up and write a book myself. Part of this, I suppose, stemmed from my father's constant chattering about the need for education, "in both areas: academics and street-smarts," he'd say.

Dad told me that although college wasn't a necessity for a young woman (he held the old-fashioned belief that marrying someone acceptable—a man of wealth and power— was still a viable path to a better life), attaining education, to the highest degree possible, was a worthy goal for anyone, and would only serve to make a woman more attractive and self-sufficient. Dad was something of a walking, talking paradox in this regard: generally speaking, he believed women had no place in the work world. That was for men only. But when it came to his daughters, well, the rules were different.

"Nothing is beyond your reach," he used to tell me. And I believed him.

Thanks in part to my father, I developed quite the affinity for reading. I could easily devour two or three books a week, most from the local library. At the time, I was too young to acquire my own library card, but when the librarian realized I was the girl who had accompanied the handsome, dark-haired John Gotti, she was more than happy to bend the rules. I could borrow any book I wanted, without ever having to worry about late fees.

CHAPTER THIRTEEN

"Tie a Yellow Ribbon"

I don't remember Dad leaving, and years later I came to believe that he left in the middle of the night because he didn't want to face us. I was only seven years old when I learned that my father went to jail. Until this point, and even after, my parents tried as hard as they could to keep my siblings and me sheltered from the harsh realities of my father's line of work.

It wasn't the first time Dad went away. My father had spent only a short time in jail after being arrested for several petty crimes as a young man. The judge took into consideration Dad's youth and his comparatively unthreatening rap sheet, which consisted of mostly low-level, nonviolent crimes like public intoxication and petty larceny. He was also married and had young children to support.

There was, however, a misunderstanding over whether he had evaded military service, which might have factored into the judge's decision. The fact was, my father simply hadn't registered for the draft, figuring that he was exempt on several counts. For one thing, he was a new father; for another, the cement mixer mishap many years earlier had cost him two toes and several broken bones in his legs, which would have precluded his passing a physical examination. So when he was questioned about why he "dodged the draft," the answers he gave were deemed satisfactory and the allegations soon disappeared.

Over the next few years, though, my father began to amass a far more impressive résumé. Accounts of this period of my parents' lives often point to my mother's father as being the savior of the family. Nothing could be further from the truth. Even in these difficult times, Mom's relationship with her parents remained frayed and tense. Although my grandfather lived a very comfortable life, I can honestly say that I have no recollection of him ever helping our family—or even offering to help. In fact, it was always the other way around.

And yet, according to FBI reports, my grandfather supposedly bought us a house and took care of the bills while my father was away. Not true. Dad would never accept a dime from anyone, in particular his father-in-law.

As A LITTLE girl, my father was my hero. He could do no wrong in my eyes. Maybe that's why, with Dad sentenced to three years in prison, Mom opted to tell us that Dad was going away on business, to "a new job, building the biggest building ever." Just like Dad, she didn't think it wise if we were there to see him off, so instead we all said our goodbyes after dinner the night before. Mom made a special meal of lasagna and roast beef.

I remember that time like it was yesterday. I hugged my father for dear life because I was scared I'd never see him again. When he told us he was going away for work, it did little to calm my fears. Even when he said that his "boss left him no choice," I was still upset with him. I wanted him home so he could take me to the park, the aquarium, and the movies—but mostly, I wanted him home so I could prance him up and down the block in front of the other kids.

I went to bed angry that night—and woke up even angrier the next morning. Mom could say little to calm me. I wouldn't speak for days. My frustration grew when we couldn't visit Dad for the first few months he was away because of inmate orientation, which of course I didn't know at the time. So I wrote him every day and usually received a return card two or three times a week. In the most beautiful penmanship, he always wrote the same message: "Be sure and help Mama. This is a very hard time for her. I love you. Love, Dad."

He was right. It was indeed a *very* hard time for Mom.

THE WEATHER CHANGED from warm to cold, and winter was rearing its ugly head the day I learned how to use food stamps. My mother did her usual grocery shopping every Saturday. She'd lug my siblings and me down to the A&P on Knickerbocker Avenue. The routine was always the same—Mom pushed one wagon, with Frank strapped in the front seat, while my sister and I took turns pushing the second wagon, with my brother John strapped in the front. We always began at the dairy aisle and worked our way up and down the other aisles, gathering only the essentials. Before Dad left, going food shopping with Mom was an errand we all enjoyed. She let us race up and down the aisles filling the wagons with the usual foods and supplies. Milk, eggs, bread, cereal, and if we behaved, she let us each choose a small box of cookies. But now that Dad was gone, Mom let us know we couldn't afford as much. It was one of the earlier signs that we were no longer lower class. Overnight, it seemed, we were back to being dirt poor and things were only getting worse.

One time Mom stood on line at the cashier and when it was her turn, she put the groceries on the conveyor belt. When all our items were rung up, Mom realized she didn't have enough cash on her. She was mortified and didn't know what to do. Mom eyed the woman behind the register and asked if she could write a check. The woman answered in a nasty tone, "We don't accept checks." Reluctantly, Mom reached inside her wallet and pulled out a book of food stamps. Although she had had them for almost a week, she had been too embarrassed and too proud to use them. She handed the cashier the book and looked around to see if anyone she knew was watching. Then the woman behind the register did the unthinkable. She reached for the microphone and yelled, "Food stamp customer at register three!" I thought Mom was going to faint. Her eyes filled with tears as she packed each brown bag with the groceries.

I WAS IN THE third grade and had one of the meanest teachers, Mrs. Murphy. She was a sixty-year-old, heavyset woman with a helmet of bleached-blond hair and the most frightening black eyes I'd ever seen. Being painfully shy was one of my shortcomings. I was always a very nervous kid—at least that's what my mother always said. And in those days I looked like a geek—I wore colorful plastic rhinestone-trimmed glasses, had skinny knock-knees, and was a straight "A" student. Put all that together and you had the makings of a colossal nerd!

One rainy October morning, I came to school with my latest assignment, an essay on who my hero was. We were expected to read our reports in front of the class that day. As you can imagine, I was beyond terrified.

I remember telling Mrs. Murphy a white lie—something about having an upset stomach. But she wasn't sympathetic. I made it through the first page of my report, stuttering and stopping most of the way. Of course, my hero was my dad and I wrote about the wonderful man he was and the wonderful job he had "building skyscrapers and office buildings in faraway places." All of the kids were fascinated—all except Ethyl Eden.

Ethyl had apparently been listening to her parents at dinnertime discussing the neighborhood gossip, and one juicy bit of news was that my father had gone to jail recently. So Ethyl—a spoiled and privileged girl from Ninety-fourth Street—yelled out that my report was a lie. She went on to tell the class that my father was *not* away building houses, he was actually "in jail."

I was devastated and heartbroken. A million questions raced through my head. *Was my father really in jail?* I stood still—absolutely frozen. I couldn't move or speak. I remember the kids' expressions going from shock to laughter, then the sound of their loud cackles drowned out any questions in my mind. They were staring at the floor around my shoes, at the puddle of yellow liquid I was standing in. I remember crying and shaking. But what I remember most was that the teacher, Mrs. Murphy, did nothing. She didn't even move to quiet the other students. All she did was stare in disbelief at the yellow puddle around me. A minute or two later she began yelling. She told me I was "a crybaby and belonged back in kindergarten." I looked at her with pleading eyes and asked if I could go to the bathroom. She said no—and forced me to clean the floor. Believe it or not, the old witch made me get the mop and clean up the mess, while the other students whispered, pointed, and laughed.

During lunch I found a place behind the handball court where I could sit alone. I hid from the other kids and cried.

After the three o'clock bell rang, I walked to the corner and crossed the street. I walked up the steps of the tiny attached house we lived in and headed straight for the bathroom to take a bath. My mother realized something was wrong right away. It was hard enough getting us to take a bath after dinner at night, and yet I was taking one in the middle of the afternoon?

I told her what had happened—every last detail. We both cried when she explained why she had lied about my father: "to protect you, Victoria." She went on to add, "I knew the truth would destroy you. Besides, sometimes the truth isn't always the best way—sometimes the truth can hurt, like now."

Of course she was right. I was too young to understand—just as Ethyl Eden was too young to be hearing that gossip from her parents.

OVER THE NEXT few months, things got even harder for Mom. She was left with four kids under the age of eight and a mountain of unpaid bills. Yet somehow she managed.

Weekly visits from my uncles, Gene and Pete, brought some monetary relief. Other income came from Mom's work as a freelance seamstress. Back in those days, it often seemed to me that my mother was the most resilient and talented woman on the planet; there was nothing she couldn't do. And it is even more impressive to me now that I realize she was completely self-taught. I even remember her building and refinishing our worn old living-room cocktail table. Better to save it than to throw it in the trash, Mom reasoned. Especially since cash was in such short supply.

As for me, I never did get over the incident with Ethyl or Mrs. Murphy. For the next few years, the kids at school called me names—they even played practical jokes on me, like hiding a box of Pampers in my cubby at school. Or bringing in a pacifier and leaving it on my desk in the morning. Mostly, though, I worried about my father. I was upset and embarrassed that he was in jail. I tried hard to convince myself that it was all a mistake. I was in denial—and became withdrawn and anxious. I even started wetting the bed, at seven years old.

CHAPTER FOURTEEN

"Daddy's Home"

I may have been young when my father went to Lewisburg, but I can vividly recall our monthly visits. The imposing structure of the prison, the guard towers, the sanitary conditions—these are things you don't ever forget. Nor do you forget what it's like to see your father trapped behind bars, like an animal.

There was a rhythm to the visits. After the prison's careful screening and scrutiny of us, my mother would lead us through a series of steel doors until we reached the visiting room. It was always packed and bustling with activity. Despite the noise and the interaction of family, it seemed to be a terribly sad place. There was always a lot of crying, with inmates holding their wives and children, rocking back and forth. Even though I was just a child I could still pick out the knock-around guys from the ordinary thugs. The guys who were "connected" were well-groomed, with slicked-back hair, white deck sneakers, and trademark tattoos: a cross with a knife through it, surrounded by rosary beads; or even a bleeding heart with a woman's name scrawled across the bottom. Dad was not particularly fond of body ink. He had only one tattoo on the back of his shoulder, of a near-naked woman kneeling. It was, he explained, a reminder of an earlier stint in prison, during which he'd utilized the services of one of the many jailhouse tattoo artists. "I was young and stupid," Dad said. "And I never let anyone mark up my body again."

FOR A CHILD, these prison visits were grueling. I remember watching my mother and feeling so sorry for her. The corrections officers treated the wives of inmates with palpable disrespect, really no better than ranchers treated cattle. It was also obvious which guards were on the take and which were not. Typically, an inmate's wife smuggled in nothing more serious than various delicacies designed to compensate for the poor quality of prison food. Pepperoni links, fresh Italian bread, small provolone cheese wheels, and freshly made mozzarella were some of the luxuries brought in by the prisoners' wives. The women would conceal these goodies inside their bras or under loose-fitting clothing that would not set off the metal detectors. In mob movies like *Good-Fellas,* similar prison scenes are depicted with much comedy, respect, and care. But in real life, there's nothing funny or easy about prison. There's nothing respectable about wives smuggling in delicacies to their inmate husbands. In real life, it's downright degrading.

My father never allowed my mother to take part in this ritual, in part because he felt it would cheapen her, but also because the risk was substantial. If she was caught smuggling contraband, the embarrassment she'd suffer as a result would have killed him. Besides, she didn't have to. The other guys whose wives did bring these things in were all too willing to offer much of it up to my father first, as a means of showing respect.

If you were a person of respect on the inside, it was quite possible to emerge from a sentence unharmed and unchanged. But it was hardly a picnic. Of course, with assistance from "compassionate" guards (those who were on the take), it was possible to enjoy the occasional good meal. Other than that, jail is depressing.

As my dad used to say, prison is prison. No one wants to be there.

DAD WENT AWAY to prison with Uncle Angelo, so each month Mom and Aunt Marie shoved bags of luggage and six kids into a beat-up Chrysler and made the three-to-four-hour drive to Pennsylvania.

Lewisburg was filled with other Mafia associates, including the Bonanno captain, Carmine Galante. Galante was serving a short sentence for loan sharking and was considered by the other inmates to be "the Warden" of Mafia row. The prison, like most others, was segregated into sections and gangs. The Italians mostly stayed in Mafia row, while the Latinos, blacks, and Irish also had their own crews. My father could care less about the so-called "administration" formed when he was in prison; he marched to his own beat. He pretty much kept to himself—and channeled his energy into self-education. Dad was self-conscious about being a high school dropout. He was determined to use his time in prison to become a well-read, well-educated man. But there was one thing that bothered him very much. Galante had many of the guards on his payroll, offering bribes to anyone in exchange for amenities and favors. Galante would arrange for these guards to sneak in forbidden items like succulent steaks, Cohiba cigars, fine wines and champagne, and recreational games like poker chips and horseracing scratch sheets so he and the other inmates could eat well and keep busy playing cards and betting on the races from prison. Dad didn't care that Galante was being pampered royally. What bothered him was that Galante kept these things for himself and a few members of his crew.

Dad was a man with undying support for the underdog. He approached Galante and asked him why he was so selfish. Dad mentioned to Galante that there were other men forced to serve much longer sentences without any luxuries or favors. Dad suggested that the Bonnano captain share some of these amenities with the other inmates. If there was one thing my father hated, it was selfishness. It reminded him of the old days of being poor and not having enough to eat for dinner, of the night his own father sat down to a steak dinner while his starving siblings sat and watched. Most of the prisoners told Dad he was crazy to question Galante's tactics.

Galante, on the other hand, was impressed with Dad's brazen and fearless demeanor—so much so that he asked my father if he wanted to join his crew. Dad turned him down, because he was loyal to Dellacroce and Gambino. But Dad did make sure that the luxuries Galante managed to acquire were shared equally with the other less fortunate inmates.

In the years Dad was at Lewisburg, the inmates grew to like and respect him so much. Just before Dad left the prison in 1972 they threw a big "farewell" bash in his honor.

*   *   *

WHILE DAD WAS in Lewisburg, I was getting ready to graduate from the sixth grade. Mom had invited Uncle Pete, Dad's older brother, and his wife, Kitty, to come in Dad's place. I was happy to see my uncle and aunt there, but I wished Dad wasn't away in jail. The ceremony took place in the school's auditorium and awards were given out in the earlier part of the ceremony. I was called several times to come up onstage and collect an award: one for "Outstanding Character," another for "Academic Excellence," and yet another for "Excellence in Physical Education." One award in particular that I received was given out not by the school but by the entire district, which encompassed thousands of students. It was called the United Federation of Teachers Award and was given to two students yearly—one male, one female—for excellence in academics. I approached the podium once again, and accepted the award. As I made my way down from the stage and back to my seat, I searched the crowded auditorium for my mother's face. She was sitting off to the right, next to Uncle Pete and Aunt Kitty. The three of them clapped the loudest for me. I smiled at them and turned to take my seat in the front row. Imagine my shock when I saw my father standing in the back of the auditorium. He was dressed so dapper in a navy suit and, boy, was he smiling.

I later learned he'd been released a few weeks early and planned on surprising me by showing up at my graduation. Even Mom didn't know he was coming home that day. My father took that award with him, resting it on the passenger seat of his car. For days, he showed it to anyone he came in contact with—bragging about how smart I was and how proud he was of me.

THE NEXT FEW years with my father home were a blessing, an actual godsend. Things started changing quickly, and for the better. We actually owned our own house—a modest, attached cape in Canarsie, Brooklyn. Moving out of rat-infested, roach-crawling railroad flats was such a step up for us, we were overjoyed. Aside from the new house, we had a shiny new Lincoln Continental—champagne and chocolate brown, the Bill Blass edition—parked in our driveway.

Our newfound lifestyle was the reward of Dad's moving up in the life after he came out of prison. Later on, I'd learn that the house and the car were gifts from his then "Boss," Carlo Gambino.

Although we thought the house was our nirvana, Dad wasn't thrilled with what he called the "shabbiness" of it. Mom had picked it out while Dad was in jail. But Dad wasn't impressed when he pulled up for the first time after being away. I remember his words were something like, "Butch [Dad's pet name for Mom], I know you tried to fix this place up with all the handmade drapes and do-it-yourself decorating, but it's a shithole. The first thing I'm going to do now that I'm home is find us somewhere decent to live."

So my father began searching for something he felt was more appropriate.

One of our neighbors in Carnarsie was an elderly Jewish

woman named Esther. She and Mom became friends early on and Esther often babysat my siblings and me when Mom had to run out. One of Esther's relatives had a serious tax problem and had to get rid of their beautiful home on Long Island. Esther told my parents the house could be had "for a song and a dance." She said it was a great bargain for anyone willing and ready to move quickly.

Dad put a deposit down on the house without even seeing it. Five thousand dollars. When we went out to see the house, we were totally awestruck. It was on a corner lot in Woodmere, a huge, white-shingled house, set back down a long winding driveway. The house itself was hidden by rows and rows of perfectly trimmed pine trees and meticulously manicured lawns. The house needed work, like new aluminum siding, wood doors, and a good paint job, but other than that, it was the most beautiful house my siblings and I had ever seen, even more beautiful than my grandfather's house in Port Chester. It was the kind of home I never imagined myself and my family ever being fortunate enough to live in.

Inside the house seemed even larger. The rooms seemed to go on forever. There were six bedrooms—enough for each of us to have our own room and one left over for guests. We'd never had guests before, though, so we didn't quite understand the meaning of a guest quarters at the time. The kitchen was huge, nearly four times the size of our current one. The cabinets were real wood, with shiny brass handles. One appliance stood out in particular—a stainless-steel dishwasher—something we'd never even seen before. My mother was immediately drawn to it—in fact, she even asked if she could "look inside." Her eyes lit up when she opened the door and saw the two plastic upper and lower racks. There was a maid's room and then some talk about hiring a live-in house-keeper, and that's when our dream came crashing into reality.

My mother, raised just as poor as my father, just couldn't get used to the idea that we could live in such lavish sur-roundings. She thought the house was too "luxurious and piggish" at the same time. She believed we would be like "fish out of water" moving from where we lived to such a place. The place we lived in at the time was a tiny, one-story row house. Like a brownstone, it was attached on both sides to other, similar houses. The rooms were closet-sized and the décor was nothing short of gaudy. As in other typical Italian homes, the living room was the focal point of the house. It was a look-but-don't-touch museum space, filled with ugly Capodimonte figurines and gold velvet couches covered in plastic slipcovers that stuck to your skin each time you sat down. In our living room, there may very well have been an invisible or imaginary velvet rope letting us know to stay out. What a joy it would have been to move to a house filled with rooms we could actually live in or use. But the mere thought completely overwhelmed my mother. Dad, not wanting to upset her, reluctantly agreed, even though the five-thousand-dollar deposit was nonrefund-able. Our excitement was short-lived. I remember the car ride back to Brooklyn—it was a mere forty minutes, but it seemed to take forever as we rode home in silence—each of us deep in thought, both resentful and angry. We had got-ten our first taste of how the "other half" lived—if only for a moment.

THOUGH HE WAS paroled in 1972, my father's life on the outside didn't last long. When he'd returned to the streets, back to the Faticos' social club, Dad learned he was to be given a promotion. Carmine Fatico had recently been indicted on loan-sharking charges and it was likely he was going to prison. He'd chosen Dad to be the acting captain, or capo, in his absence. As a result, Dad quickly became familiar with both adversaries and allies along the way. One such adversary was the "Don" himself, Carlo Gambino.

Gambino had recently suffered a tragic loss. A group claiming to be the "Westies," an Irish gang originating out of Hell's Kitchen in Manhattan, had kidnapped his nephew. They demanded one hundred grand in ransom. Gambino agreed to pay and wanted his nephew back safely. For the moment, he'd arranged for his nephew's wife to pay the ransom. Gambino delivered the full amount, but the kidnappers killed his nephew, anyway. It was the actions of one of the most ruthless gangs around—an act of savagery that left every wiseguy from New York to Las Vegas craving revenge. The thugs responsible for such an unspeakable act would be made to pay. Gambino reached out for Gotti, the young man he'd been hearing so much about. Ironically, Dad was not yet even a "made man." Gambino had issued a "no buttons" restriction a few years earlier and his orders still stood. But he was very impressed with my father and made it his business to keep the young "buck" close to him. He wanted the man responsible for killing his nephew brought to him—alive.

Dad, Angelo Ruggiero, and one of Gambino's soldiers, Ralph Galione, were personally picked by Gambino to carry out his revenge. They found out the man responsible for killing the Don's nephew was James McBratney, a member of the Westies gang. Gambino's men found him one night at Snoope's Bar and Grill in Staten Island. The three men entered the bar pretending to be detectives, claiming they had a warrant for McBratney's arrest—a believable ruse, as McBratney was always in trouble with the law and had been arrested numerous times. But that night, McBratney resisted. He ignored the men and became belligerent. What happened next was not part of the plan. Galione pulled out a small pistol and shot McBratney at close range, killing him. The three men fled the scene. Dad and Ruggiero were soon identified from photos that police officers provided to eyewitnesses. They heard they were being hunted and went on the lam. It was as if Dad was in prison again. Money was scarce, bills piled up once again, and Mom grew increasingly depressed. As young as I was, I remember the many times that Mom would wake us in the middle of the night, telling us to "dress quickly." Then we all shoved into my uncle Pete's car and hours later we'd arrive at some nondescript motel in New Jersey. Dad would be waiting, pacing the floors nervously until we arrived. We wouldn't stay longer than overnight, so as not to draw unwanted attention to the motel and to Dad. He was on the lam and had to stay "underground" until things cooled off. This period lasted about a year, until Dad was arrested in a Queens bar. He'd deliberately let himself get caught. Gambino, meanwhile, had been busy arranging top-notch legal counsel. Roy Cohn was hired to get Dad and Angelo the best possible deal, which by the way wasn't that hard to do. Back in the seventies, even until the mid-eighties, the police, even the FBI, rarely bothered "made" men—or any organized crime guys—mostly because law enforcement welcomed the extra protection the

Mafia provided. The streets were calm and quiet, and it was a rare occasion if chaos broke out. Some cops looked the other way because they were on the take. But most of law enforcement deliberately adhered to the rules; mobsters took care of their own territories and, if need be, reprimanded anyone who dared mess with their rules and regulations. If a mob hit or mob war took place, it was thought to be a "casualty of the job." It went with the territory—and every man who signed on for that lifestyle signed on for the risk as well. In the case of Gambino's nephew being kidnapped, even the cops were outraged and wanted to see justice played out.

In the end, Cohn managed to get my father and Angelo two years in prison. The charge was later dropped from murder to attempted manslaughter. Galione, who actually pulled the trigger, was never seen or heard from again. Most in the life believe he was killed on Don Carlo's orders for botching the carefully planned event. Both Dad and Ruggiero were sent to Green Haven Prison in upstate New York in 1974. This time, Dad was automatically initiated as "the Warden" of "Mafia row." But on the streets, where it mattered most, word soon spread that John Gotti had officially earned his "bonus"—a term used when a man became a wiseguy or goodfella.

By now, Dad had found a father figure in Dellacroce. The two became inseparable. Dellacroce took Dad under his wing and made him his protégé. And this pleased Dad. He believed Dellacroce was a "man's man," and few of the elders had that impact on my father. Dellacroce stayed in close contact with Dad while he was in Green Haven, using cards and letters and many prison visits to brief my father in his way. And for Dad having the support and respect of a man in the life like Dellacroce was money in the bank as far as climbing to the top of the underworld went.

While he was in jail, Dad started making plans—he would no longer be kept down. Most of the men in his life fell short of achieving any greatness. His own father had made little of himself, just drink, fight, and screw around. Dad didn't recall too many success stories involving the men he'd known. But he was determined to change that. He may not have been born into privilege or wealth, but he was determined to achieve greatness, one way or another. Street life was the only life Dad knew and respected. He learned the rules and regulations and laws of the land early on. He bucked the system and cheered on the little guy. He believed the government was nothing more than a "hypocritical pack of liars" with selfish agendas. He believed the "little people" were deliberately being suppressed and denied their God-given right to govern their own communities and provide for their own families. He believed the politicians were selfish pigs and liars, who would do or say anything to get in office. He believed these men hid behind a wall of deceit and treachery. Mobsters never denied their profession; politicians pretended to be upstanding and legitimate. Mobsters stole, killed, and cheated; politicians did the same. Mobsters went to jail. Politicians went to the White House.

Dad believed the politicians and the laws they helped make were all "hypocritical bullshit"—and he believed it was definitely time for change.

Dellacroce was leadership material, as far as Dad was concerned. A man who represented and supported the "little people"—a man John Gotti respected and wanted to be like.

CHAPTER FIFTEEN

"The House of Pain"

The Gotti home where we would ultimately settle turned out to be a four-bedroom cape in Howard Beach, Queens. Mom found the modest home not more than six blocks from where Uncle Angelo and Aunt Marie moved with their now-burgeoning family. Growing up, we almost always lived near the Ruggieros. Dad and Uncle Angelo were *that* close. My aunt and uncle had three children of their own, with a fourth on the way. My father was finishing the stint at Green Haven for the Gambino incident when we moved to Queens in 1975. He joined us a year later in mid-1976. It was then that John Gotti was formally inducted into the mob. He had finally become a "made" guy.

It was the mid-seventies and things weren't so prosperous for my father out on the streets. There wasn't much money to be made, especially given the Gambino no-drugs policy, which Dad felt strongly about. The other families may have turned a "blind eye and deaf ear" to this ruling by the Commission, but for Dad, drugs were off-limits for his guys. So while other crews reaped the rewards from this particularly lucrative area, my dad's crew went hungry for a little while, mostly dabbling in running numbers and gambling dens. The drawback of the latter was my father's penchant for gambling himself—he had a weakness for *any* game.

Football and ponies were his favorites; he loved getting a good tip from some of his friends who themselves were horse owners. And as far as football went, Dad always loved to root for the underdog, the team that was destined to lose by the bookies' standards and had wide point spreads. It had little to do with winning, as my father once told me, "and all to do with watching the team with pure heart rush to victory." Besides, he'd add, "When you bet the underdog and the team wins, it's usually a *big* payout, and that's what gambling's all about—winning big rather than a few dollars here and there. It makes the game that much more exciting when the stakes are higher." My father was a notoriously unlucky gambler, though.

Dad's bad gambling habit wasn't so much of a problem in the early days, as he didn't have much to gamble with. But when we moved up economically, from lower to middle class, his habit began to interfere with his standards of living and even played a role when the bills were due. Rather than ever admit he didn't have the money, he'd make sure that Mom had the house money every Saturday—even if it meant walking around with nothing in his pockets. I also learned that my father's exorbitant gambling habits stemmed from anxiety and nervousness, as well as anger. In this state, he would bet well beyond his means—practically on every game that day or week, be it pro-ball, college games, the Belmont Stakes, or any horse race. Often a losing streak put my father in a financial bind.

123

Dad's gambling habits didn't sit too well with my mother, either, and they fought constantly about it. But in the end she really had little say in the matter. It wasn't as if my father came home from a nine-to-five job each week and handed over a predictable paycheck to cover the household expenses, so she really never knew just how much he was betting. All she knew was that he was providing.

Dad believed that if a man couldn't provide for his family it was a "sign of weakness," or the guy was just "plain irresponsible." I guess living hand-to-mouth as a child had taught him that. Another belief my father had was that when it came to a woman—especially a wife going out to work—it was "a sign of embarrassment on a man, as people would then assume that man couldn't pay his bills at home or provide enough for his family to survive comfortably."

Dad was always resentful that his mother was forced to work. He believed a woman's place was at home with her family, in the kitchen and taking care of her house. He believed a woman should never be involved in financial matters—that was a man's job. But Mom was always scared. She feared something might happen to Dad and then she wouldn't be able to support her children.

That's why my mother always saved whatever extra money my father gave her for herself. She would deposit the money in the bank each week, even if it was a small sum. My mother was never like the other women married to men in the "life," either. While these wives always showed off some newly acquired diamond trinket or a new fur coat, Mom got more excited over a set of pots and pans. And while my mother was always a well-dressed woman, she was never high-maintenance or a show-off. I always respected my mother for this and was proud of just how unspoiled she was. Another important lesson Mom taught us had to do with love; she could turn into a flesh-eating monster if anyone harmed her kids.

When I was twelve years old my mother sent me to buy a few things from the local grocery store. The store was only nine blocks away, yet back then it seemed like I'd walked miles to get to what we commonly referred to as "the Boulevard"—Crossbay Boulevard. I made it to the store, and bought all the ingredients on the list. I even had a few quarters left over from the ten-dollar bill that Mom had given to me. I decided to use the change for a rainbow-flavored Italian ice. I walked the two avenues over to Gino's Pizzeria, got my ice, and headed home.

At the corner I noticed a man riding a beat-up bike. He was watching me with dark beady eyes. He was dressed shabbily and sporting a scruffy beard. I had noticed him waiting outside the pizzeria while I was getting the ice and also noticed him following slowly behind me when I left the store. But it wasn't until I saw him ride slowly to the corner, stop, turn back to look at me, and then wait at the light until I caught up that I got scared.

Sensing imminent danger, I turned around in a panic and headed back in the other direction. I kept walking until I reached the neighborhood hardware store.

The strange man was now stopped, perched in front of the store at a fire hydrant, waiting. His creepy eyes flashed from one end of the block to the other. I strolled up and down the aisles and created enough suspicion that the two employees took notice of me almost immediately. They both approached me and asked what I was looking for. But I was so nervous I couldn't think straight, much less talk.

I glanced out the window in the front of the store and saw the man still outside sitting on his bike, puffing on a cigarette; his eyes were fixed on the front entrance of the store. I should have blurted out something like, "Please call my parents," but because we had just moved to the neighborhood, I couldn't remember our phone number. Then like a ray of sunshine someone I knew, a neighbor's mother, entered the hardware store. She noticed me, as I'd been to her house a few times, especially when we had school projects to do. Her daughter was also named Vicki, so we became friends the first time we met in class at Junior High School 202.

The woman, Mrs. Mona, called out to me almost immediately, asking how I was doing and wondering why I looked so scared. It was then that I became hysterical—crying and speaking at the same time. I told her the guy waiting outside had followed me for blocks.

Mrs. Mona ordered me to wait there in the store while she went outside and approached the man. I saw her yelling and pointing her finger as the man turned his bike around and sped off down the boulevard. Seconds later she came back in the store again and grabbed me by the hand. Before we left she asked if I wanted to call my mother and for the life of me I still could not remember my phone number. But then again I was so nervous and terrified, I could barely remember my own name.

When Mrs. Mona pulled up to my house, I spotted my mother, who, at the time, was nearly eight months' pregnant with my youngest brother, Peter. I became hysterical again,

I nearly jumped out of Mrs. Mona's car while it was still moving. My mother was busy gardening in the front yard. She noticed the terrified look in my eyes almost immediately and came running toward the car. I could hardly speak around the lump in my throat, so Mrs. Mona explained the chain of events. My mother—all four feet of her—sprang into action: she grabbed the nearest weapon she could find, my brother's baseball bat, and asked Mrs. Mona to drive us back to the boulevard. Mrs. Mona, noticing my mother's condition, begged her not to go. She explained that she'd already scared the man off and told him that if she ever saw him again "lurking around Crossbay Boulevard, she would call the police." Still, this wasn't good enough for my mother. She had four kids to raise on her own while her husband was on the lam and heading to jail soon, another baby on the way, and no patience for anyone causing trouble with her family.

Mom charged for the car and forced Mrs. Mona to drive her, us, back to the boulevard. I remember praying that we didn't see the man. I was that scared that my mother would lose it and do something stupid. She was angry, near hysterical. God knows she wanted to rip this man's eyes out—it was written all over her face. I was scared she'd seriously hurt him and end up in jail, like my father—or worse, hurt herself and the baby she was carrying.

Needless to say, my prayers were answered and we never found the guy. Mrs. Mona *was* right—she'd scared the life out of him with her threats. I had no doubt he was a pedophile. And less than six months later, he was finally arrested after he attacked a girl who was blocks from her house. I was so relieved the jerk was finally caught. But what impacted me the most was the way Mom had behaved. She literally sat down and cried for nearly an hour after we got home.

Growing up in a home, having no parents or anyone to love her, had left Mom cold and somewhat empty inside—except when it came to her kids. She wasn't the type of mother who hugged us or often told us how much she loved us, like some parents did. She didn't know how. But if one of us got sick or injured, she would nurse us better than a doctor. If one of us was ever in need of protection or in trouble, she'd come to our aid like a superhero. As she cried, I kept asking her, "What's wrong?" But she just kept shaking her head. Finally, she turned to me and said, "I'm just so scared. I'm so scared one day I am going to lose one of you—I just know it." Mom always had it in her head—an uneasy feeling she was going to lose one of her kids. She called it "mother's intuition."

Dad came home two weeks later, and was getting ready to go back to jail. On November 9, a few days before he was due to surrender, Mom went into labor and delivered her fifth child, another son, Peter Joseph Gotti.

WHEN DAD LEFT for prison, the baby was just a few weeks old and Mom had not yet fully recuperated from the delivery. Yet she pulled herself together and did her best under the depressing circumstances. As in the past, my mother found it very difficult to survive without my father around, but not impossible. She had five children now to care for.

The monthly visits to see my father weren't a walk in the

park, either. As much as she wanted to see him, the strain of the long drive—often leaving in the middle of the night—was hard on all of us. We were stuffed into a broken-down, dilapidated old car, its trunk filled with luggage and care packages for my father. Because my father and his "Goombah," Uncle Angelo, were away in prison together, these monthly visits were almost always shared with my aunt Marie and her young children—so you can imagine just how crammed we all were sitting in that car for hours. Often, when we'd arrive, my father and uncle would be waiting at a big table where we would all sit together. It would turn out to be more of a family picnic or gathering than a prison visit. There was always so much laughter, and most times we all left the visit feeling happy and fulfilled. But one visit in particular did not go as smoothly, and to this day I *still* have nightmares just thinking about it!

During the visit, Aunt Marie was telling a story of an incident at a neighborhood store that had ended with her and my mother arguing with the store's owner. This made my father see red. One of his traditional and staunch rules was that a woman *never* argues with a man—that was a man's job, especially if that particular woman had a husband. Marie just didn't think before she began telling the story, which infuriated both of my parents, for different reasons. One word led to another and soon everyone was yelling. Only after one of the prison guards came over did things quiet down. My father was so upset that he ended the visit an hour earlier than scheduled. No one even said good-bye. Dad and Uncle Angelo quietly followed the guard back to their cells, while another guard led the rest of us to the prison parking lot.

129

Needless to say, Mom and Aunt Marie argued all the way back to the car. Things turned so ugly that my aunt refused to ride in the car back to Brooklyn. She called a car service instead. Lord knows what that fare must have been in those days. It was the end of a close, twenty-year friendship.

The day my father came home from Green Haven in 1976, my sister, Angel, and I were going to a friend's birthday party. We had a small close circle of friends we both shared, and often went to the same parties. When Dad first arrived home, after exchanging kisses and hugs, Dad and Mom decided to go out to dinner to celebrate Dad's release. Of course, Mom decided I would stay home and babysit. I protested and Daddy, always a pushover, gave me my way. He agreed to let me go to the party, providing I came home at a reasonable hour. Usually Mom and Dad went to dinner around 8 P.M. That night, Dad agreed they would go later, so as to let me enjoy some of the party. I was to be home at 10 P.M. sharp.

Imagine my father's shock when I came stumbling up to the house later that night, so drunk I could barely walk. I had my first beer . . . well, actually three, maybe four. Having heard around the neighborhood earlier that day that John Gotti was home from prison, the two guys who gave me a ride home from the party were afraid to drop me off in front of my house. Instead, they let me out of the car at the corner and my father watched as I stumbled down the block like a drunken sailor. When I was ten or so feet from him, I could see the rage and confusion in his eyes. By now, my mother had come outside. It was nearly 10:30, and she was upset that I was late. The two of them had been pacing the floor for half an hour waiting for me. That was my first mistake. Dad had trusted me, even gave me the opportunity to go to the party, providing I be home early to babysit, and I blew it, big-time. My mother thought she was coming outside to reprimand me for being late; little did she know I was inebriated as well. When she saw me wobbling, I thought she was going to have a heart attack. She started screaming at me. My father stood stunned, shaking his head. The last thing I remember before Mom threw me in the shower with my clothes on was Dad mumbling something like, "Butch, what the hell has gone on here while I was away?"

They never did go out to dinner that night.

I remember sitting at the dinner table the next night; I wasn't feeling well at all. I had a raging hangover and I thought I was dying. Dad took one look at me and said, "Last night you felt like Superman, right?" I didn't dare answer. Then he added, "But today you feel like death, right?" Still I didn't answer. "Your mother and I were up pretty late last night trying to decide what punishment to give you. I say, you already learned your lesson, judging by the way you look and feel today. What do you think? Do you agree?" I couldn't even look at him. All I did was nod.

We never discussed the incident again.

CHAPTER SIXTEEN

"He's So Shy"

Every young girl looks forward to turning sixteen. This age represents becoming a woman, especially in Italian culture, and is celebrated by a lavish Sweet Sixteen party. My father had recently been released from Green Haven Prison, so my Sweet Sixteen was celebrated on an even greater scale. To my amazement the party was like a small but grand wedding. We lived a middle-class life in Queens, in a modest home, in a small and close-knit community, so the elaborate party was a big surprise to me. The party was held at a well-known and very elegant wedding hall called the Queens Terrace on Queens Boulevard.

My father had invited hundreds of guests, even family members from as far away as Boca Raton, Florida. Men arrived dressed in fine, expensive Italian suits with matching silk ties and pocket hankies, while the women were clad in beautiful, costly dresses and gowns. We didn't live this way every day—parties like that were not the norm. Ironically, my grandmother Faye won the New Jersey lottery. The prize was a million dollars. She offered to pay Dad back the ten thousand he'd lent her years earlier, but he refused it. Grandma also offered to buy each of us expensive gifts, but

Mom wouldn't allow her to. When my grandmother heard about my Sweet Sixteen, she offered to help pay for the party—but Dad wouldn't hear of it. Both my parents encouraged Faye to use the money to live the life she'd always wanted to. She bought a condo in St. Petersburg, Florida, and moved out of New York less than a month after winning the lottery.

Dad was rising in the ranks. Carlo Gambino had died several months earlier and Paul Castellano, his brother-in-law, was now head of the Gambino Family. While in prison my father had time, lots of time, to start making plans for when he was released. The prison housed some mobsters Dad knew from the streets, men he'd come across once or twice in the life. He carefully observed these men, looking for weaknesses and strong points. It was time to build his own crew—time to handpick men who were willing to lay their lives down for the life. Dad looked for those who had certain qualities necessary to successfully help him to begin his rise to the top of the Family. Strength was important, as muscle and brawn always served tough guys well. But loyalty, trust, and intellect were *most* important. Especially loyalty. John Gotti sought out men he believed could be trusted till the end, men who would adhere to and honor La Cosa Nostra's code of ethics religiously. Only a few passed muster and some of these men came with a checkered past. Most of them had served time in prison. This was important to Dad, as he needed to know his men could withstand the rigors of prison life, the trials of being in captivity and not breaking or cracking. Some of them practiced tactics my father was staunchly against—such as doing or dealing drugs. Dad made his position clear from the start. If they joined up with him, they would be given a "pass" for what they did in the past. They were to begin a new life and were given a clean slate, erased of prior imperfections or sins. If these men agreed to join up with Dad, they had to follow his rules. One such man was Anthony "Tony Roach" Rampino. Tony was a tall man, nearly six and a half feet tall. And he wasn't pretty. Let's just say he earned his moniker, "Tony Roach," because of his appearance. Tony had a criminal record as long as his arm, but he also had a well-earned reputation for loyalty and for getting any job done successfully using whatever force necessary. Tony was mild-mannered and quiet for the most part. But when provoked, he definitely rose to the occasion. Dad liked him from the start. They'd met in prison and Dad kept a close eye on him. When both men reached the end of their sentence, Dad asked Tony if he wanted to join his crew. Of course Tony accepted. It was considered good luck to pal around with John Gotti in those days. To be part of his crew was an honor.

These men were taught by my father. There were rules . . . and then there were Gotti's rules. Dad taught his men to listen, obey, and learn. He also taught them to be mindful of the "old order." He believed that rules, especially Mafia rules and codes, were meant to be followed to a "T." He believed these same rules were only to be broken under extreme circumstances. Dad was "old school" even when it came to mob politics.

The night of my Sweet Sixteen, it was obvious to me and many others that John Gotti went to prison a powerful force and came out even more powerful. I remember some of my girlfriends' reactions as Dad and many well-dressed men huddled in a corner to discuss business. Some of the girls

passed comments like, "All those men are connected"—
a term used to describe a man affiliated with the life.
These girls actually seemed impressed by that lifestyle or
way of living. I never understood this—and while it awed
them, it saddened and terrified me. I wondered in silence
if they ever really knew about the ugliness of it all. Just as
impressed as my girlfriends were, so were my guy friends.
They were also afraid and didn't dare ask me out. As if
puberty wasn't hard enough! With his men put carefully
in place, Dad was ready to conquer the streets. That night
indicated change—in Dad, in life, our life—and I was terrified.

It was that night I also realized two important facts
about my father. First, he was determined to give us everything he never had while growing up, and second, under the
tough and self-confident demeanor he always put forward,
he was actually shy. Toward the middle of the night, the
emcee announced a "special dance" between father and
daughter, just after the traditional sixteen-candle lighting
ceremony, in which the young hostess chooses the sixteen
people closest to her, with the last candle being lit by the
most special person in her life. I chose my parents. When
the dance was announced, my father literally cringed. I
remember him loosening his tie and then wiping beads of
sweat from his forehead with his silk hanky. I tried urging
him while standing on the dance floor, but to no avail. He
leaned in closer to my mother and I saw him whisper, then
nod. Seconds later my brother John appeared to rescue me
from my misery and obvious embarrassment, a role, I would
later learn, my brother was quite good at—and always
prepared for. There was always an unspoken camaraderie

between all the Gotti kids; we were always there for each other, in good times and in bad. We all learned early on the difficulties of living in the Gotti household. It was an unspoken rule between each of us and in the end, no matter what, blood was thicker than water.

My brother and I swirled around the floor to Elvis's "The Wonder of You." All I could do was cry. I tried so hard to hold back the tears and I leaned my head into my brother's shoulder in an effort to hide my embarrassment and hurt from the crowded room. Dad could greet all these men, but not dance with me? I wasn't that important.

I was angry with my father for weeks—until my mother sat me down and explained why I was left on the dance floor during one of the most important nights of my life. It had to do with my father's loathing of being the center of attention. This was ironic, as many people assumed my father loved the spotlight. Oh, and there was one more reason Dad would not dance with me that night. He didn't know how.

CHAPTER SEVENTEEN

"I Miss You Like Crazy"

Football was a passion for the men in the Gotti household. My father and brothers were die-hard Jets fans. Dad would buy tickets and take the boys as often as he could during football season. When it wasn't possible to attend a game, the Gotti men would stay at home, feasting on Mom's delicious food, while cheering on their favorite team from the living room sofa. My twelve-year-old brother, Frankie, adored the sport more than anyone else. He would spend hours each day practicing his moves and exercises to improve his ability. Since kindergarten, he was obsessed with playing on the Lynvet's team, a junior varsity league from Queens. The home field was an empty patch of green on Crossbay Boulevard just to the right of the exit for the Belt Parkway.

Every time Frankie would pass the Lynvet's home turf, he'd press his face up against the car window, his eyes glued on the players scrambling around the field, and smile from ear to ear. We often teased him about this, especially the fact that he often fell asleep wearing his New York Jets helmet (autographed by Joe Namath). Frank was always a big boy. He was average in height, but a bit overweight. Any sports fanatic knows the guidelines for weight maintenance in pro sports. But who would think the rules were just as strict for Little League teams?

The day before tryouts for the Lynvet's team, Frankie was so excited he tried on his team uniform at least a dozen times before Mom forced him to take it off and "keep it off." Mom took Frankie to the field that Saturday morning. My parents had discussed this a few nights earlier and had decided there would be too much pressure on Frank if Dad were present. They were right. Frank did great that morning. But he was crushed when the coach, calling out the names of the boys who made the team, didn't call his name.

My mother went to find out why. Imagine her shock when the man rudely said, "Your son is too fat to play ball." Mom was devastated and Frankie was embarrassed. The two of them drove home in silence. Frankie asked Mom not to tell Dad he didn't make the team; he believed he'd let my father down. Mom explained to him the coach was just plain rude, but this did little to ease the hurt and disappointment for Frankie. Mom praised his efforts, told him how proud she was of him, and tried to make him feel better. Still, when they pulled up to our driveway, Frank went directly inside and straight up to his room.

I felt horrible when Mom told me about this later on. He was such a good, kind, and compassionate boy—it pained me to know someone would hurt him. Mom decided it best to keep this from Dad. That night, when Dad came home, she only said, "The team was too full" and there was no room for Frankie this season. This news confused and upset my father.

Imagine the rage Dad felt when he learned the truth

a few days later. One of the teammates' fathers ran into Dad at the newsstand one night and told Dad what had really happened the day of tryouts. Dad was furious. He waited until the following week and on Saturday he got up early and went to the ball field. My father asked the coach to "take a walk" with him. Needless to say, the man was reprimanded for his inexcusable behavior, especially since my brother had a complex about his weight to begin with. It was bad enough that the kids at school teased him and called him hurtful names; it was another for an adult to do the same.

Later that day, Dad returned home and had a talk with Mom. A few minutes later the phone rang. It was the coach, calling to speak to Frankie. He'd called to say that one of the kids had taken ill and there was an empty spot on the team, and asked, "Are you still interested in joining, Frank?" *Interested?* It was my brother's dream come true! I'll never forget Frank's adorable face when he danced around the room that day. It's a memory that remains so clear and fresh in my mind.

Two days before the first practice, Frankie was so excited he couldn't eat or sleep. All he thought about was running the field and playing with his other teammates. The day before the first practice, he was so excited, he took a shower and spent more time than he normally did fussing with his appearance. He came running into my room and asked if he could borrow my hair dryer. I, too, was in a rush. I was already late for my first class. I told him he had to wait until I was done before he could use the dryer. He was so impatient that he left the house with wet hair. Frankie went to school as usual—except, unlike most days, he had

139

a spring in his step. Later that afternoon, after school, he met a few neighborhood friends and went out to play. He couldn't wait to tell them the news. He'd finally made the team.

I was seventeen and in my first year of college at St. John's University. I had skipped a year in high school because of good grades. On the afternoon of March 18, 1980, I was at school late that day and I missed my usual ride home. I had to call my grandfather to pick me up.

Believe it or not, Grandpa may not have been much of a father, but he became a good grandfather many years later. I don't know if Dad could ever completely forgive his father for his terrifying childhood, but once he had his own family, Dad chose to put all of that behind him. I believe what prompted this decision was my grandfather's treatment of my siblings and me. When Dad was in prison, my grandfather often stopped by the house to check on us and he always asked Mom if we needed anything. He couldn't offer much financially, but when it came to babysitting and driving us here and there, he was more than happy to help. I believe my father found it in his heart to make peace with his father and move on.

As a means of doing "the right thing," my father always sent Grandpa some money each week. "Just enough to place his racetrack bets and have his few drinks every night," my dad would say. I also knew my father paid my grandfather's rent, which was now for a two-bedroom apartment on Liberty Avenue, just around the corner from the Bergin Hunt and Fish Club. Family was so important to Dad, and even though he'd had many violent confrontations with his father, he didn't want to prevent us from having a grandfather. Plus, with Grandpa close by, Dad could keep an eye on him.

When we reached Crossbay Boulevard, in Howard Beach, I begged my grandfather to stop at the local McDonald's even though dinner was usually 5 P.M. I was starving and needed something, even a small order of fries, to sustain me.

Coming out of McDonald's, I saw Frankie horsing around with his friends; all of them were on bicycles. I stopped and said something to him like, "It's late and you know you have to be home for dinner at five or Mommy will be pissed." He nodded and took off down the avenue toward home. Grandpa and I passed the group after we took a right turn down 160th Avenue.

Mom was in the kitchen, preparing dinner and feeding my baby brother, Peter, then four years old. It was easier to feed him before dinner, before the rest of us actually began eating, as he loved to entertain and often played with his food.

I arrived home ten minutes late, threw my school bag to the side of the steps, and ran upstairs to quickly change and head back to the kitchen to do my usual chores. I set the table first, then finished preparing the pasta and pork chops that Mom had started earlier in the day. I also relieved Mom and finished feeding Peter, who was sitting contently in his child safety seat, his face covered in red sauce and his chair's tabletop stained with his red fingerprints.

The phone rang four times before I was able to wipe my hands clean on a nearby dish towel and pick up the receiver hanging on the wall in the hall just outside the kitchen. It was a close friend of my sister's. Her voice was frantic and quick: "Vicki, this is Marie Lucisano—your brother's had an accident. Don't worry." She went on to add, "He's okay —I think he just broke his leg." She also asked me not to tell my mother and instructed me to come to her house right away.

I dropped the plate I was holding into the sink and grabbed my sneakers. Just as I was frantically tying my shoes, my mother came flying down the stairs, sensing something was wrong. "What's going on?" she screamed.

It took me a moment before I could answer, then I said, "Frankie's been hit by a car. Marie Lucisano called. It happened in front of her house." Before I could even stand up, Mom was outside the door running the four or so blocks to the Lucisanos' house on Eighty-seventh Street.

By the time she got there, the ambulance was already on the scene and things were far worse that just a broken leg. My brother had borrowed another kid's minibike and was riding in a construction site near the side of the road. But that dreadful day, a drunk driver was speeding down the avenue and struck my brother. He dragged him some two hundred feet before angry neighbors stopped the car, pounced on his hood, and stopped him from crossing the avenue. All the while, he had no clue he was dragging my brother beneath his wheels.

"Don't you even realize you have a kid under the wheels of your fuckin' car?" one neighbor, Ted Friedman, recalled yelling out.

According to the neighbor, the driver, John Favara, then stopped the car. Another neighbor reached in and grabbed his keys, shutting the ignition off and pointed to my brother's near-lifeless body under the front wheels. My brother's blood seemed to leave a trail down the entire block, leading up to the now-parked car. Favara jumped from the car and started yelling, "What the fuck was he doing in the street?" According to the neighbor, "The driver of the car was angry, not remorseful." Only when Marie Lucisano shouted, "Oh my God, that's Angel Gotti's brother," did Favara calm down.

Ted Friedman later told me the guy was belligerent—a real asshole until he realized the kid trapped under his wheels was John Gotti's son.

Favara then appeared to be "dazed and confused," according to eyewitnesses.

When my mother arrived, the Howard Beach Fire Department was already on the scene and working on my brother. My mother ran to him, knelt and was cradling his head, screaming his name over and over, "Frankie, it's Mommy—can you hear me? Frankie, Mommy's here." Mom would later tell me that he seemed scared beyond belief. Of all the things she could remember, it was "the look of abject fear in his eyes." His clothes—a sky-blue leather jacket with a brown long-sleeved T-shirt underneath, and an old pair of jeans—were covered with blood, tissue, and bone fragments. The firefighters cut away at his clothes and loaded him onto a gurney. The only person allowed to ride with him in the ambulance was my mother.

The ambulance arrived at the hospital and Frankie was rushed inside to the trauma unit. The hospital officials waited until my father arrived. They believed it was wise to tell him first that my brother had died. The doctors didn't have the stomach to tell my mother—even though she'd suspected as much. Minutes before Dad arrived, according to one eyewitness, Mario Borrito—Frankie Boy's best friend—my mother started screaming at Frankie, yelling

143

and cursing because he was on the bike at all. Mom hated minibikes; she called them "death traps." She warned John and Frankie over and over to never ride one. She said she always had a feeling, some sort of premonition, that one of her children would die tragically. As a result, she was always reluctant about certain things. But Frankie ignored her and it had cost him his life. Mario's father, also at the hospital, later told me it was "heartbreaking" to watch.

My father nearly collapsed when he was first told that Frankie was hit by a car. He got the call in the middle of a meeting at the Bergin Hunt and Fish Club in Ozone Park, Queens.

My father said the hardest thing he ever had to do was tell my mother that their son was dead. He told me that just seeing her sitting in the waiting room, just outside the trauma unit, shaken and looking like a ghost, made him afraid for "the first time in my whole life." He knew how she'd react, like any mother would. He said he "felt no emotion that day" and that "it was as if he was on automatic pilot," especially when he had to identify his own son's body in the morgue.

I had stayed at home throughout the ordeal, making sure the rest of the Gotti clan—my sister and youngest brother—had the dinner my mother had started. I was told to "hold down the fort." I was the most responsible of the clan and often left in charge of the other kids. I did just that. Dad stayed at the hospital. Besides having to identify Frankie's body, there were reports and procedures that needed to be done. Uncle Pete drove Mom home. When I first saw her face, the blank look and pale pallor, I knew she was in shock. She walked into the kitchen and started folding laundry from a nearby bin. She didn't say a word.

I asked her where Frankie was and if he was okay. She didn't answer—so I asked her again. Still no answer. Her silence terrified me and I started screaming, "Where's my brother?" over and over. Finally, Uncle Pete blurted out, "He's dead. Frankie's dead." That's when it really hit Mom and she lost it. Uncle Pete had to hold her arms down and literally drag her up to the master bedroom—she was screaming and kicking the entire time.

I was shocked—so shocked I didn't move from the hallway, grabbing on to the banister for support—ignoring my brother Peter's screams for attention. I couldn't comprehend what I'd just been told. I couldn't believe what I'd just heard my uncle say. Dead? Frankie? My younger brother, gone? It was all too much for me to handle. I remember watching my mother pass Frankie's room, and she broke down. She cried into Uncle Pete's arms, holding on to him for dear life. Her sobs resonated throughout the house, cries for the son she'd just lost.

MY FATHER HAD to force himself to face the fact that his boy was dead. He went through the motions of everyday life. There were things that were expected of him. He had to plan his son's burial. He bought a crypt inside St. John's Cemetery in Queens—a threesome, should something ever happen to either him or my mother—as he didn't want his boy to be alone. My mother, on the other hand, was literally out of it. She was deeply medicated, from a doctor who'd paid a house call hours after the accident. Still, she was not sedated enough to sleep.

We all heard the crash, and then blood-curdling

screams. My mother had awakened later that night from a drug-induced haze, and realizing that her son was indeed gone, smashed the mirrored vanity in the master bathroom and then attempted to cut herself with the jagged edges from the broken mirror.

Once again my father had the doctor visit, this time increasing her medicine to a more powerful dose. She was still wild with grief, so much that she tried to take her life again. This time, she was smarter. She swallowed a fistful of pills. Fortunately, my father had made a point of checking on Mom every half hour. He went back and forth from his newfound grieving spot, a recliner in his private den that doubled as a TV room when he wasn't home, to the master bedroom. He would sit there deep in thought, pretending to watch a ball game or the news, while his mind was filled with grief. He struggled to come to grips with it. I remember him running from my parents' bedroom, carrying my mother in his arms, her limp form looking more like a broken doll than a grown woman.

He rushed her to a local doctor's private home, just around the corner. My mother needed her stomach pumped and different medications to stabilize her before he took her back home, this time making sure that I would monitor her four-times-a-day dosage. She refused to eat. She just slept, completely lost in the drug-induced slumber the doctor had prescribed.

I also had to take over all my mother's day-to-day tasks, from keeping the house maintained, to looking after my youngest brother, making meals, and cleaning up the house at night. Due to the sudden tragedy, a lot of relatives came and went that night. My sister, Angel, being the most sociable out of all of us, did her best to keep these guests comfortable. My brother John was away at military school in upstate New York, so Dad sent two of his "associates" to retrieve him. Later on, John would tell me that he knew someone was seriously ill, or even worse, dead, when the school chaplain came to tell him that he was going home for the week. John said that as soon as he saw two of my father's closest friends, Charlie and Bobby, arrive to pick him up, he assumed it was my mother who had passed away and the mere thought drove him crazy with grief the entire two-hour-plus ride back to Queens. No one spoke in the car. Both men had been told not to tell John anything. My father wanted to tell John himself.

I remember sitting at my bedroom window that night, long after I'd put Peter to sleep, waiting for John to arrive. The moment the car pulled into the driveway Dad met my brother outside. They walked down the street and Dad told John that his little brother, his best friend, had been killed earlier that day. I watched in horror as my brother John collapsed with grief. He would have hit the pavement, except my father was there to catch him. They embraced and had a long cry. The sight was devastating for me.

Dad came inside first. John couldn't bring himself to come in. He couldn't bear to face Mom. He stayed outside, shivering in the cold night air, and had a moment to himself. I continued to watch him, and it broke my heart all over again.

As for my mother, she slept all that night and most of the following day. But then she became restless again. The night before my brother's wake, she somehow convinced my father's younger, rebellious brother, Uncle Vinny, to help her escape through an open window in the bedroom and take her to the funeral parlor a few miles from the house, because she believed her "baby was cold and needed a blanket." She couldn't bear the thought that he wasn't at home with the rest of her brood, asleep in his bed.

We knew the owners of the funeral home very well, and out of pity, I'm sure, they allowed my uncle and mother entry late that night and gave her access to my brother. She covered Frankie's lifeless body with a heavy wool blanket. The sight of her son embalmed and lying in a coffin destroyed her to the core.

The next day, the funeral was surreal. It was as if nothing, even my brother's death, was real. Thousands of people came and each expressed his or her deepest sympathies, leaving behind mass cards and offers of help with the cooking, cleaning, and shopping. Meanwhile, my father remained stoic and stiff; a blank expression covered his face. He was standing watch over my little brother's coffin as if he were a guardsman in the Queen's court. He greeted those he knew with forced smiles of graciousness and those he didn't know with polite half-smiles and thank yous. I'd never before witnessed my father so distraught or emotionless as I did then.

THE FACT THAT a neighbor, John Favara, had hit my brother was horrific. Favara, whose backyard abutted ours, was known throughout the neighborhood as a disruptive drunk. He was a man who over the years had prompted many calls to the police from other neighbors due to his inappropriate behavior.

It was a well-known fact that he ruled his house like

a tyrant. I knew this firsthand, as I was friendly with his adopted son, Scott. There is *no doubt* in my mind that he was drinking the day he hit and killed my brother. Being intoxicated would certainly explain why neighbors who witnessed the accident had to chase down his car and nearly jump on his hood to get him to stop. He didn't even realize he had hit a boy and was dragging his body down the street. Favara emerged from the car looking bewildered and confused—"not right in his mind" was the way the neighbors described him to the police. And when Favara complained of chest pains at the scene, the cops, who were more concerned with my brother's welfare, released him to his wife's care.

His wife put her husband in her car and immediately removed him from the scene. She told the cops that she would take her husband to the emergency room. The cops, knowing at this point that the boy lying in the street was John Gotti's son, thought this was best in an effort to keep the peace.

I talked to my father about Favara late one night shortly after the accident. I was sitting by the front bay window in my father's den, crying for nearly an hour as I waited for Dad to return from the funeral home. He walked in and found me. The first thing he said was, "We need to be strong for Mama. You do understand that she's suffered a great loss." As always, he was thinking of everyone else before himself. I continued crying, hardly able to look at him as he continued.

"It was an accident," my father said through a raspy, cracked voice, desperately trying hard to maintain his composure. I wasn't sure if he was trying to convince me or himself. The realization that Frankie's death was anything

149

other than an accident would have sent him over the edge. He was displaying the stoic demeanor he preached to each of us while we were growing up. I barely spoke to him, except to say, "That man killed my brother! How can you be so forgiving? How can you be so strong?"

I remember his eyes, as black as coal and as empty as the devil without redemption, when he responded, "It was an accident, Vicki, an awful accident." I ran crying from the room knowing what a bad man Favara was, shaking my head and screaming, "That's a lie. A damn lie!" But I wasn't surprised. Even my mother expressed sorrow when rumors surfaced that Favara may have had a heart attack.

At the same time, she wanted to believe it was an accident—she didn't want to believe that Favara was a cold monster.

I ran upstairs to my room, not wanting to push my father any further. I had my theories and he was entitled to his, as much as I didn't agree with them. Minutes later he followed me upstairs and knocked lightly at my door, so as not to wake Mom. I let him in and he sat in a white wicker chair in the corner of my bedroom. He started to explain how one of the officers who had been at the scene of the accident told him at the hospital that the "neighbor involved had been complaining of chest pains."

I will *never* forget my father's face when he said this, not as long as I live. He truly believed this and even added something like, "We've already had one tragedy; we don't need another. If this man has a heart attack, there will be two tragedies, two families torn apart."

I was surprised—no, shocked—at Dad's reaction. I wondered in silence how he could be so understanding. I was sick with grief and angry about the death of my brother, and I imagined my father was even sicker and beyond angry. I wanted revenge. I wanted someone to pay for taking my brother's life. Anger and grief aside for the moment, Dad was a reasonable man. If someone crossed him and he knew they had, there was going to be trouble and retaliation. But if he believed the act or tragic event wasn't deliberate or intentional, he would set aside the rage and wallow in his own pool of misery.

I put my hands over my ears in an effort to muffle his words and the sound of his voice. When he saw he wasn't making any progress with me, he threw his hands up in the air; he was too broken up to argue. Exasperated, he left the room, quietly closing the door behind him.

AFTER THE BURIAL, the days and nights played out like a dream. It was a nightmare I prayed I would wake up from. Instead, I stayed home from school and continued doing the household chores and caring for my mother and youngest brother. Housekeeper, nursemaid, and cook were the three hats I wore at various times of the day, leaving little time for me to dwell on my brother's death. One thing I thought about over and over was the blow-dryer, how Frankie wanted to use it the morning he was killed. I felt so guilty. (I still have that hair dryer tucked away in a keepsake box. For obvious reasons, I could never throw it out.) Then, I didn't even have the energy to express the anger that was bubbling up and about to erupt, especially when I got an unexpected knock on the door. The boy who had lent my brother the minibike was standing on my doorstep. Kevin McMahon wasn't at my home to express sympathy or to offer his condolences. He was there to ask me, "Who is going to pay for my bike?" I couldn't believe my ears and stepped outside so that no one inside the house could hear us. I let him know that I thought he was "utterly disgusting and unfeeling." I told him to "beat it." I also told Kevin that given the fact that he'd been told numerous times not to allow Frankie on his minibike, he was lucky that all he was getting from me was a warning. Then I slammed the door.

A FEW NIGHTS LATER, I heard a commotion coming from John Favara's house across the way. There was loud music and even louder laughter coming from Favara's backyard. I glanced out the sliding-glass doors in the dining room and saw that he and his friends were sitting out back and were in the midst of some sort of party. I thought I was seeing things! A party? I decided to take a closer look. I crept outside the door, into the backyard, and walked slowly and silently to the fence that separated our property lines where we had lived for nearly five years. Sure as I was standing there in the flesh, so was Favara. He held a bottle of beer in one hand and a hot dog in the other. There were mostly men present, and most were dressed in Members Only jackets. It was the end of March and still pretty cold outside. They were all laughing. Talking and laughing. The very sight enraged me and tore at my heart. I didn't expect the man to be broken up beyond repair, but this was a far cry from what I deemed a normal, feeling, and compassionate man who had suffered "chest pains at the scene of the accident."

As the anger built up inside me, my heart began to

race and my head started to pound. My hands were cold and clammy and within seconds my entire body broke out into a cold sweat. My mind kept flashing to the sight of my brother's lifeless body in the wooden coffin my father had picked out. Then the images changed to the package, wrapped neatly in a brown bag with twine tied around it, filled with my brother's clothes, the outfit he had to be cut out of before the paramedics could begin working on him. Most of the cut-up fabric was covered in blood, tissue, and bone fragments. The package had awkwardly been delivered by one of the hospital workers to my father in the waiting room, where he'd come after being at the morgue to identify his son.

Standing in the yard, not taking notice of the cool temperatures nor the slapping winds, my body and mind were burning with the quest for revenge. I was only a teenager, perhaps too young to even understand death itself, but I knew enough to know that this man felt absolutely no remorse. I knew enough to know if that were me, I could hardly get through a day without wanting to die of guilt because I had ended such a young and promising life. Yet this man was enjoying a backyard barbecue with his friends, laughing and drinking as if nothing had happened.

I crept back inside the house as quietly as I had come out, not wanting to make my presence known, especially to my mother sleeping upstairs, nearly comatose from enough medication to put down a horse. As I closed the sliding-glass door slowly, I heard my mother's bedroom door open. Knowing my father was in the den, I went into an absolute panic. She barely made the eleven or so stairs down to the first level of the house, while grabbing tightly to the wrought-iron handrail for dear life. She walked into the kitchen and found me loading the dishwasher. I was making as much noise as I could in an attempt to drown out the noise coming from the backyard. But my actions were in vain and my mother was immediately drawn to the yard like a moth to a flame. I tried stopping her. I even stood right in front of her and took hold of her shoulders, saying, "Mom, you need your rest, you need to go back to bed!"

She didn't hear me. As far as she was concerned, I wasn't even there. She looked crazed—her eyes were wide open and darting around the room. I found out later that she'd heard the noise emanating from the yard minutes earlier and when she'd stumbled out of bed to the back window and stared down and saw the neighbor and his friends having a party, she was beside herself. My mother looked as if she'd seen the devil himself. I did the only thing I could do under such circumstances. I ran and got my father. In the minute or so it took to get him awake, on his feet, and into the kitchen, Mom had already made her way outside. She was standing against the fence, dressed in a flannel nightgown, her eyes filled with hate, disbelief, and grief.

Favara took notice of her. Instead of getting up and going inside his house, which would have been the smart thing to do, he shot her a smug smile. Then he grinned. If I had not been there to witness this myself, I would never have believed it. But Favara never expected my father to push through the trees and retrieve my mother. Thankfully, Dad didn't see the smug smile and grin. Fortunately, one of Favara's guests had the sense to turn off the music when they spotted my mother. My father didn't say a word; he just guided Mom back inside the house.

❖ ❖ ❖

WHEN MOM WAS sure that my father was sound asleep beside her, she crawled out of bed and made her way back downstairs. This time she avoided the kitchen, even the backyard. Instead, carrying a baseball bat, she headed out the front door and made her way around the corner to the neighbor's house. I heard the screen door slam shut and I knew it was Mom. I grabbed my robe and chased after her. Around the corner in Favara's driveway was, as far as my mother was concerned, "the murder weapon"—a late-model, shit-brown-colored Oldsmobile, with a dented right fender and badly damaged quarter panel. The man didn't even have the decency to hide or even clean the car after the accident. My mother saw blood—her son's blood now dried and caked on the car—and went crazy. She began banging the bat against the car with great force, and within minutes Favara came out of the house, looking dazed.

I found my mother standing in the driveway still wielding the bat. She was just inches from Favara. He was pointing a finger at my mother and staring at me—screaming things like, "Get this crazy woman off my property!" His remark, along with that smug look he had on his face, is something I've had to witness a million times in my dreams over the next thirty years. Then he looked at me, yelled, "What the hell was her son doing in the fuckin' street?"

His last remark sent my mother into an even crazier state. She lunged at him, the bat missing Favara only by inches. Once, twice, three times. Each time she only narrowly missed him. He was quick on his feet. For a moment I froze—even I was afraid of Mom, afraid of what she might do.

"She's fuckin' crazy!" Favara yelled over and over. The scene was getting louder and I imagined one of the neighbors would call the police. I needed to get Mom out of there, fast!

I will admit that I, too, could have killed him with my own hands that night, that's how much rage I felt. But my protective nature came out and my first reaction was to get hold of my mother, calm her down, and get her safely back to the house and to bed, where she belonged. While we walked around the corner, my right arm wrapped around my mother and my left carrying the bat, Favara continued to rant and rave about his car and who was going to pay for the damages.

I managed to get my mother back inside the house and back to bed without disturbing anyone, including my father. The next morning when my father came downstairs to the breakfast table and found me feeding Peter, he said, "Did something happen last night?" I couldn't look at him. So with my back to him I said, "No, nothing unusual." He nodded his head and with a puzzled and mostly confused look on his face said, "I thought I heard fighting coming from down the block." I didn't answer—I just shrugged my shoulders.

My father did of course find out that there had been a commotion. I told him the truth, and boy, was he angry— mostly with me. He said things like, "Mama just lost a son and knows no better. You, on the other hand, should!" He told me I should have called him the minute I saw Mom leave the house. As tears rolled down the sides of my face, he weakened his stance and continued, "I know you're suffering a loss, too, he was your brother, but the one thing *we* need to do is keep our wits about ourselves. Do you hear me?"

I realized he was right. Still, the grief made us feel empty. My whole family, especially my mother, felt a huge void that could never be filled, even years later.

Our entire lives had changed overnight. My siblings and I walked on eggshells whenever Mom or Dad were present, desperately afraid of saying or doing the wrong thing that might trigger a memory or thought of my brother, especially on holidays. Regardless, Frankie Boy was on their minds constantly. My father visited the cemetery every day. He would sit there sometimes for hours while my mother walked around like a zombie.

She was getting worse by the day, and Dad grew despondent. He believed that a few weeks away from home, being surrounded by what little family Mom had left, would do her some good, so he arranged a trip to Florida. Dad, Mom, and my brother Peter left early in the morning. Because Dad hated flying, we always traveled in two groups—on two different flights because he believed if the plane crashed, he would lose his entire family. Dad couldn't imagine that.

But he made one exception when he took Mom to Florida in 1980. Dad was more frazzled over Mom's state of mind after Frankie's death than he was about flying. He had hoped her father could help.

During this time, with my parents in Florida, Favara went missing.

According to the FBI, he was last seen being beaten and stuffed into a van. I remember the FBI coming to the door only days after Mom and Dad returned home from

Florida. They came to see Dad, but because Mom was in the kitchen, they started asking her questions. Simple ones like "How was your trip?" and "How are you feeling?" The two men seemed nervous—even anxious. It was obvious that they were affected by my brother's death. One of the agents said he had a ten-year-old boy and couldn't imagine the thought that something might happen to him. Mom only nodded and left the room. When Dad came downstairs, he ushered the two men outside—he didn't want to talk in front of any of us. Dad and the two men spoke only for a few minutes. I heard one of the officers tell my father that Favara was missing. I heard my father say "Really?" There was another minute of conversation and then Dad said, "I wish I could help you gentlemen, but I'm sorry. I know nothing about this."

Soon after, so many theories surfaced: Favara was shot and his body buried under a parking lot; Favara was stuffed in John Carneglia's (an associate of Dad's) car crusher on Fountain Avenue; Favara was kidnapped and taken to a nearby basement, tortured, and then killed, his body dissolved in acid, all in retaliation for my brother's death. I believe Favara *is* dead. I was told years later, by someone "in the know," that someone close to my father—outraged by my brother's death, Favara's callous behavior after the accident, and my father's grief—killed Favara. I believe this person felt he was doing a tremendous favor for my father. No mob-sanctioned hit. That's the truth.

If it were indeed a mob-sanctioned hit, at least one of the many government witnesses would have knowledge of where Favara's body is—yet no one has offered any credible information to this day.

One witness claimed the body was in one location and the FBI dug up the site for days, finding no trace of Favara, while another claimed the remains were in another location, a rumored mob graveyard, and once again that site was dug up. Yes, there were bodies found, but not Favara's. Also, the many rats who have testified in recent years all have totally different stories about the suspected murder of John Favara. No two stories match.

In retrospect, I have always had mixed emotions about the disappearance of Favara. Hearing the horrible details about the accident, imagining my brother's lifeless body mangled and on the street, and witnessing firsthand Favara's cruel actions have sent me over the edge on more than one occasion.

Besides taking my baby brother away from me, his actions destroyed my parents and left them empty and cold. It destroyed my family, my life. A person can't help being bitter. Nearly thirty years later, I still find it difficult to speak about Frankie Boy without tearing up. Normally, I could never take a human life, but if someone hurt my child, the rules would change. It's human nature to protect those you love. It's human nature to want revenge against someone who hurts those you love. And then there's the guilt. And the knowledge that two wrongs don't make a right.

I only wish Favara had shown some remorse—some respect. I believe he would be alive today if he had. Because in the end, Dad was right—two families were destroyed.

CHAPTER EIGHTEEN

"Rumor Has It"

I met my first serious boyfriend, Carmine Agnello, in 1980, the same year that my brother was killed. We met three months before the accident. Mutual friends introduced us, and I didn't know much about him except that he was a popular guy around the neighborhood. I treaded the waters slowly, but I grew to like him early on, much to the surprise of those who knew me best. He was different from the guys I usually dated, and he was handsome in a dark and brooding way. There was a little young, mischievous, and scruffy Marlon Brando in him.

Carmine was not formally educated, but I convinced myself that what he lacked in academics he more than made up for in business savvy. He had street smarts like my dad. He owned his own auto parts business and was quite successful. He drove fancy cars: Cadillacs, Lincoln Town Cars, and even a Mercedes. He took me to expensive restaurants and gave me beautiful diamond jewelry. What girl doesn't love diamonds?

Well, little did I know that he supposedly came with a checkered past. Besides running the biggest auto parts yard in Queens, it was heavily rumored that he participated in what was called "insurance jobs." This was something my father had heard about Carmine early on from an associate of his, John Carneglia, who was also in the auto parts business and was a competitor of Carmine's. Back then, Brooklyn and Queens were two of the riskiest boroughs in which to own a car. Stolen car rings were cropping up everywhere. These rings profited mostly from insurance jobs. Car thieves labeled these cars "tag jobs." The car owners would buy expensive luxury cars like Porsches, Mercedes, and Corvettes. When they could no longer afford the payments or they simply grew tired of the car, they contacted someone involved in a stolen car ring and arranged to have their car taken. Someone would show up late at night and pick up the car using a key supplied by the owner. These cars were taken to a junkyard, stripped of their valuable parts (which were later sold for extra money), and put in a car crusher. The compacted steel was sold to a metal shredder and then shipped overseas. The owner was instructed to wait at least a week before reporting the car stolen.

Carmine would often show up in various luxury cars. A flashy yellow Corvette. A fully loaded black BMW. Even a two-month-old beige Rolls-Royce. When I asked him who these cars belonged to, he would just look away and mumble something about helping a friend with some repairs. I was young and stupid. I believed him. My father did not.

I questioned Carmine and his answers made sense to me at the time. He'd claim that Carneglia was spreading false rumors. Carmine told me Carneglia was jealous of him "because he was a better businessman." He added that his auto parts business was making much more money than

Carneglia's. Again, I was young and stupid. I *wanted* to believe him.

My father issued me a stern and firm warning: I was *never* to see or even so much as say hello to Carmine Agnello ever again. Dad had hoped I would marry a Jewish doctor or lawyer. I wasn't head-over-heels in love with Carmine, but I saw this as an opportunity to rebel against my father for the first time in my life.

Coincidentally, Carmine was robbed, beaten, and nearly killed a few months later. He was at a red light, not far from his auto parts business, when he was attacked by a group of young men. One of these men was later identified as Peter Zucaro (later he became a government witness). Immediately the neighborhood began gossiping about how my father was responsible for the attack. This wasn't true. The incident had nothing to do with me, and everything to do with an ex-girlfriend. During their nearly two-year relationship, she had been caught cheating on him with another guy—one of the guys who would later attack him.

Carmine had retaliated by going out with the sister of the guy his ex-girlfriend was cheating with. The girl claimed Carmine even beat her up once. Soon, it turned into a gang war. Carmine wrecked the Lindenwood Diner during one of these heated rumbles. What Carmine didn't realize was that the Lindenwood Diner was John Carneglia's main hangout, his regular meeting place. Of course, the incident enraged Carneglia—enough so that he sent Zucaro and a few others to teach Carmine a lesson he wouldn't forget. My father had nothing to do with the beating or the cause, and it definitely had nothing to do with me. But for years people gossiped that Dad was behind it. Supposedly, Carmine had beaten me up and John Gotti sought revenge. Not true.

Further evidence of this came less than a month after the beating when my brother Frankie died and Carmine showed up at the wake to pay his respects. Carmine became enraged when the guys who had issued him the beating arrived not too long after him. The men, all in their early twenties, were Carneglia's errand boys. Carmine left rather quickly. But everyone soon realized there was no way Carmine would have showed up at John Gotti's son's funeral if Gotti had been responsible for the attack. But, sadly, the rumor still circulated and caused my family much grief years later.

For two years, Carmine and I continued to see each other behind my father's back. This was something no other guy would ever dare do when it came to John Gotti. That must have impressed me back then, the fact that Carmine was risking his life to date me.

THE NIGHT BEFORE my eighteenth birthday, my father asked me what I wanted as a gift. I asked him to give me permission to date Carmine. Once again he refused. He told me that it "was for my own good." I ran from my father and cried well into the night and insisted I would not show up at my own eighteenth birthday dinner, which was being hosted by my father at Ruggiero's, a fancy Manhattan restaurant. My father was livid, as was my mother. She always had a soft spot for Carmine and really hoped my father would finally give in and allow me to date him. She, too, was sick of the sneaking around and all of the lies. At my mother's insistence, Carmine went to see my father a few hours before the birthday dinner. He and I had had a brief conversation earlier in the day and we both agreed that we were tired of going behind my father's back. We decided Carmine would approach my father for the last time and if my father still said "No," we would just end it.

Carmine showed up at the Bergin Hunt and Fish Club and asked to see my father. He was ushered inside a few minutes later and led to the back room, where my father was sitting behind his desk, smoking a cigar as usual. Carmine was nervous and said, "Mr. Gotti, I am here to ask your permission to date your daughter."

My father didn't bat an eyelash, just stared back at Carmine. When my father finally spoke, all he said was, "If you don't think I've known all along that you and my daughter have been seeing each other on the sneak for over two years, well then, you're dumber than I thought." Carmine told me, "You could have heard a pin drop," the silence after that was so deafening. Carmine bowed his head. He really believed he was going to be killed.

My father continued, "I can't stop my daughter from doing what she wants. She's that strong-willed. If this is what she wants, then so be it. But I will tell you this: If I ever find out you take her to inappropriate places like bars and clubs, or mistreat her in *any* way, I will come looking for you."

Carmine thanked him and left the room quickly. He was thrilled he'd made it out of there alive and that he had my father's blessing. When Carmine called me, my mother and I nearly fell off the sofa when he announced, "He said *yes*!" My eighteenth birthday wish had come true.

The news spread around the neighborhood so quickly that everyone was talking about me and Carmine—most people were happy for the two of us. Some were not. My father's blessing meant that guys like Zucaro were now forced to "bow down" to Carmine. Overnight, it seemed Carmine went from being persona non grata to John Gotti's new and favorite protégé.

In the meantime, my father remained very on-guard where Carmine was concerned. He realized early on that forbidding me to date Carmine only propelled me to do it even more. With Carmine, he figured if he gave me enough rope I'd hang myself. Dad believed I would eventually "wake up" and see this for myself. What he didn't realize was that girls my age found men like Carmine exciting. He was tough, dark, and daring, and I found these traits very attractive. I really believed marrying a doctor, lawyer, or accountant was a path to a boring and mundane life. How stupid I was.

DURING THESE YEARS, Dad and Neil Dellacroce became nearly inseparable. My father realized his older, wiser mentor was a wealth of information as far as the life went, and Dad became utterly enthralled with Neil. The men were so close that vicious rumors began to swirl. One rumor in particular had to do with an affair between Dad and Neil's daughter Rosemary, a married forty-year-old housewife. Dad was seen coming and going from Neil's house in Staten Island so often that those who loved gossip and lies started spreading rumors of an affair. Rosemary and her family lived with Neil. Dad may not have been a saint, but I would bet the farm there was nothing going on between Neil's daughter and my father. Dad played by the book when it came to the life. Pissing off the man he idolized and respected above all other men was not something Dad would have even thought about.

Years later, the lies and rumors grew. One "rat," Michael DeLeonardo, testified at my brother John's trial that Dad had an affair with Neil's daughter and as a result shared a "love child" with her. DeLeonardo told a packed courtroom that John had confided in him years earlier about Rosemary. Definitely not true. My brother would never repeat such a scandalous rumor—especially to an outsider. It was hurtful for us as a family. I can't imagine what it did to Rosemary's teenage daughter. Although I have to say, I was quite surprised at my mother's reaction. When the rumor first surfaced and reporters shoved microphones in her face, she said, "I don't believe it. But if I'm wrong, I would welcome this Gotti love child with open arms. Anyone with the same DNA as John Gotti would be accepted with open arms." There never was a DNA test done.

DAD'S LOYALTY AND support of Dellacroce came with a hefty price, too. Their relationship became troublesome when politics caused Dellacroce and Paul Castellano to drift apart both personally and professionally. When Dellacroce was passed up by Carlo Gambino and Paul was made the new Boss of All Bosses, Dellacroce took the slight quietly, like a man. He didn't so much as grumble about it, whereas Dad was furious and let everyone know it. Under the old regime, rules were rules and loyalty was valued above all else. My father believed the insult was reason enough to go to war. But Dellacroce calmed his young protégé and insisted there was nothing to be done.

Usually, after a boss died, the position was automatically passed on to the underboss. This was done mainly to ensure that the Family would be run properly and to stave off a possible mutiny from any of the overzealous captains waiting in the wings. Gambino made his decision based on nepotism—he wanted the organization to remain within his blood lineage. Castellano was married to Gambino's sister, Katherine—and as a result he remained close to Carlo over the years.

Castellano came from a family of butchers. And using the influential connections of organized crime, he built a profitable empire for himself and his sons that extended to many major supermarket chains like Key Food and Waldbaum's. America's white-bread food meccas were stocked with Castellano's meats. Even household names like Frank Purdue sought Castellano's advice on many occasions—and his help. When Purdue couldn't get his chicken product on supermarket shelves, he "reached out" to Castellano. Years later, Purdue told FBI agents he did so because Castellano was "the Godfather."

After Castellano was given the position of boss, rumors started swirling. Men high up in the Commission went to see Dellacroce. These men were unhappy with Gambino's choice of a successor. They were even less happy with Castellano's favoritism toward his personal driver, Thomas Bilotti. It was rumored that Paul was grooming Bilotti to take Dellacroce's place. This did not sit well with others involved in the organization. But there was little they could do.

Gambino had made his decision—his brother-in-law, Paul Castellano, was the new boss.

My father continued his obligation and dedication to the life. In the early 1980s he expanded his gambling interests and set up a formal "betting parlor" around the corner from the Bergin Hunt and Fish Club in Ozone Park. The new parlor was in a larger brick building with an apartment on the second floor. It was appropriately called Our Friends Social Club, "Our Friends" being slang for "goodfellas," a term associated only with "made" guys in the life. Dellacroce remained mostly at the Ravenite Social Club in Little Italy. His headquarters also had a two-story brick façade with an apartment above the club. The landmark structure was a historic mob hangout, dating back to Albert Anastasia and Lucky Luciano. In those days, both hangouts went unnoticed to passersby or tourists. Only neighborhood residents knew that these nondescript storefronts housed the toughest mobsters in New York, and people, mostly curiosity seekers, from all walks of life were attracted to these social clubs. Young and impressionable women from different neighborhoods would get dolled up at night, pile into a car, and cruise the mob hangouts all night long, hoping to be noticed or, better yet, invited in. Men not affiliated with these clubs prayed they could get invited inside, even join one of the card games or conversations over espresso and cannolis, just so they could race back to their friends and brag about having been granted entry to the underworld. Celebrities were also intrigued by Dad and his world, even Marlon Brando. Once Brando was having dinner with Matthew Broderick and Dad happened to be at the same restaurant in Little Italy. Brando sent Broderick over to Dad's table to ask if Dad would join them for a drink. Dad declined. He wasn't into celebrity worship. Just the same, he was polite to Broderick and even sent a bottle of champagne over to their table.

When Dad was leaving, he was approached by Broderick one more time, who told him, "It would be an honor if Marlon could say hello." Dad was stubborn, but he was not rude. Finally, he allowed Brando inside the Ravenite Social Club in Little Italy. That night, the reel-life Godfather came face-to-face with the real-life Godfather.

CHAPTER NINETEEN

"Hot Child in the City"

I was raised in a strict, traditional fashion to believe that a woman grew up, got married, and had children. In Italian culture, women were considered second-class citizens, similar to the way Muslim women are treated. In Italian households, women were relegated to the kitchen. Cooking and taking care of children were the only requirements needed to become a "respectable wife." But being an ambitious young woman, I wanted more—a formal education and even a career. Unfortunately, my plans were curtailed when I learned that I was suffering from dysplasia, a common female condition that usually develops later in life after a woman has had multiple childbirths. But I was only eighteen, a student at St. John's University and still a virgin when I was first diagnosed with the condition. I had begun to get what were called dysmenorrheic or irregular periods. One such cycle lasted longer than a month. As a result I became anemic. There was nothing doctors could do to stop the bleeding, and nothing they could do until the bleeding stopped. I was forced to undergo testing and have invasive biopsies. When the results came back, they weren't good. A week later, my mother and I were summoned to the doctor's office in Manhasset, Long Island.

The look on Dr. Frances Stern's face as she perused my file said it all, especially when she read the lab report. She described the condition to my mother, speaking as if I wasn't in the room. She explained the different levels of the condition, and categorized me as "moderate-to-severe." She said that there was a "very good chance your daughter will need a hysterectomy before she is twenty-five." I was despondent. I desperately wanted children.

Dr. Stern went on to explain that if left untreated, the abnormality would almost certainly "develop into full-blown uterine cancer." My mother had had a hysterectomy in her early thirties because of the same problem, and Dr. Stern confirmed that it was a hereditary condition. She went over the list of treatment options: "cryosurgery, or freezing of the pre-cancerous cells; laser surgery to burn off whatever was left over." Neither sounded appealing to me, and I was still worried about a hysterectomy and the prospect that I might never have children.

I wanted what every young girl did at that age—I wanted it all. Prince Charming, a big beautiful house with a white picket fence, and lots and lots of kids. I also wanted a career as well.

At that moment I just sat there and stared straight ahead. I pretended that I was listening. All I could think about was how much Carmine was always talking about having kids, a son in particular. The doctor's words left me speechless. I was hardly able to take in exactly what she was saying. But some things I'd heard loud and clear.

"If young Victoria wants children, I suggest that she gets married early and starts working on having a family as soon as possible."

I had been dating Carmine for nearly three years now

and we had been talking about getting engaged. And I knew Carmine was even shopping for a diamond.

Sitting beside my mother facing the doctor, I pretty much blocked out most of what she had said.

I had a lot of decision-making to do. Besides marriage, education was very important to me. I wanted to study law and go on to write legal thrillers. It had only taken one class in Criminal Justice to solidify my decision. Because I had skipped senior year, I was barely seventeen when I started college. My father was thrilled with my interest in law, and the fact that I wanted to be a writer, but Carmine was not as excited. He felt threatened and was very insecure when it came to my education. The mere thought that I might one day be even bigger than him professionally crushed him and his rather large ego. So he had given me an ultimatum: "Marriage or law school! I want a stay-at-home wife raising my kids." I had been so upset, I couldn't concentrate on my classes any longer. As fate would have it, he got his wish.

I WENT HOME FROM the doctor's office with a heavy heart. I had some decisions to make. After careful consideration, I decided to get married and start a family. I wanted a career—but I wanted a family more. I decided to tell Dad I was not going to law school. He was crushed, and refused to speak to me for weeks. And when he finally did, he looked for ways to change my mind. He didn't argue with the doctor. In the end, he blamed Carmine for the choice I'd made. Dad cursed the day he'd given Carmine and me his blessing to date.

It was then that Dad started really plotting to break Carmine and me up.

CHAPTER TWENTY

"Smokin' in the Boys' Room"

Aside from my health issues, there were other problems brewing in the Gotti household. These problems concerned my brother John, who was finishing his education at New York Military Academy. My parents received a phone call that John had not been attending his classes on a regular basis. He was still acting out as a result of Frankie's death. This infuriated my mother. She was used to keeping things from my father that concerned John, mostly out of fear that Dad would seriously hurt him one day, but this matter she brought to my dad almost immediately. And Dad made a special trip up to the military academy.

John had been sent away to school because my parents were both afraid that if he stayed home he would get mixed up with the wrong crowd. They believed my brother needed rigid structure and discipline. Mom had started to see a side to John when he was an adolescent that she was not happy with. He was staying out later than usual and going to bars and clubs. Mom was afraid that John might grow to like "street life" so much that he would follow in Dad's footsteps. That was the last thing she wanted for her oldest son.

Dad believed that New York Military Academy was a fine and respectable institution. I'm sure my father's choice had much to do with the fact that Aniello Dellacroce's nephew had graduated from the military academy. O'Neill raved about the school. My father considered it "honorable" to have *his* son walk down the same path.

My brother's reaction to the news that he was going to the military academy was to rebel. John's behavior started to change markedly for the worse. He began by changing his physical appearance with daily workouts in the school gym and a new wardrobe of fancy "Sunday" suits that replaced his usual attire of comfortable jeans or track suits. Even his taste in women changed. He went from dating the plain girl next door to being seen with the prettiest, flashiest girls in town. On weekends whenever he was home, he went out to the hottest nightspots with a different piece of arm candy each weekend. He also began enjoying the respect he received that went along with being John Gotti's son.

I realized early on just how tough it must have been for John. Every son wants to grow up and fill his father's shoes or carry on the family trade and name. But in my brother's situation, he wasn't just any son, with any ordinary father. Still, John was prepared to fight the urge. I can tell you that as far back as I can remember, my brother never wanted to grow up and fall victim to my father's lifestyle. John would often speak to me about this when we were growing up. My father made his wishes clear early on that he did *not* want my brother to follow in his footsteps, but at the same time it was the only life John knew. It was the only trade that he was privy to. John believed that the only way he would really gain my father's respect was to enter into the same life. Years later, I still believe my brother thought it was expected of him. I also believe John's change in behavior served as a means of getting my father's attention.

This behavior did not sit well with my mother. She especially despised the bevy of newfound friends John had suddenly started to hang around with. They were local wannabe tough guys.

When Dad was called up to school because John was skipping classes, all hell broke loose. My father hit John for the first time. He punched him in the face, he was that angry.

But the incident did little to scare John. In fact, he "acted out" even more. The following weekend my brother, tired of waiting for his monthly leave, had a friend call the academy pretending to be a relative. He'd told the dean there was a "crisis at home" and that "John had to leave." With a permission slip in hand, my brother boarded the bus and headed back to Queens. He had already made arrangements to stay at a friend's house. It was 1981; he was seventeen at the time and knew all the neighborhood hangouts. He decided to get off the Greyhound bus at 161st Avenue and Crossbay Boulevard in Howard Beach. It was a bus stop in front of a small card and cigarette shop called Party-Time. John entered the store, bought a few things, and headed to the back of the store to play a few games of pinball. He couldn't imagine that our sister, Angel, would walk in to buy a pack of cigarettes just moments later. The owner of the shop, Mike, knew our family and said to Angel, "Imagine my luck, seeing two Gottis on the same night." Knowing I was home sick, Angel recalled that she was quite perplexed. Mike told her that my brother was "just

175

in" and that he "could swear he was still in the back playing pinball," so my sister went to the back of the store to see for herself. But by then, hearing his sister's voice, John had slipped out the back and was hiding in the parking lot.

My sister figured Mike was just confused and left. When she returned home for dinner she mentioned something to my mother about whether John was expected home that weekend or not. Seeing my mother's surprised reaction, Angel realized too late that she'd opened a can of worms that was sure to get my brother an ass-whipping.

Angel ran upstairs to tell me. She felt really bad about ratting him out. Things got even worse when Mom called the school and found out John was not there.

Within minutes my mother had my father and his associates combing the streets looking for my brother.

The neighboring town, Ozone Park, or "O.Z." as it was called back then, had been at war with the "spoiled" and more privileged kids of Howard Beach. Really, the whole mess started because a girl from Ozone Park began dating a boy from Howard Beach. In those days the town ruffians did not take kindly to their enemies moving in on their territory, especially their girls. Because of this fiasco, on the weekend before my brother John's "illegal" leave from school there had been a serious street fight between the two towns. More than six or seven carloads of O.Z. guys had stormed one of the popular Howard Beach hangouts, the Big Bow-Wow, wielding baseball bats and crowbars and beating up many of the neighborhood regulars who were hanging out that night. Out of retaliation, the following night, seven or eight carloads of guys from Howard Beach had quietly entered Ozone Park, creeping into their well-known hangout the

Candy Corner, a candy store just next door to the Brooklyn-Queens borderline. This was where mostly made guys and their gophers hung out. The Howard Beach kids did similar damage as the Ozone Park guys had done the night before. It became an ongoing situation in desperate need of defusing. In fact, the streets became so hostile that my father ordered my sister and me to stay at home until things were under control again.

As my brother stood hiding outside, waiting for my sister to pull away from Party-Time that night, a van filled with Ozone Park guys had pulled up, jumped out, and mistaken my brother for another kid who looked something like him. There was no way my brother could have been a part of this neighborhood war, as he was away at school when all the trouble began. Nevertheless, the guys from Ozone Park beat him up badly, enough that the store owner had to call an ambulance. From what Mike later told my father about that evening, my brother "didn't even see the beating coming." The owner told Dad that "a bunch of big, burly kids jumped out of the van and just started beating up on him with bats, crowbars, sticks, and anything they could find." Mike even told my father that one kid picked up an old hubcap and began hitting my brother over the head and in the face with it.

After Mike grabbed a shotgun he kept hidden behind the counter, he called an ambulance, and then he called my mother. He ran out back, fired two shots into the air, and scared the kids off my brother.

To say my father did not take the incident well is an understatement. An attack on anyone he knew—anyone associated with him—was completely against the rules. But

177

an assault on his son, his heir apparent, and with no reason at all, was a complete declaration of war by his standards. It didn't matter that the street punks who had done it were merely kids—Dad believed that the kids from O.Z. answered to a higher authority.

These thugs had a hangout just next door to a social club in West Ozone Park where captains within various families, especially the Colombo Crime Family, could be found. The Colombos were these kids' mentors, just as the Fatico brothers had been my father's when he was just a teenager himself. Therefore my father saw these men as responsible for the behavior of the boys.

My mother was the first to learn of the incident from Mike, the candy store owner. She immediately called my father's social club in East Ozone Park but he wasn't there; he was at a dinner meeting in the city that night. The two rival clubs were less than a few miles apart, but those few miles might just as well have been worlds, as most of the men shared dissimilar views and allegiances. When Dad finally got Mom on the phone, he needed to know just how badly my brother had been hurt. When Mom answered in hysterics it sent my father further over the edge. The second phone call my father made was to his social club, alerting every man there to be "ready for action."

My father raced home from Manhattan in record time. When he walked in the door and took one look at my brother John's face, grotesquely distorted, his blood began to boil. I can honestly say that the only other time I'd seen him so angry was just after my younger brother's death. John was lying on the living room sofa when Dad came in. Immediately Dad began to question him, but my brother could hardly speak—his mouth was so enlarged it was painful to talk. His eyes were swollen shut and terribly bruised, and his nose seemed like it was spread in two across each side of his face. He also had scratches and bruises covering the rest of his face and body. Luckily, the store owner had come to the house to make sure my brother was okay, and to let my parents know exactly what had happened. He starting describing how a "carload of punks had been driving, cruising up and down the boulevard for what seemed a little over an hour looking for trouble." That was all my father needed to hear. He dialed the social club once again.

"Jimmy," he shouted to "Jimmy-Butch," who answered the phones at the club, "get *all* the boys you can muster together to meet me down at the social club." Just before he hung up he shouted into the phone, "If you see any young punks, any of the regular derelicts hanging out on the avenue, break their legs with a baseball bat. Make sure you tell them it's from me, John Gotti!"

My father didn't give any thought to mob politics that night; in fact, he was so blinded by his rage that anyone unfortunate enough to get in his way was doomed.

Three unfortunate men remained in the Colombo social club; the rest had already fled when they heard my father was on the way. After Dad beat the three men to a pulp, he left them a message: "Go back and tell your boss that this is just an example of my rage. For every punch my son took, ten guys will fall!" Dad then made his way back outside the social club, where dozens of his men stood at the ready, looking up and down the avenue for any signs of life, men, or teenagers. The streets were deserted.

°   °   °

IN THE WEEKS that followed, fear spread so rapidly throughout both neighborhoods that the streets were like a ghost town at night, nearly mimicking the days of 1977 when the "Son of Sam" held the five boroughs captive with his murderous spree. Older teenagers vacated their usual hangouts or cruising routes, and stayed locked inside their houses. This was especially true for those who had participated in the savage beating that nearly killed my brother. They knew it was just a matter of time before my father caught up with them or before their elders did.

Once the elders were involved, numerous "sit-downs" took place. The leaders of the other social club immediately admitted wrong and were made to pay restitution. This was generally a fine, and a hefty one at that, from their own pockets as a means of teaching these men a solid lesson in controlling their future soldiers and associates. But that wasn't enough for my father; he wanted names. He wanted these young men taught a valuable lesson for what they had done, and my father didn't believe that the elders would handle it with nearly enough force as he would.

In fact, every time he looked at my brother's face, it made him more enraged. He would say things to my brother like, "I'd like to get all the guys who did this to you that night in one room, at one time. Then I'd let you take each one of them one at a time, like a *real* tough guy would, and let you teach them a lesson." My brother didn't seem to mind, either. He was filled with rage as well. Ever since the beating, he'd become withdrawn and short-fused. He just happened to be in the wrong place at the wrong time. The attack mixed with the grief over losing his brother just a few months earlier made for a powerful and deadly mix of emotions. That's what had all of us even more concerned than my father's own dangerous anger.

IT WASN'T UNTIL my father got his wish and the key attackers were brought to him, offering formal apologies and begging for their lives, that he even managed one restful night of sleep. As a means of teaching my brother John a lesson, Dad forced him to fight each boy, under fair circumstances. No one had the advantage of a weapon or the element of surprise. The incident had more to do with pride than anything else. I may not have agreed with my father's tactics or approach back then, but now, after raising three sons on my own, I *fully* understand, at least.

TWO WEEKS AFTER the incident with John, Mom received a phone call from the St. Petersberg, Florida, fire department—Grandma Faye had been found dead in her condo just hours earlier. Mom believes Grandma knew she was going to die, because the fire chief found a letter addressed to Mom on the bedside table. It was just a few words: "I'm sorry and I love you."

Grandma also left a signed check—a donation made out to the fire department, with instructions to call Mom after her death. There was also an envelope filled with papers, also addressed to Mom.

Ironically, Grandma had willed the million dollars she had won in the lottery to Mom—her only child.

CHAPTER TWENTY-ONE

"Volare"

My brother John graduated from New York Military School on a warm, balmy day in June 1982. We had left Queens hours before the official graduation ceremony was to begin so as not to be late. My father could not have been more proud of his son that day.

The military graduation was a beautiful event with an awards ceremony, the traditional valedictorian speech, and a marching band. It was to be the beginning of the rest of John's life. And my father had plans for him. John had two choices: going to college, or going directly to work. John chose to go to work.

My father was not thrilled. He had hoped John would choose college. But rather than force my brother through another four years of school, Dad decided to help him start his own business, something small without a large overhead or huge responsibilities.

The business was a trucking company, Sampson Trucking. My father asked John to take my sister Angel's fiancé, Louis, in as a small partner. Dad believed it was a good idea since Angel and Louis planned to marry the following year.

Sampson Trucking started out slow, but in no time at all

it became quite successful, as more and more people signed contracts in an effort to score brownie points with my dad. The company brought in quite a bit of revenue and made for a sound investment during the first few years. Then the problems began. My future brother-in-law's eyes became what Dad called "green with envy," and he wanted an even bigger piece of the pie. Louis believed he was entitled to the same amount of money as John. He'd invested nothing but wanted half of all the profits.

At that time my future brother-in-law began living and enjoying the fast life, but we all thought he was living beyond his means. My brother John tried to reason with him, but to no avail.

Soon the in-house fighting began. Other problems occurred as well. The FBI was watching Dad more closely, and John as well. Everyone who did business with Sampson Trucking was getting harassed. Companies were forced to hand over their accounting books and many were soon audited by the IRS. These companies were legitimate businesses and soon even the most loyal customers were afraid to do business with John. Sampson lost a lot of revenue, quickly. The company was closed in less than three years.

With my brother John out of work, my father realized he needed to help him get involved with another business endeavor, and fast. He desperately wanted to keep him off the streets. So Dad reached out to a friend in the carpenters' union. The friend was able to get my brother into the union and secure him a good contractor's position. John worked at this job for a few years, commuting back and forth to Astoria, Queens, every morning and evening, five days a week.

He really seemed to enjoy it. John was happy and Dad was even happier.

HOWEVER, ONE AREA of constant bickering between John and my dad was over the company my brother chose to keep. Sure, he had his usual cast of pals that he'd known since grade school, but once in a while he would bring around a new friend that my father didn't like, saying that he "didn't look right." And he was usually right, as in the case of Johnny Alite, an Albanian kid from the wrong side of the tracks whom everyone said was "trouble with a capital T."

Every one of us was suspicious of this newcomer, most of all Carmine. He literally hated him and told me that he "didn't trust him." Mostly, Carmine didn't like the way Alite looked at me. He was sure the guy had a crush on me. Johnny Alite was someone who seemed to appear from out of nowhere, without history or roots. Alite said very little about his upbringing or his present living conditions. This automatically sent up red flags. Many people—mostly my brother's childhood friends—grew extremely suspicious of Alite's sneaky nature, and tried to warn my brother.

Still, John and Alite spent a lot of time together, mostly horsing around and in the end always getting into trouble. Because of this, Mom also hated Alite. John refused to see the bad in Alite, and in time, others set aside their suspicions and learned to accept him as a means of pleasing my brother—even Carmine. He asked Alite to be an usher at our upcoming wedding. I wasn't keen about that. But we decided early on to have a "King's Wedding." I didn't want a formal wedding party filled with bridesmaids in long frilly dresses. Instead, the wedding party would consist only of men, twenty-six male friends and relatives.

As the wedding grew closer, more and more rumors began to surface about Alite. John became involved in many fights, mostly barroom brawls. One fight even led to John and Alite getting arrested. The charges were later dropped, but my parents were beyond angry. Rumors also began flying around the neighborhood that Alite was dealing drugs—and robbing drug dealers. Alite denied everything. He always managed to convince my brother that he shared the same "no-drugs" policy as John and my father.

I, on the other hand, was of the belief that where there's smoke, there's fire. I brought this up to my brother several times. I would tell him over and over that people in the neighborhood were talking. John would always go back to Alite and threaten him, telling him on many occasions that if these rumors were true, he "would be chased, permanently."

CHAPTER TWENTY-TWO

"She's a Brick House"

We all grow up with nicknames; some that are downright insulting, especially for a teenager. In my case I was called "Vicki Body" and "Brick House." I was called this because I wore a D-cup bra. You get the picture. To most girls this might have been a godsend, but it wasn't to me. I became really self-conscious and tried my best to minimize what God had given me.

Every day, I woke at 7 A.M., for class. I had two close friends, Vickie Estevez and Marie Koumbis. Because it was the early eighties and Vickie was a redhead; Marie, a blonde; and me, then a brunette, we were dubbed "Charlie's Angels" by everyone in school. It didn't help matters that we drove to school in a brand-new silver Corvette. It belonged to Marie, a gift from her father for her sixteenth birthday.

One morning, I took my usual shower and found a lump in my left breast. When the girls got there I told them to leave without me. I caught a bus and was nearly an hour late for my first class. For the next three weeks, all I thought about was the lump—and whether it was cancerous. I didn't tell anyone, not even my mother. I don't know why but I was embarrassed. I went about my everyday life as if I never noticed the lump. It didn't go away, but it didn't grow any bigger, either.

ONE MONTH LATER, I woke up with excruciating pain. But even worse was what I saw when I looked in the mirror just before showering—my entire right side, from the bottom of my stomach to the top of my shoulder, had turned a bluish-purplish yellow. I also felt feverish and dizzy. Stupidly, I showered and dressed for school. I had missed a lot of classes when Frankie died, and I needed to get my attendance up.

I was only in school for one class before one of my teachers sent me to the medical office. The nurse called my mother and then an ambulance. Within minutes, I was taken to Long Island Jewish Medical Center. I was diagnosed with having a tumor that had somehow developed into a hot abscess. It burst and was spreading poison throughout my body. The surgery was quick and nothing short of barbaric. They needed to cut me open immediately, remove the abscess, and start drains to get rid of the poisonous fluid trapped inside.

I only vaguely remember the commotion in the operating room or the actual cutting and draining, mainly the pain and the sound of my own screams. My mother was at my side, holding my hand. This was difficult, since the nurses had me strapped down to a gurney.

For the next thirty minutes, as the doctor and team of nurses cut open the area, removed the tumor and abscess, and stuffed two pieces of gauze inside of me, my mother kept wiping the beads of sweat from my forehead. I finally passed out from the Valium the doctor had given me. When I woke up, the procedure was over. I was wrapped with bandages and gauze covering my entire torso. I stayed in the hospital for a few days. It was later determined by a breast specialist that I had the start of breast disease, something that I learned ran in my family on my mother's side.

Dad was very upset. With each passing day, he became more paranoid that something bad was going to happen to me. He couldn't bear to lose another child. My brother's death had a profound effect on him, one that changed him permanently. He began to hover over me and became a real pain in the ass. Everywhere I went, everything I did became his business. I could barely leave the house without being grilled about where I was going and who I was going with. It was driving me insane. If I had any doubts about getting married, my father's behavior quickly put them to rest. I would do anything to get away from home and away from the constant scrutiny and nagging.

CHAPTER TWENTY-THREE

"Like a Virgin"

Growing up in such a traditional household meant strict rules and regulations, especially when it came to issues like a woman's reputation. This was a subject not open for discussion, at least where my father was concerned. He believed a woman's virginity was "her greatest asset, only to be given away to the right man." Once a woman was spoiled, that was the end. She had little or no chance at finding a husband. He instilled these traditions and beliefs in my sister and me at a young age.

Dad used to tell us that "wild girls with a reputation were used for only one thing: a good time. On the other hand, those young women smart enough to save themselves for marriage, or the *right* man, would always win the brass ring in the end."

So I practiced what I had been taught and saved myself for the man I knew would be my husband. I was eighteen years old when I lost my virginity to Carmine. I already had an engagement ring on my finger, so I assumed it was safe to sleep with him.

Unfortunately for me, I got pregnant less than a year before the wedding. I had made a mistake. Like millions of other young girls, I believed it wouldn't happen to me. I walked around for weeks completely numb. I must have bought ten over-the-counter pregnancy tests. Each time the pink line appeared, I managed to convince myself that there had to be a mistake.

But my body was already going through noticeable changes: swollen breasts and growing abdomen, rapid and unpredictable mood swings, extreme fatigue, and crying fits. I could no longer focus on my studies. I even distanced myself from my closest friends and family members. My mother was still affected by losing Frankie less than two years earlier and was not in any condition to sit down and talk to me about sex and teen pregnancy. I was completely lost. The only person I'd told was my fiancé. Of course, he flipped out.

The wedding was planned, but I could not bring myself to tell my father about the pregnancy. I felt that I had failed him. I was now, as he used to tell Angel and me, "damaged goods." I also feared what he would do to my fiancé. I imagined every worst scenario—from my father beating him beyond recognition even to killing him for ruining his little girl. I imagined that the embarrassment of my pregnancy would cause my father to do the unthinkable.

To be absolutely sure I was pregnant, I made an appointment with a neighborhood ob-gyn who had a reputation for being discreet. I made the appointment under an assumed name just in case. He confirmed what I already knew, but there seemed to be a problem. After the doctor examined me, he'd asked me questions like "When was your last period?" and "Do you notice any pain on the right side?" I had, but I just assumed it was normal and came with being pregnant. The doctor handed me a prescription for prenatal vitamins and a piece of paper on which was scribbled a bunch of different blood tests that he wanted done immediately.

I went home thinking the worst. *Was the baby deformed? Was there something wrong with me?* I had to slap myself in the face to snap out of it. I went about doing my usual chores of setting the table, helping to get dinner served, and cleaning up the dishes. Later that night, a sudden and violent wave of nausea swept over me. I went running for the hall bathroom and threw up. While hugging the bowl, I passed out. Thank God my mother had seen me run for the bathroom. When she came knocking on the door and received no answer, she started banging and yelling. Eventually, she picked the lock with a knife and found me on the bathroom floor. She called my father and Carmine and let them both know she was taking me to the emergency room at Long Island Jewish Medical Center.

At the hospital I was handed a cup and asked to pee in it. I realized they would certainly run a pregnancy test and so I filled the cup with mostly water. This was stupid, I now realize. Carmine was pacing back and forth in the waiting room. He came in to see me a number of times and asked me if we should tell my mother about my pregnancy. Or he wondered whether or not he should hightail it before my father arrived and things turned "messy"? I said no to both questions, stupid me. I was scared.

The intern came back with the results and told my mother that I was pregnant. She said the nausea and vomiting and stomach pain were all early symptoms of pregnancy. My mother was shocked, to say the least. I remember her saying, "This is something we'll talk about when we get home." And then she warned me, "We are *not* going to tell your father when he gets here. We will tell him you have a stomach virus, perhaps food poisoning. He will kill Carmine." She was probably right.

By the time my father arrived, I was ready to be released. My mother just shut him up with a quick "I'll tell you everything in the car on the ride home. In the meantime, let Carmine drive Vicki home in his car."

When we got home, Carmine asked me if he should come inside. I immediately said, "No. This is something I have to do alone. Maybe you can come back and speak to my parents tomorrow." Besides, I was also starting to feel worse and just wanted to lie down. When I went inside, my mother didn't say a word about the pregnancy. All she said was "Go to bed."

Three hours later, after tossing and turning, I woke up and went into the bathroom, turned on the light, and saw that my stomach was four times its normal size and growing. When I peed bright red, I yelled for my mother.

We snuck out like two thieves in the night without Dad knowing and Mom rushed me back to the hospital. The doctors soon determined that I had an ectopic pregnancy. The fetus was growing inside my right tube, and after twelve weeks my tube had ruptured and I was bleeding internally. I needed emergency surgery. My mother signed all the papers and called my fiancé.

When I woke up in recovery, the first person I saw was Carmine. He was crying and just behind him was my mother, looking utterly exhausted. I remember Mom kissing me on my forehead. I was relieved when both of them told me that I was going to be fine, and that the surgery was a success. Of course, neither mentioned the fact that my right tube and part of my ovary had to be removed, yet another obstacle to having children.

Now that I was awake, the doctor came to see me. Dr. Wallace explained that during the procedure they had encountered some trouble with my heart. She told me that I'd suffered a few bouts of arrhythmias and that once or twice my blood pressure had nearly bottomed out, making a complicated situation even worse. Dr. Wallace did her best to reassure us that there may not be anything to worry about, but that I would need to undergo some tests.

After three days of cardiac tests, I was diagnosed with a serious arrhythmia problem brought on by a disease called cardiomyopathy, an infection of the heart wall or muscle.

Using my prior medical history as a road map, the doctor concluded that I must have contracted the disease after a simple dental cleaning years earlier. The dentist was not aware that I had been born with a condition called Mitral Valve Prolapse, more commonly known as MVP. The condition affects mostly women, and is usually more bothersome than dangerous. But the risk of a serious infection is always present. Because of this, women with MVP are usually pre-medicated with a high dose of antibiotics before any dental procedure. I was put on cardiac medications like Digoxin to strengthen the contractions of my heart and Tenormin to regulate my rhythm.

My real concern was the effect this would have on my parents. They had been through so much in such a short time. I really worried about their well-being. My mother cried, while my father kept his sorrow bottled up inside as usual. He stood stoically as the doctor told him I might need more than medications, and that my quality of life could be affected.

We didn't talk much about the pregnancy. But Mom did suggest that perhaps the pregnancy was "a blessing in disguise," as without it we wouldn't have found out about my bad heart. Maybe she was right. But I was thinking more about the ass-whipping I was spared from. I feared Dad a lot more than I did a bad heart back in those days!

LITTLE DID WE know my father already had his suspicions, having found one of the many pregnancy tests in my room. Being a neat freak, Dad often did a routine inspection to check our rooms as well as the rest of the house to make sure "we were keeping up with our chores." I'm sure when he found the pregnancy test, he was crushed. Yet he never even mentioned it to me.

I could also tell by the way he looked at me and the questions he asked me when he came to visit me later that day that he knew something. I found it difficult to even look at him. I'd never lied to him before. But I realized my mother was probably right; telling my father would only further complicate the situation, especially since Carmine and I were due to get married in less than a year.

WHILE ALL THIS was going on, my brother John continued his foray into the life, which surprised me. Even though John had the luxury of a formal education at a prestigious military academy, he would always revisit our early years in

Brooklyn when we were dirt-poor, while our father was in prison and our mother struggled to raise five children. But then again, watching Dad dress up in fancy suits, having late-night meetings at social clubs, did begin to appeal to John. He saw all the good the life had to offer, and he was always protected against the bad. I'm sure the most attractive part was the respect my father received from everyone around him, and the obvious financial opportunities weren't bad, either.

I heard the rumors of my brother John wanting to be a part of the life. I remember the anger and confusion I felt. I was mad at my father for allowing something he'd sworn he would *never* allow, "no matter what." I was confused in the end about why my father did in fact allow this to happen, especially given his dreams of having his sons grow up to be legitimate later on in their lives. I wasn't the only one upset, either.

I remember an argument between my mother and father one night over John. My mother was deeply disturbed that he opted not to go to college and was quite fearful that he would find his way into the lifestyle she had come to loathe. It was one thing to be forced to sit back and "mind your business" when it came to what her husband did for a living, but it was a different story when it came to her own son. She wanted better for him.

It was bad enough that she lived in fear each time my father walked out the door, not knowing if he would come home that night, either because he was arrested or worse, killed. But being forced to sit back and watch her oldest son put himself in harm's way after already losing a son was devastating. That night my father had tried his best to alleviate her fears and concerns and ended the argument with the promise to my mother that my brother "would always be safe." Needless to say, Dad's promise did little to calm her. I, on the other hand, wasn't so easy to bullshit. I loved my father and all of his redeeming qualities—but I hated his lifestyle and everything associated with the life and what it had to offer. I was tired of worrying about whether or not my father could go back to jail or worse, be killed. I was tired of keeping my anger and resentment bottled up inside. Most of all, I was tired of sitting back and watching history repeat itself. I was determined to talk some sense into my brother. But, after countless discussions, it was obvious his mind was made up. John really believed it was expected of him to follow in Dad's footsteps. Dad was a complex man to begin with, and after Frankie's death, he became even harder to understand. He grew colder and more distant. There was little any of us could do to reach him. Unfortunately, John found a way.

IT WAS NOT all bad news for my family in the early eighties. We were getting ready for the first Gotti wedding, Angel's. My sister and I behaved like two schoolgirls; shopping for a wedding gown, the perfect invites, and bridal party favors. We were always close growing up. Sharing a bedroom made us closer. I was happy for my sister. No one deserved to be happier than her. But I was also scared. I didn't want my own room—I didn't want to be left behind. I set aside my unhappiness, though, and watched my sister shine. It was a lavish event at La Mer in Brooklyn. There were nearly six hundred guests; Dad never did anything on a small scale in those days. Generally the hall was large enough to host three weddings at a time. But Dad rented all three floors, so Angel's wedding was the only affair that day. She and Louis Albano were married on a sunny day in September 1983. I was the maid of honor. Unlike my wedding plans, Angel had a full male and female bridal party. Because we had three floors of guests, the bride and groom as well as the bridal party had to be announced on all three floors. Angel was exhausted after dancing the first dance three times!

It was the first important Gotti gathering since Frankie's death, and it was a real tearjerker. Every time a sad song played we all cried. When a special toast was made in memory of Frankie, my sister and I ran to the bathroom in tears. Mom was also inconsolable, while Dad wore his best poker face and tried hard to be an affable and charming host. Yet another sign of Dad's rise in the life was the obvious ass-kicking going on during the wedding. Men, hundreds at a time, would line up to pay homage to Dad—maybe even get a word or two with him. A lot of these men viewed weddings as a forum for any special needs they might have—like settling "a beef" or some financial wrongdoing. I remember, when I was younger, all the chaos that always went on whenever Dad attended a wedding or a funeral. There was always a line of men and women hoping to see him. Some would even gather around his table waiting for him to get up so they could grab his ear. The night of my sister's wedding was no different. I felt so many emotions when Angel got married. I knew it was supposed to be a happy occasion, but I couldn't get past my own fears. Angel and I used to confide in each other, late at night, before bed. We had thousands of conversations about life—our life. Mostly, we talked about Dad—about how scared we both were because he was in the mob. With Angel leaving, I had no one to confide in, no one to tell me things would be fine. Sure, there was always the telephone, but it wasn't the same. My sister was moving out and moving on and I was terrified. But I was too embarrassed to tell her or anyone else how I felt. Instead, I smiled and pretended to be happy.

Angel and Louis had a peaceful and relaxing honeymoon in Aruba, and less than four months later, my sister announced she was pregnant. Dad was ecstatic!

CHAPTER TWENTY-FOUR

"This Magic Moment"

I t was a sunny and unseasonably warm Sunday on December 9, 1984, when I married Carmine Agnello. I had always wanted a Christmas wedding, with the few girls in the wedding party (my matron of honor and two flower girls) to be outfitted in classic red ball gowns, while the all-male or "King's Wedding" party wore black tuxes and tails, trimmed with red cummerbunds and bow ties.

As with any couple getting ready to tie the knot and going through a year of preparations and planning, the two of us did our fair share of arguing. In the months before the wedding it seemed as if we fought daily. The littlest thing would set off the bickering and fighting. My soon-to-be mother-in-law had gone way over her allotted number of invited guests. My gown was too big. And we couldn't even agree on a honeymoon destination, let alone a place to live after we got married. In the end we found a perfect "starter home" in Atlantic Beach, Long Island. It was surrounded by the most incredible views of the bay and the Atlantic Ocean.

The day of my wedding, my father, my sister, Angel, and I rode to Saint Mary Gate of Heaven Church in Ozone Park in a vintage white Bentley. We rode the entire way in silence, all very much deep in thought that day, especially my father and me. It's no secret that he was convinced I was making a mistake, probably the "biggest mistake of my life." He used those exact words. To this day I believe he was still plotting in the car on the way to church, how to get the ceremony called off. I was filled with a twisted and mixed-up bundle of emotions, ranging from nervousness to anxiety to uncertainty to plain old cold feet.

When we arrived there were people everywhere, lining the steps of the church and standing down 101st Avenue as far as the eye could see. My body was wracked with nervous energy and my mind was racing with thoughts of fleeing. I felt uncomfortable sitting in such an extravagant car dressed in a ridiculously expensive wedding gown, being stared at by thousands of onlookers while flashbulbs popped.

It was twenty minutes past noon and the ceremony was scheduled to begin promptly at 12:30, but the groom and his family had not yet arrived. I remember my father's face—his expression was as stiff as stone, his eyes glaring. Even I was scared. He always believed in being on time for everything and today was no exception. *Especially today!* He checked his Rolex repeatedly before turning to me and saying, "I'm giving Carmine five more minutes. Then I'm calling off the wedding and hunting him down like a wild animal. Who does he think he's playing with?"

Tears welled in my eyes as I realized things were going terribly wrong. I was in an absolute state of panic. I had little time or even room inside of me to even consider the second thoughts I'd been having all morning. I sat and prayed in silence for some sign from God. Just a few minutes later, a dirty old tow truck pulled up to the church with Carmine in the passenger side and his brother Mike at the wheel. Behind the tow truck was Marie Agnello in her Chevy Nova, with her daughter and two of her sisters. The fleet of limos sent to pick up my fiancé and his family had never arrived. When they realized it was getting really late, they had the sense to jump in their own cars and make their own way to the church.

My father adjusted his bow tie and the lapels to his custom-made tuxedo, then turned to me and said, "Too bad. I was just coming to terms with the notion this wedding wasn't to be. I was really enjoying the images of what I was going to do to Carmine when I caught him."

My father exited the Bentley, and had a few words with one of his friends, Tony Moscatello, about how he had screwed up the limo situation. I got out of the car and nearly made it to the church steps and then disaster number two occurred. My expensive designer gown split down the back! The teeth on both sides of the zipper broke. Angel shoved me back in the car and dried my tears with a Kleenex. Meanwhile, Dad sent one of his men to find a seamstress—fast! Luckily, Uncle Angelo's mother, Grandma Emma, as we called her, was one of the best seamstresses around. She always carried a travel-sized sewing kit with her and was able to sew the zipper back together. In less than five minutes, I was ready to go, but not before Grandma Emma issued me a stern warning: "Whatever you do, don't try to unzip this dress. If you need to go to the bathroom or take it off, do so over your head." I was so grateful she'd fixed my dress, I cried tears of joy.

We finally made our way up the church steps and inside the back of the church, where we stood for a moment or two, waiting for the organ music to begin. It was a moment I will never forget as long as I live. Dad turned to me and with a look of sincerity and eyes filled with tears, said, "Vicki, you *still* don't have to do this if you don't want to. We could call the whole thing off and change the affair into an elaborate Christmas party. We could go home and you could change into something more appropriate and we could just have fun tonight." Believe me, I was tempted—God knows there were many signs telling me to run—but we'd come this far and now with the entire church filled with people, I just bit the bullet and kissed my father on the cheek, told him I loved him, and we walked down the aisle.

HONESTLY, I WOULD rather have been a guest at my own wedding. I hardly remember having five minutes to myself. There were so many guests, most of whom I didn't know, and my father insisted on introducing me to each and every one of them. The procession line seemed never-ending.

Most guests were eager to trade an envelope stuffed with cash in exchange for a handshake, a thank you, even a word or two with my father. In 1984, my father was the man to watch as far as members of the life were concerned. By now, my father had caught the eye and personal attention of many high-ranking members of the Commission. The day I got married, mostly all of them were in attendance. The guests, the lavish affair, the celebrity performers—it was just like a scene right out of *The Godfather*.

I hardly knew two hundred people out of the fifteen hundred guests in attendance. Greeting each guest was exhausting! Halfway through the affair, I decided to take a break. I felt a bit light-headed; my palms were sweaty and my heart was racing. I found it very difficult to breathe. Because of my recently diagnosed "bad heart," I was put on cardiac medication. Sometimes this medication made me feel worse than my heart did. I excused myself and headed straight to the bride's suite. The room was empty and I was happy for the privacy. I went to the vanity and splashed some cold water on my face, hoping it would calm my nerves.

I sat down on the velvet sofa and laid my head back and closed my eyes for a minute or two. While I was resting, there was a knock on the door. I heard the door open and standing in the doorway was one of the groomsmen—my brother John's friend Johnny Alite. He had come to tell me that my father was looking for me. I nodded. I had expected Dad to send someone to look for me.

"Please tell my father I'll be right out." He nodded, but instead of leaving he entered the room and stood just inches from me, as if he thought I might try to escape through an open window or something. I had to laugh. "Well, what more do you want? I told you I'd be right out." I stood up and at that moment our eyes met. He was a good-looking man and it was easy to understand why he had a reputation as a womanizer. We stood face-to-face, eyes locking and both of us with our hands on our hips. We stared at each other for a few seconds, then I said, "What?" I wasn't sure why he was standing and watching me so closely. But then, in one swoop, he grabbed me around my waist and pulled me closer to him and whispered, "You are the most beautiful girl I've ever seen."

Maybe it was the champagne, or just feeling flattered,

but all I could do was smile and say, "Thank you." That's when he reached down and did the unthinkable, the unexpected, and unimaginable. He kissed me, long and hard, on the mouth. I was stunned. I remember thinking, *On my wedding day? Is this guy crazy? Does he realize my new husband will break him in half? Not to mention my brother, or worse, my father?*

I pushed him away and took a step back. It was clear he'd had a lot to drink. I convinced myself it was sheer drunken stupidity but I was still shocked.

The wedding went off without a further hitch and truly was *the* event of the season. It was all anyone could talk about for weeks to come. Meanwhile, Carmine and I spent our honeymoon in Acapulco and Las Vegas. We stayed at the beautiful and intimate Las Brisas Resort, a mountainside of villas so private each couple had their own pool just outside their villa.

We left on the seventh day and headed to Las Vegas. When we arrived at the MGM Grand, we were quickly ushered to a beautiful suite on the top floor. We stayed in the first night and then spent the next morning at the pool. The second night we went to dinner and to see Siegfried and Roy perform. At the end of every day, Dad would call the hotel to check in. He was pleased we were having a great time.

Later on, Carmine went into the casino to gamble—while I made a beeline for the exclusive shops in the hotel lobby. When I returned to the suite, I was surprised to find Carmine there, sitting on the sofa with his head cradled in his hands. When he looked up and saw my arms filled with shopping bags, he nearly collapsed.

When he announced that he'd lost seventeen thousand dollars, *I* nearly collapsed! When he told me he had "absolutely no money left," I really did fall on the floor! We didn't even have enough money for breakfast the next morning. I was sick with worry. Carmine begged me not to call my father, so I called my brother John instead. He tried his best to calm me down and promised me he would wire some money to keep us comfortable for the rest of the trip. Then he warned me to "keep Carmine away from the tables."

Instead of wiring the money, my brother shocked both of us by showing up in person the next day. I was so surprised when I opened the door and saw him staring back at me. More shockingly, standing next to him was Johnny Alite. He was someone I definitely wasn't happy to see, especially on my honeymoon.

The next few days were extremely awkward for me, to say the least. Everywhere I turned Alite was there. He looked for every chance he could to be alone with me, even if it was just to walk me down to the lobby. I let him know I wasn't amused by his obvious crush, and I assured him my husband wouldn't be too thrilled, either. If Carmine found out about Alite's interest in me, he would surely break him in two. This seemed to put him off, at least temporarily. Later that night Carmine and I had dinner plans, so my brother and Alite took off for the casino. By the time I got out of the shower, my husband had left the suite and followed them downstairs. I was furious. I waited for over an hour and a half, and when he finally returned he had that same look of dread on his face he had when he had lost all our money days earlier. It didn't take me long to realize that whatever relief money John had brought to Vegas was now gone. In fact, Carmine, my brother, and Alite took turns blaming each other. This time I was furious and let *everyone* know it. I slammed the door in their faces and cried myself to sleep. The next morning I wasn't surprised to learn my brother and Alite had caught an early-morning flight back to New York. My brother didn't even say good-bye. He was that embarrassed.

Carmine and I fought all the way back to New York. I wouldn't even sit next to him on the plane. I had the flight attendant change my seat and sat on the opposite side of the aircraft. When we landed I returned home to my parents' house. I told my father our house was not yet ready, but my mother knew better. It was that night I realized I'd definitely made a mistake by marrying Carmine Agnello.

I spent three nights at my parents' house in my old familiar room. Carmine stayed at his mother's house. I was anxious and depressed and didn't know how to tell my father that he had been right. I worked myself into such a frenzy I made myself sick. After I couldn't even keep clear broth down, my mother took me to the doctor. That's when I found out I was pregnant.

CHAPTER TWENTY-FIVE

"Don't They Know It's the End of the World"

'll never forget my father's face when I announced that I got pregnant on my honeymoon and I was going to have a baby. His expression was a mask of excitement and fear. He was thrilled about the prospect of having a second grandchild on the way. My sister was due in June and I was due in late August. But at the same time, he was worried sick my heart wouldn't sustain the rigorous trials of pregnancy, and especially the birth. It didn't help matters that my mother was also concerned and shared this openly in front of the entire family that Sunday in early January. Ironically, Mom had recently watched the movie *Steel Magnolias* starring Julia Roberts and Sally Field. For anyone who hasn't seen the movie, it's a tearjerker about a young girl (Roberts) battling Type 1 diabetes. She gets pregnant and, against her doctor's advice, has a baby—and dies just after childbirth. Mom went on to tell Dad all about the movie.

The pregnancy really pushed my father's fears into high gear. He asked me all kinds of questions—"Does the doctor think pregnancy is wise in your condition?" and "Do you feel strong enough to go through this?" Lastly he said, "Let Mama call the doctor in the morning and schedule all the necessary tests." As if I wasn't capable of doing this myself?

His last comment sent me over the edge. For the first time in weeks I was over-the-moon with joy, and now every ounce of happiness was being drained by the second. I wanted the baby so badly. Ever since the doctor had mentioned I might not be able to have children, it was all I thought about and it made me realize just how badly I wanted to be a mother.

The pregnancy did not go well. Even though the doctors hovered over me like hawks and I had two standing appointments each month as opposed to the normal one, I began spotting from the early weeks after conception. When the bleeding continued for days and then weeks, the doctor ordered me to bed. I was to remain there for the better part of the day and night, only getting up for meals or to go to the bathroom.

The doctor examined me about six months into the pregnancy, and seemed very concerned about the size and position of the baby. She hospitalized me for a battery of tests. I was diagnosed with gestational diabetes and my cardiologist was called in. He found that the pregnancy was placing too much of a strain on my already damaged heart. The increase in blood flow commonly associated with pregnancy was proving to be too much for my heart to handle. I was kept in and out of the hospital for nearly a month. After I was released I remained bedridden again, only this time I was only allowed to be on my feet to go to the bathroom.

By early summer the weather was still showing no signs of warming up and each morning felt cold and damp. One Monday morning I woke up colder than usual and climbed out of bed to get a heavier blanket. While I was up, I went to the bathroom. It was early and still dark outside. I don't know why I didn't put the light on. Lord knows I've gone over this question in my mind for years, wondering if it would have made a difference. I walked into the bathroom and didn't see the small puddle of water left over from my husband's bath just a half hour earlier. I slipped and fell down. I remember feeling nothing at first, then a sharp and sudden pain shooting across my abdomen. It felt as if my stomach and the baby were caught in a viselike grip and then released. Though the pain was gone I was still afraid to move. So I sat for a few minutes and tried to catch my breath.

The anxiety slowly passed and I felt normal again. As I reached up for the door handle I saw the bright red stain on my nightgown and I knew something was seriously wrong. I crawled out of the bathroom and before I dialed 911, I called my mother. I wasn't making any sense. I was hysterical and breathing fast and hard. I shouted, "Something's wrong, Mom. Something's very wrong."

My mother called the ambulance and I was taken to Long Beach Memorial Hospital. I was taken in through the emergency room on a stretcher.

My mother and husband arrived first and I started crying with relief at the sight of their worried faces. The doctor came in and announced I would need to be admitted because I'd had my show (a mixture of blood and fluid that preludes labor) and could be going into labor soon. He told us that the baby and I were fine. After a few tests and several uneventful hours, he released me.

The moment I arrived home I called my regular doctor. She was very upset that I had been released. She was also suspicious about the show and the fate of my pregnancy. She ordered me to meet her at Long Island Jewish Medical Center, where I was scheduled to give birth when the due date arrived. I was immediately admitted and told I was to stay overnight, just for observation. If nothing happened in the next twenty-four hours the doctor would release me the following afternoon.

I had a peaceful night and slept until nine the next morning. When I woke the nurse was standing by my bed, waiting to take my vitals. I asked if I could use the bathroom first. As I got out of bed, I suddenly felt strange. The room seemed like it was spinning. There was a quick sharp pain in my lower abdomen and then a gush of water. I was mortified and ran to the bathroom, but the flow wouldn't stop. I assumed I'd peed my pants. The nurse summoned the doctor.

When Dr. Stern arrived she had the same glum look on her face as the day before. She explained that the flow was amniotic fluid and that the baby and I might be in danger. The best-case scenario would be if the "mucus plug" replenished itself and early labor did not begin. It was a long shot, but we hoped for the best. She went on to explain about the seriousness of early labor. The baby's eyes were not yet fully developed, and neither were the lungs. She seemed most concerned, though, about whether or not I would develop a fever. If an infection developed it would be serious. Then the bombshell: I was told a decision would have to be made about whose life should be saved if there were complications, the baby's or mine? There was a paper to be signed by the family. A choice had to be made.

I was crying so hard at this point I couldn't call anyone.

(Clockwise) John, me, Mom, Frank, and Angel in the 1970s.

Mom and Dad with Baby Angel.

John and Frank.

"Mr. Muscle" John and me in the backyard, Canarsie, Brooklyn.

William "Willie Boy" Johnson, an unknown companion, and Uncle Genie outside the social club, Ozone Park, Queens.

Dad, Miami in the 1970s.

Mom, Peter at six months old, and me.

The Gotti clan at dinner, mid-1970s.

Dad and Angel on her wedding day, September 1983.

ABOVE: Dad and Frank, Mother's Day, 1985.

LEFT: Dad and John (in military school uniform).

My wedding day.

Dad and me—I was bawling my eyes out!

John (second from left) and his childhood pals.

On the way to meet Dad for our weekly outing—he sent a limo every week to see/spend the day with the kids.

The last picture of me and Carmine together as husband and wife.

John and all the gang, Christmas, 1990. These group shots were always taken for Dad's benefit.

Mom and me at a heart fund-raiser I hosted.

Peter, me, and John.

My three snazzy dressers!

Fans and mourners lining the streets of Ozone Park, Queens, during Dad's funeral procession.

So Dr. Stern did. Within the hour my family had arrived. My mother was nervously pacing the floor, and my father anxiously inquired about my condition over and over. Carmine sat solemnly in a nearby chair. The doctor told my parents and my husband that the baby was a girl. She was small and the delivery would be difficult. Later that night my mother was exhausted and I asked my husband to drive her home. My father wanted to stay longer. He told me later that he had a strong feeling something terrible was going to happen.

I assured everyone I was okay and forced them all to go home and get some rest. I was exhausted and craved sleep. My father was the last to leave, around 11 P.M. I drifted off to sleep almost immediately. Then I was awakened a few hours later with excruciating pain. I was sweating profusely and my forehead was burning. The nurse summoned the doctor and the next thing I knew chaos broke out around me.

The next few hours were filled with distorted images and voices. I remember the excruciating pain and the loud screams I made. It felt like my insides were being ripped apart. I passed out from the pain after about an hour, just as the baby was kicking up a storm inside me.

I woke up around 10 A.M. to find a nurse standing beside my bed. The first thing I reached for was my stomach—the swollen mass was gone. Images flashed before my eyes of the labor and delivery just hours before. But the outcome was a complete blur. I had no clue what had happened after I lost conciousness. I was scared and alone. I looked up at the nurse. She stared back at me, then said, "Do you want your baby baptized?"

Being a Catholic, I nodded yes.

"Would you like to see her?" she added.

I could hardly wait. I wondered where my parents and my husband were. The night nurse had called everyone once labor had started and once again everyone raced back to the hospital.

The nurse left the room and headed to the nursery. She returned a few minutes later wheeling a small, well-lit incubator. I hoisted myself up and cradled my arms to receive my daughter, wishing my parents and husband were there to see her as well. I waited for the nurse to hand her to me, but the woman just stood there staring. A few seconds later she left the room, with a confused look in her eyes.

I turned the white cotton blanket swaddling the baby over to one side and noticed my daughter was lying completely still. The tips of her lips were blue and her skin was a pasty gray. I reached inside the bin and lifted the baby into my arms. It was only then that I realized she was dead.

I started screaming so loud the entire nursing staff came running to my room. They stood at the door staring at me. I was crying and my body was shaking with grief. One nurse shouted to the other, "Oh my God, didn't anyone tell her?" Quickly she reached for the baby and took the small bundle from my arms. A slight mass of dark hair capped her head and her tiny fingers were perfectly formed. She was a beautiful girl with tiny perfect features and a small, perfectly formed body that was as stiff as a plastic doll. I ached, the pain was so bad.

The nurse said, "I'm so sorry, someone should have told you," as she took the baby away from me.

A few minutes later my father appeared, looking both disheveled and anxious. It didn't look like he had slept. I later learned he'd been downstairs in the hospital lounge, waiting for me to wake. One of the nurses had the foresight to run and tell him what had happened in my room with the baby. He took the elevator and raced to my room. When he looked at me with tired, dark eyes, his heart nearly broke. Before he spoke to me, he walked to the door and asked a nearby nurse to "get the doctor right away." She nodded. Then he whispered, "Can I ask why my daughter is still on the labor and delivery floor?" His eyes moved to the newborn babies being wheeled out of the nursery for their regular feedings.

She nodded in agreement, then shrugged her shoulders. "I was told early this morning your daughter was to be moved to the surgical floor ASAP. I guess they were waiting for an available bed."

The nurse left the room and shut the door behind her. My father looked clumsy and awkward; sensitive as he was, he had a great deal of difficulty expressing it. He sat down on the bed beside me and reached for my hand. "I'm sorry, Vicki, the baby didn't make it."

There were a few moments of silence, and then I started sobbing again. I fought hard to hold back my tears, especially in front of the man who'd always taught me that crying was "for those who were weak." My father would tell me often throughout my childhood to "never cry over simple things like a scraped knee or a bad test grade." He would end the lesson by letting me know I should "save the tears for when *really* necessary." I turned my head slightly to the side so he couldn't see my tears, but he moved in closer to me and whispered, "Go on, cry."

I spent the next three days in the hospital. The day I was sent home, the baby was to be buried at St. John's Cemetery in Queens. Dad had made the arrangements; the crypt was

213

to be close to Frankie Boy's. I gave my daughter the name I had picked out the day I learned I was pregnant—Justine Gotti Agnello.

Everyone thought it would be too much for me, but I insisted on being there. The mass was nearly an hour long and I cried the entire time. I remember holding my hands on my stomach, waiting for any sign of life—a kick, a poke, or a twist. But nothing came. My belly was empty, just like my heart.

I returned home and locked myself in the baby's room—a beautifully decorated bedroom with bright colors splashed across the walls. The floor was covered in a bright red carpet and in the corner sat a life-sized stuffed clown, a gift from my father during my sixth month of pregnancy. I disconnected the phone lines and double-bolted the front door in an effort to keep all the sympathetic guests away, even my parents. Most of all, I couldn't bear to see my sister, Angel. She was due to give birth any day. I was angry and selfish. I wondered why this had to happen to *my* baby? I couldn't face anyone.

I stayed locked in the room for many days and nights following the burial. Even my husband couldn't speak to me or lure me from the baby's room. My parents were frightened. My father insisted on seeing me, even though I refused. He pushed his way inside the house one night and took the stairs two at a time. When he opened the baby's room door he nearly fell down when he saw what I looked like. I was still sleeping on the floor, curled up into a ball and clinging to the stuffed clown. My father sat down on the floor and began his speech. He told me he understood my grief—and he did. He told me I had a right to be angry—and I was. He told me I had to get back to the real world—but I couldn't.

The following week, my father arranged for an infertility specialist to fly in from Boston to see me at Columbia Presbyterian Hospital. His diagnosis was not something I wanted to hear: the delivery was a difficult one that had damaged my reproductive organs. "The chances of your carrying a baby to full term is slim to none," he told me.

I was devastated. My husband sat next to me, visibly squirming. I ran from the doctor's office hysterical, so my husband thought it best he take me to my parents' rather than our home. When I got there I broke down in front of my mother and father. I could see it in their eyes; they, too, were crushed. Later, my mother admitted to me that she'd cried herself to sleep that night—begging God to give me a child, one child. She knew how much having children meant to me.

The following week, my father sent for my husband and insisted Carmine take me away on a cruise. He believed I needed a rest from all that had happened. We left for the Caribbean on a Friday and returned on the following Friday. Other than being quiet and restful, it did little to sway or change my depressed state. At this point I'd become so sick with grief, I couldn't eat or keep anything down. The day after we returned, my mother took me to see the doctor and asked her to prescribe something for my stomach. The doctor did some routine tests and could hardly contain her excitement when she returned to the examining room with a piece of litmus paper in her right hand.

"Well, I can't believe it myself. You're not sick—you're pregnant!"

CHAPTER TWENTY-SIX

"Fly Me to the Moon"

t was 1985 and the name John Gotti seemed to be on every OCTF (Organized Crime Task Force) agent's lips. The use of street canaries and bugging devices of various mob-connected associates had led the agents to believe that John Gotti was the up-and-coming guy to watch in the Mafia. Even the media began devoting much time and space to coverage of the mob in an effort to familiarize the public with the enigma that was John Gotti. Reporters portrayed my father as a "modern-day Robin Hood," even further propelling the public's fascination with John Gotti and romanticizing the mob. Everyone wanted to meet John Gotti, have dinner with him, or even a "quick audience"—especially celebrities. Pro athletes seemed enamored of my father. Often when I went to football or baseball games, they would come off the field just to meet me—and then ask about Dad. Jason Giambi, Mike Piazza, and Jason Kidd were among the list. Actor Steven Seagal often showed up at the social club, as did Tony Danza and Mike Tyson.

One night I was invited to have dinner with Sean Penn. We met in his restaurant, Man Ray. He was so fascinated by Dad that the dinner lasted hours, and we went to three different places throughout the night. I walked in the door at nearly 6 A.M. Sean had asked question after question about my father—and only when I could no longer stay awake did the night end.

Even Liz Taylor had met Dad in a restaurant. Though the *National Enquirer* claimed that they were dating and superimposed their likenesses together to make it appear as if they were crossing the street arm-in-arm, they really had met only briefly. Robert De Niro wanted to do a movie about Dad, as did Sylvester Stallone. Despite all the attention, Dad was not impressed with celebrities. He was always affable and accommodating when he met anyone, but he wasn't into pretentiousness. He wasn't a phony. Besides, he never had the time for random meetings, and he was shy about being introduced to new people.

Week after week, articles came out about my father. Well-respected publications like *New York* magazine and *Time* magazine ran articles about the Mafia. *Time* even featured my father on the cover—a first for the otherwise politically driven magazine. The public loved stories about John Gotti and his crew. Why wouldn't they? He wore two-thousand-dollar Brioni suits. He had "movie-star" good looks, a cross between James Dean and Clark Gable. He held court, telling unending, witty stories, and had a perfect memory. His smile lit up a room and he walked with a swagger that stood out on any crowded street. The public ate him up by the spoonful and couldn't seem to get enough. It drove the FBI and members of law enforcement crazy!

While the press and the public elevated Dad's celebrity, the streets became even darker.

Life for the Gotti family began to take a drastic change—gone were the days of privacy and calm. Everything a Gotti did somehow managed to garner unwanted and unnecessary attention. Everything we did was magnified under a microscope. It was not a transformation any of us Gotti kids welcomed. Overnight, it seemed, we went from being low-key and unpretentious, as my father had insisted on, to being very publicly exposed. Each of us willingly or not was dissected by the New York papers on a weekly basis, from the moment one of us was spotted with Dad. This continued and grew, much to my father's dismay. Believe it or not, Dad was staunchly against unwanted publicity. He feared it would awaken or arouse many degenerates looking for money—especially when it came to his kids or grandkids. Someone might get an idea in his or her head in an attempt to get their hands on some cash—an idea like kidnapping. I believe the Gambino kidnapping tragedy did this to Dad and greatly unnerved him. Dad figured if someone was brazen enough to go after Carlo Gambino's nephew, it could happen to anyone. As a result, Dad was always on guard as to where we went and who we were with. And as much as he could, he kept us out of the public eye.

MEANWHILE, PAUL CASTELLANO'S reputation was growing throughout the Mafia kingdom as a tyrant and a selfish boss. As a result, most men within the organization were leery of his leadership. Even Castellano's own loyal soldiers began questioning his leadership abilities. Some men openly defected to Dellacroce's side. They felt more secure working under someone of the "old order." And no matter what politics dictated, in their minds the real boss was Neil. My father was one of those men. Politically, he answered to Paul—but his loyalty always remained with Neil. Dad believed that Neil was a "man's man," with many admirable qualities.

Uncle Angelo had a brother, Salvatore, who was known as a ruffian by most men in the streets. It was rumored he was involved with some major drug dealers. Because of this, Sallie was excluded from the family—there was a strict "no drugs" bar for any members, punishable by death. He had his share of legal issues as a result of his lifestyle, and law enforcement had been after him for years. Tired of living life on the lam, Sallie had decided to surrender. But en route to turning himself in, both Salvatore Ruggiero and his wife, Stephanie, were killed in a private plane crash on their way from Florida to New York.

The accident distressed Uncle Angelo beyond words and he set out to Florida to tie up any loose ends with his brother's estate. The couple had two small children, Jamie and Danielle, both of whom were supposed to be on the flight, but at the last minute Stephanie had decided to leave the children behind. My uncle Angelo was now in charge of the children's welfare and their financial assets. Supposedly, there was an estimated $3 to $4 million of Sal Ruggiero's money still out on the streets, waiting to be collected. However, by involving himself with Sal's estate, Angelo opened the doors to much scrutiny. Law enforcement officials believed Angelo had "stepped into his brother Salvatore's footsteps." This was an allegation that Angelo had vehemently denied.

With the help of Uncle Genie, Angelo went to Florida,

collected the children and their things, tied up a few real estate matters, and returned to New York. While trying to put his brother's estate in order, Angelo decided the money on the street rightfully belonged to his brother's estate—to his brother's kids. The moment he set about trying to collect these debts, he and my uncle Genie were arrested. Their involvement in Sal's business caused them to be implicated in the sinister world of drugs. My father was *livid*. Dad walked around in such a constant enraged state that few people would dare to cross him. To make matters worse, Paul Castellano, the "Big Boss," insinuated that he would hold my father "accountable" for this "outside act of defiance" in violating the drug policy. If Angelo's and Genie's actions were found to be anything more than money collecting, the two men would be killed. It was yet another factor in the ongoing personal war between my father and Paul.

My father stuck by his brother and best friend, defending them as best he could given the circumstances. He went to meetings on both men's behalf to see Paul and reassured him of their innocence. But Paul wanted confirmation; he wanted access to personal tapes acquired by the FBI to be used in the case. These were tapes that my father had no control over. Yet he pressed Angelo daily. On some tapes Angelo was heard bad-mouthing Paul and some others he deemed "selfish" or "greedy," and there was no way he wanted the boss to hear his rants. Angelo also claimed that many of his dear friends would be "thrown under a bus" if these tapes got out. My father agreed, but told Angelo that a compromise would have to be made. My father met with Paul many times in an effort to calm matters, but each time the meetings ended on a sour and unresolved note. With Neil and my father still a threat to him, Paul remained on guard. Another thorn in Paul's side was the fact that Dad was growing far too popular with many of the "higher-ups" in the Family. I'm convinced Paul had hoped Dad would refuse to follow protocol when it came down to the tapes. He'd hoped there would be destruction, perhaps bloodshed. I believe Castellano wanted a reason to kill Dellacroce and my father.

The so-called "Big Paul" tapes were acquired after FBI agents planted bugs inside Angelo's house, in a dinette booth where he was known to have early morning meetings with associates, as well as on each of the phones in his house, including his young daughter's pink Princess phone in her bedroom. The FBI had used "breaking and entering" to set the bugs in place, a tactic even law enforcement sources agreed was "dirty." The notion "innocent until proven guilty" went out the window when it came to organized crime. Angelo suspected that the FBI was listening to his conversations using phone bugs, so he had a security expert called in to "sweep" his house and car clean. The FBI knew the expert was coming and so they turned off their mikes that day. The guy appreciated the work and needed to justify the exorbitant thousand-dollar fee he charged. So he told my uncle his house was indeed bugged. But he calmed Angelo down by assuring him that he had removed the mikes. Outside my uncle's home in Cedarhurst, Long Island, the FBI grabbed the security expert and threatened him for revealing their bugs. The man pleaded for his life and told the agents he only lied to Angelo. He said he never really found any bugs.

Unfortunately, Uncle Angelo believed the man and

believed he had no reason to be afraid about speaking "freely" in his own home from then on—something my father would never do. Dad believed that speaking on phones was careless and stupid, and speaking in one's own home was even worse.

Even the FBI was aware of this and never attempted to bug our house. They knew my father never conducted any meetings in his home and rarely spoke on the phone to anyone except his driver.

Still, my father realized he had a mess on his hands—a mess that would require much skill and intervention to keep everyone happy. Dellacroce stepped in and went to bat for my father and his crew members. It was no secret that Paul and Neil were rivals, and the ever-present feud between them was really starting to heat up. Dad attended meeting after meeting, with Dellacroce as his closest advisor and supporter. Dellacroce, in fact, even stood up to Paul on many occasions, having never forgotten the way he was passed over when Castellano was made boss. Neil was also convinced my father was innocent of whatever acts his men perpetrated. Neil also believed Paul was using the tapes as an excuse to screw Gotti. He believed the tapes were not incriminating, but rather embarrassing to Ruggiero—still, Dellacroce also respected the Commission's rules. During one conversation at Neil's home, he told Ruggiero that he agreed with my father; "a compromise would have to be reached." Neil took Angelo's side, but at the same time, knew what breaking the rules of the Commission would bring. Even my father strongly urged Ruggiero to hand over the tapes. Dad agreed with Dellacroce and didn't think these tapes were worth a possible mob war. As it was, these tapes were compromising many others as well as Ruggiero. Dad and Dellacroce were at risk as well. Rumors began to surface that Paul wanted both Dellacroce and my father dead and was conspiring behind their backs. Paul knew Dellacroce would always be resentful because Paul was made boss—and Paul knew Gotti would always stand behind Dellacroce. He blamed his decision on the tape fiasco, but anyone in the know knew it had more to do with the ever-present fear that Dellacroce and Gotti represented. Not too long after the tape situation surfaced, Dellacroce was diagnosed with terminal cancer. This devastated Dad. He loved Neil like a father. From then on, any other meetings concerning the tapes took place at Neil's home, at his sickbed.

Despite mob politics, Dellacroce believed Dad should not be forced into a position of walking away from his closest men. Dellacroce was overheard asking my father, "You want me to tell Paul to go fuck himself, I will. But then we need to be ready for war. Does anybody really want this?"

The answer, of course, was no.

In the end, a decision was made—one that utterly broke my father's heart. Angelo's and Genie's lives would be spared, but Dad had to "distance" himself from them—the two people he was closest with. It was not something my father wanted to do, but he was a man of his word, who really believed in that life and followed the rules by the book.

Setting aside his two close confidants was not easy for my father. His moods became more volatile. There were additional rumors on the streets—Paul was not content in just letting sleeping dogs lie; he wanted more. With his mentor, Neil Dellacroce, gravely ill and his closest confidant,

Angelo, now "distanced," Dad was left in a vulnerable position. He walked around in a constant state of unease. For the first time in his life, Dad was forced to look over his shoulder—and suspicious of anyone he came in contact with.

To compound matters, Uncle Angelo was diagnosed with lung cancer. It was deemed advanced and terminal, at stage four. Even though Dad had distanced himself from his childhood pal, he felt the grief of losing someone so important to him. Angelo's condition rapidly deteriorated. He was hospitalized a short time later and his only request was to see Dad. My father fought many demons in his decision-making process. If he followed his heart and went to see Angelo, the Commission would soon find out. Dad didn't care about being reminded about the earlier deal he'd made to spare Angelo's life. Dad was mostly concerned about how other men in the street would perceive him as possibly weak and easy if he went against his own words, his own rules. He was expected to set an example. In the end Dad did not go. When Uncle Angelo died, the last words on his lips were "Tell Johnny I love him."

When Dad was told, he bowed his head solemnly and went into a deep, dark place in private. He stayed home for the next three days, locked in his bedroom. He didn't answer calls and wouldn't see any visitors. The wake lasted two days—Angelo's body was in repose at Stephen's Funeral Home, a few blocks from the Bergin Hunt and Fish Club. It came as no surprise to me when one of the funeral directors told me that Dad was seen leaving the funeral home at 10:45 P.M. on the second night of the wake. He'd slipped in and out of a side entrance, well after the crowd of mourners had left. I knew there was no way my father would let Uncle Angelo exit this world without saying good-bye. After all, the two were closer than brothers.

It didn't help matters that not too long after that, Dad got the phone call that Neil had died. He went peacefully in his sleep on December 2, 1985. His funeral was befitting a Mafia boss, and Dad had his mentor entombed in a crypt in St. John's Cemetery, not more than a few feet from Frankie Boy's crypt. But the last insult from Paul came when he deliberately avoided Neil's wake. This was the greatest slight imaginable in the life.

While this turmoil was going on, other members of other families were expressing their disdain and dislike of Paul Castellano. Behind Paul's back, many men grumbled, even those in high positions in that life. Heads of other families, captains of important and influential crews, and many soldiers supported a mutiny against "Big Paul" Castellano.

More meetings were arranged by the Commission to discuss the topic of Paul's leadership and why every crew was "now starving." Many men showed up for these secret meetings, unhappy with the newly anointed boss—a man put in his position because of marriage and family ties. In the months that followed, most of the leaders or capos under Paul let their frustrations be known. During numerous secret meetings these men shared their gripes with the Family's underboss, Dellacroce, before his death. They claimed Paul was taking more money from them than ever before. They also claimed that Paul was a hypocrite—that he was involved with known drug dealers, members of the Bonnano Family, despite the staunch "no drugs" policy the Gambino Family adhered to. These men were said to be kicking up some of their profits to Paul in exchange for favors and good placement in the Commission. Castellano was also involved with the ruthless gang the Westies. Paul often handed these gang members work he needed done, much to the resentment of his own men. It didn't help matters much that Paul was recently arrested for what later became called "the Commission Case," and was facing a lengthy jail sentence. If he was convicted, the future of the Family seemed grave to his loyal underlings—especially since Paul intended to hand over control of the Family to his inexperienced driver, Thomas Bilotti. This bit of news was the last straw as far as some members of the Commission were concerned. Now, with Dellacroce dead, there was no one who would go to bat for these loyal men when it came to Big Paul. Most of them, as well as my father, knew Paul wanted John Gotti and some of his crew members out of the way. Without Neil, they were moving targets. One of these disgruntled men was Sammy Gravano. At one such meeting he was complaining to the other members about how Paul was dividing the Family in two—those who supported Dellacroce and those who supported Paul. The Gambino Family was supposed to be *one* Family—strong and loyal—and Gravano's gripes were heard loud and clear by other members of the Commission.

The issues with Paul were discussed and the Commission cast their vote. All the men who were in leadership positions agreed—all except one man, Vincent "the Chin" Gigante, from the Genovese Family. But the majority ruled and Paul's fate was decided.

It was a typical December afternoon in 1985, cold, gray, and windy outside. I remember thinking it was going to snow. I was five months' pregnant with my second child and was following doctor's orders to stay in bed for most of the day, getting up only if necessary and drinking lots of fluids. My second pregnancy was not an easy one, but I was determined to give birth to a healthy baby. So I took to complete bed rest from my fifth month onward. My sister, Angel, had delivered the first Gotti grandchild in June of '85. He was appropriately named Frank. Now it was my turn, and I was determined to add a healthy baby to the burgeoning Gotti brood.

It was Christmastime, the most joyous season in New York City. Castellano was heading to a business dinner with his trusted bodyguard and constant companion, Thomas Bilotti. The dinner was planned at a usual spot for Paul, Sparks Steakhouse on Forty-sixth Street in Midtown. According to witnesses, as his car pulled up to the curb and he and Bilotti got out, a group of men dressed in long overcoats and furry Russian hats approached and opened fire, killing Castellano and Billoti instantly.

I remember watching the news and seeing the breaking story. My heart skipped a beat. It was a time of uncertainty for the mob. There were reports in the newspapers almost daily about mob wars and threats on certain men. One such report stated that there was to be an attempt on my father's life—a report, though false, that had all of us especially worried. It was the always present fear that accompanied the lifestyle and kept our family members on guard.

When I first heard of the double murder, the announcer said only one victim's name had been released, Paul Castellano. The other victim was not yet identified. I froze, thinking it was my father. I tried to call my mother—it was a constant busy signal, and I must have pressed redial ten times. So against doctor's orders, I grabbed my car keys and headed to Queens to my parents' home to find out what was going on.

When I arrived, everyone in the house was standing around the television, watching for the latest news report. Just like me, they thought my father might have been the other victim. Then the phone rang. A part of me didn't want to pick it up for fear of horrible news; the other part of me desperately wanted to grab the phone in the hopes it would be my father—it was. I was so relieved, I started crying. This angered Dad. He shouted into the receiver, "Are you crazy? Has everyone gone crazy?" He said he was at the Bergin Hunt and Fish Club in Ozone Park and ended the conversation with "Tell Mama I'll be home in a few hours." Then he hung up. It was forty minutes after the shooting. Later that night I ended up in the emergency room. Once again, I had started bleeding mid-trimester, and the doctors believed the unexpected stress was the cause. They kept me overnight for observation.

Within a few days the reporters were in full swing. Everyone had my father tapped as Paul's executioner. The fact that there were news reports showing lots of well-dressed men arriving at the Ravenite Social Club in Little Italy to pay homage to my father gave even further evidence that he was involved in the murders. It was later learned that the very same Commission that had voted Paul Castellano be "removed" had also decided that my father take his place. A boss cannot be killed without the votes of the Commission, so reports that the hit was planned primarily by my father were in no way accurate. Shortly after the Castellano murder, there was more heat. As with any major uprising within the ranks, there were those who were not happy with the change. One such person decided to take matters into his own hands and let the world, especially members in the life, know of his discontent. He did this in an explosive manner.

The message came in the form of a car bomb. In 1986, Frank DeCicco, then underboss for the Gambino Family, was killed as he approached his car. Pieces of him littered the Brooklyn street, in front of the Veterans and Friends Social Club—a known hangout of Sammy Gravano. De-Cicco's car was reduced to nothing but smoking shreds. The explosion had literally rocked the entire block. DeCicco was a longtime friend of my father's as well as a close confidant of Castellano. Many believed he had betrayed Paul and had taken part in the plot to kill him.

Obviously, the murder of DeCicco brought fears of an all-out war. Was this killing an isolated incident, a renegade event, or the opening salvo in a new gang war? Rumors spread that Vincent "the Chin" Gigante was sending a message of disdain over Paul's death, while others speculated that the car bombing was not related to organized crime at all. Given the nature of the bomb—one with a handheld remote control and the sophisticated mechanism attached to it—whoever had orchestrated the hit had access to top-of-the-line technology, such as the government. Some people insist the Feds planted the bomb in an effort to kill John Gotti (as Dad was rumored to have canceled a last-minute appointment with DeCicco that day) or perhaps to weaken the entire organization. At the moment, it didn't matter. Panic hit the streets. The men in the life were up in arms, ready for war. If the bombing was meant to be a message that Gotti should watch his back, it didn't work. Dad, standing tall, visited every social club and mob-gathering place throughout the metropolitan area, to rally his men and assure them that those responsible for the DeCicco killing would be found and appropriately dealt with.

He drove in his own car by himself to each location, demonstrating no fear and no retreat. As always, he led by example.

"We are the Gambino Family, and nobody, anywhere, anytime, is going to fuck with us" was the promise he made. All challengers would be answered; power and honor would be maintained. Those Family men, wary, nervous, who heard the chief's message were reassured by his strength and by his words. They knew he would never ask any of them to do something that he himself had not already done and would do again.

Panic and fear went looking for a new address. It was back to business as usual.

CHAPTER TWENTY-SEVEN

"I Fought the Law, and the Law Won"

In 1984, a minor incident by Gotti standards ended up splashed across the front page of every paper in New York. On the way home from a late-night card game, my father had his driver and friend, Bartholomew "Bobby" Borriello, drop him and another friend, Frank Colletta, off at the Cozy Corner Bar in Queens to make a phone call. The car was double-parked outside, blocking the street. While they were in the bar, a truck pulled up and began beeping incessantly. Colletta came out to see what the commotion was about and my father soon followed.

My father was not in a patient mood that day, as he told me and my family after the incident. The driver continued to lay on his horn. When he saw Dad and Colletta, he jumped from the truck and approached them, shouting.

The truck driver, Romual Piecyk, continued his rant against the double-parked car. Colletta pushed the man back, and in the scuffle, the man's pay for that week was ripped from his pocket. My father told him to "Get the fuck out of here." Piecyk left and went to the police, and a few minutes later they were at the bar, arresting my father.

Dad was charged with felony assault and theft, but he

was released on bail. He returned home later that night and went straight to bed. The next morning all the newspapers had stories about the incident and my father's arrest. It was all anyone talked about that day, and even more so in the days to come, for when Piecyk learned who my father was, he decided he had messed with the wrong guy. By the time the case went to trial, he wanted the charges dropped and claimed Gotti was the wrong guy. Piecyk claimed that by then the incident was so long ago that he didn't remember who was involved in the scuffle. The headline in the *Daily News* the next day was priceless: "I FORGOTTI."

When questioned later by reporters, Piecyk not only insisted he wanted the charges against my father dropped but also told them that the FBI had contacted him. He claimed the agents tried hard to convince him to press charges against my father, and made threats that if he didn't, they'd press charges against him. Piecyk even wrote a letter to my mother and me stating, "They [FBI] did all they could to make me press charges against John." The Queens DA's office even considered perjury charges against Piecyk, but eventually decided against it. They had bigger issues to deal with.

The Piecyk incident was the first of four trials my father was about to endure. With that out of the way, my father had his next trial to worry about, which was scheduled to start just two weeks later on April 7, 1986. It was a RICO case, and anyone who knew anything about RICO knew that this would be a tough charge to beat. To make matters even harder for Dad, the FBI as well as the Queens DA's office wanted in; both wanted to be the first to get Gotti.

Meanwhile, one day after Dad's trial began, I went

into labor. My water broke while I was at my parents' home awaiting news of the first day of the trial. At first I thought I'd wet my pants and ran to the bathroom, flushed with embarrassment. But when the painful contractions began, everyone went into a full-on panic. The baby was over a month early and everyone feared the worst. When I arrived at the hospital, there was a full staff waiting, including two neonatal specialists in case the baby was in distress. My sister, Angel, came with Carmine and me to offer support and calm my fears. During the fourteen-hour labor, Angel tried her best to keep me distracted from all the pain and commotion that was going on in the hospital. At one point she made me laugh so hard, I really *did* pee my pants! Dad found out a few minutes after he left the courthouse and raced to Long Island Jewish Medical Center. Nine hours later I gave birth to a baby boy. He was a mere five pounds. When the doctor told my father that the baby and I were healthy and resting, he was ecstatic! He stayed at the hospital, just staring at his grandson for nearly twelve hours. Dad visited daily for the next few days. He was in such a good mood, he ordered dinner every night from all the finest restaurants in Manhattan for the entire hospital staff. He also passed out hundred-dollar tips to anyone who entered my room. Even the janitor couldn't wait to mop up every afternoon around two. Enough flowers to fill two hospital rooms arrived from all over the country. It seemed everyone wanted to congratulate John Gotti on the birth of his second grandson.

It wasn't until a few days later I learned that the premature birth had resulted in a severe left eye and left foot deformity. The pediatrician came by to examine my son, and the moment he suspected there were problems, the doctor sent for all the appropriate specialists. It took two surgeries to correct the lazy muscles and poor vision in his eye, and one surgery to correct his club foot. He was also forced to wear a patch over his left eye and a leg brace for the next three years. No matter—Carmine Gotti Agnello was truly a blessing from God.

Meanwhile, the trial continued. The prosecutors assigned to the case were John Gleeson and Diane Giacalone from the Queens DA's office. Giacalone was the more outspoken of the two and let the media know early on that she intended to use every resource to get a conviction of Gotti. Giacalone had grown up next to the Bergin Hunt and Fish Club in Ozone Park, Queens—my father's known hangout. She knew exactly what she was dealing with, and also seemed to have a personal vendetta against my father—at least that's what most reporters said. Also, she favored red suits for court and was dubbed "the Lady in Red" during the trial.

Giacolone was at odds with the FBI from the start. Not only because she was trying to steal their thunder, but also because she made some telling mistakes early on. The most profound mistake was that Giacolone exposed a rat, a member of my father's crew, "Willie Boy" Johnson. He was an informant, unbeknownst to anyone except the FBI for nearly twenty years. He had been arrested at a young age for being involved in a drug deal, and rather than go to jail, he agreed to become a rat. For the next twenty or so years, Willie Boy played both sides. He gave the FBI just enough information to keep himself out of jail, yet not enough to indict anyone on anything more serious than bookmaking and loan sharking. The FBI warned Giacalone about exposing

Johnson—they did not want to lose a key informer on the inside, and they especially did not want to be responsible for getting Johnson killed.

In the middle of an important bail hearing just following the arrests of my father and his associates, Giacalone announced to the packed courtroom that bail should be denied given that the defendants would attempt to intimidate witnesses and use the same threatening tactics that got Dad's earlier case dropped. She used Johnson as backup ammunition and announced that he was a federal witness. The courtroom was in an uproar. All eyes were on Willie Boy, including my father's. While FBI agents shook their heads in disbelief, Giacalone continued her argument. In the end, Giacolone won, but at a very heavy cost. Many men on the street went into a panic, wondering what Johnson had divulged about them and whether or not they would be arrested, too. Giacalone's revelation had put Johnson in grave danger. Predictably, Johnson was later shot and killed as he walked down a Brooklyn street.

The case continued with the DA and the FBI constantly criticizing each other. It was a battle of the wills to see who could successfully "get Gotti." In the meantime, the case also continued to unravel. One of Giacalone's key witnesses disappeared from a hotel room on the eve of testimony. He left a note scribbled on a hotel pad saying, "Sorry, I've changed my mind. Good-bye and thanks." His whereabouts were unknown. Another witness, Matthew Traynor, a self-confessed bank robber, was supposed to testify against my father and provide a correlation between the rising boss and the other defendants. Traynor was caught in many lies while being grilled and prepped by the prosecutors and was later disqualified, but not before doing irreparable damage to Giacalone's case. On February 2, Traynor took the stand and told the jury that the DA had promised him many things in exchange for his testimony. He told a packed courtroom that Giacalone offered him a pair of her panties when he told her he wanted to get laid. Traynor also said that a DEA supervisor provided him with drugs while he was in prison and that one time he was so wasted during a meeting with law enforcement officials that he puked on Giacalone's desk. It seemed like quite a coincidence to my father's lawyers that the other DA's wife worked at a hospital and had easy access to any drug she wanted. They subpoenaed the hospital records of John Gleeson's wife. Notes between the DA and the witness were discovered, one reading, "Sometimes you make me so darn mad, I forget how happy you make me the rest of the time." This badly embarrassed Giacalone and the state. The case was in tatters. Then news reports claimed that Giacalone was involved in secret meetings concerning a television movie about John Gotti and the case called *Getting Gotti*. Lorraine Bracco was to play the ambitious DA.

THE JURY DELIBERATED only four days and returned a "not guilty" verdict. The Queens DA's office was despondent, but the FBI was gloating. They realized Gotti was still up for grabs and theirs for the taking if they could only put together an airtight case.

Meanwhile, the trial propelled my father to even larger-than-life status, on the streets and in the media. He was dubbed "the Teflon Don," and "the Dapper Don," because hardly anyone ever beat a RICO case, and certainly not with as much style as John Gotti.

I WAS NOT PRESENT at the trial and relied on news reports and conversations with my father to keep me informed. Because my father was so old-fashioned, women were never allowed in the courtroom.

At the end of his second trial for RICO, I couldn't take the suspense or the agony of waiting at home once the jury was out. So on the morning most reporters suspected that a verdict would be reached, I went to the courthouse in Lower Manhattan and snuck in through a side entrance.

As I was making my way inside, a crowd of reporters recognized me and gave chase. Little did I know that Dad had decided to exit through the same side entrance to avoid the media melee. We came face-to-face and his expression was mixed with anger and joy. He was ecstatic about the victory but angry that I had defied him. I thought he was going to kill me, right then and there on the courthouse steps. The look in his eyes said it all. Instead, he ushered me to the waiting Mercedes at the curb, waving politely to reporters and fans. We pulled away from the courthouse and he never brought the incident up again. Perhaps it had much to do with the fact that I was pregnant again. I'd found out when Carmine was not yet two months old. My doctors called it another "miracle."

I delivered another baby boy on May 5, 1987. He was a robust seven pounds and had swollen cheeks. Dad took one look at him and immediately took to calling him "Chipmunk." Appropriately, he was named after my father—John

Gotti Agnello. Not only did he look like Dad, the two shared similar personalities as well. He was an independent, easy-to-please baby, and as early as his crib days, he exhibited leadership qualities and always looked out for his older brother, Carmine. And the family was still growing; my sister, Angel, and I once again had been pregnant at the same time. She gave birth in September 1987 to a girl, Victoria Gotti Albano. Dad couldn't be happier watching his brood continue to grow.

CHAPTER TWENTY-EIGHT

"Speak Softly Love"

I t was Christmas Eve, 1988. Last-minute shoppers filled the city streets, wide-eyed children held hands with their parents, eager for the gifts of Christmas Day. Church bells rang, as did cash registers. Sadly, there are so often monetary motives behind traditions, on both sides of the law. I've learned that nothing is what it seems to be, not even the most celebrated holiday.

Christmas is for many the celebration of the birth of a savior, a time of peace on earth and goodwill toward men— but for my brother John, this particular Christmas Eve was a celebration of his own official rebirth as a gangster.

He was to be inducted into the Family, La Cosa Nostra, or whatever the media and the government calls it. We referred to it as the life.

My brother and a few other soon-to-be made men who were being brought in that day were leaving the old existence and being reborn into another world. They would no longer be civilians—they were getting a passport stamped for travel in the dark realms of the criminal underworld.

Every one of them being inducted that day was extremely proud to be where they were standing. All men at the time of the ceremony are excited and hopefully ready to take on the responsibilities and dangers. It is supposed to be an honorable induction, one to be proud of.

Back then, my brother John stood dressed in his best suit, wearing a red tie for luck, in a dimly lit apartment on Mulberry Street in Manhattan. More than a dozen others, hard men in expensive suits, stood with him. They were the elder statesmen of organized crime, come to take part in this time-honored ceremony. They had come to welcome the new blood into the organization.

John was handed a picture to hold in the palm of his hands—a picture of a saint—that had received a drop of blood from his father's finger, pricked by a knife. The picture was burned while an oath of loyalty was recited. John pledged that he would hope to burn like the picture if he were ever to betray La Cosa Nostra.

"Getting made" is a Sicilian ceremony that has its basis in Catholicism, but it certainly wasn't in church that the government learned of the conduct of the initiation.

These ceremonies don't take place at a catering hall, and there are no photographers. They take place in a small Lower Manhattan apartment. The ceremony is somber and dramatic—maybe like Christmas is supposed to be.

John felt that he was being officially welcomed into a sacred brotherhood—a mutually protective society where men looked out for each other and for each other's families, an organization that ironically mirrored a military organization, complete with its captains, lieutenants, and soldiers and its own code of conduct. In a sense, they were like Robin Hood and his Merry Men, as many of them did take from the rich and often gave to the poor, while lining their own pockets of course. That, also, is a part of their history.

H OW OFTEN—IN HISTORY, in mythology—is the outsider, the outlaw, lionized and idolized?

It isn't hard to understand, really. It's about the awe of the common downtrodden man, and the uncommon strong ones who stand up to the system that treads upon the average citizen; the respect for those who never bow their heads or bend their knees to neither king nor cardinal. Leaders of all kinds are men set apart, be they artists or assassins, cops or criminals. What sets them apart is often feared *and* respected. Often, men desire, secretly or openly, to emulate those special ones, set apart. It is not merely the desire for their power; it is the wish for their degree of freedom from outside rule, their desire for such a rebellious nature and the freedom to wear it visibly on the outside of their skin as opposed to hiding it deep within their souls.

History reveals that the Mafia was originally created (at least in part) for the protection of people and to establish an unofficial system of justice, when the ruling powers spit on the average citizen, when there was no justice for the poor in the courts or the Church.

This perception of honor among those who could fairly be called thieves might seem strange to those whose view of the life comes from newspaper clippings by outsider journalists, or Department of Justice press releases. How could anyone be proud to be a mobster? How could anyone joyfully embrace membership in an organization dedicated to criminality?

Remember, the brotherhood concept was what gave the

241

mob *meaning*. It was the sense of belonging, of being a part of something larger than their individual selves, that motivated mobsters more than just money. It originated in Sicily, and found its way to America. People were tired of being oppressed, of living under tyrannical rule. It was an uprising over what they believed to be their lack of civil rights and proper protection.

The activities that gave rise to the income to support those in the brotherhood, albeit illegal, were not substantially different from the revenue-raising methods of government, or the actions of so-called legitimate business. It took great financial means to initiate and keep up such an organization. The only way the common people could raise funds was by working and taking part in criminal activity. These criminal acts were often committed against the rich, commonly referred to as "piggish aristrocrats."

When an unofficial organization demands money for protection, it is extortion. When the government takes a percentage of your income, for protection (police department), your purchases, your sales, your house, your phone bill, your electric bill, that's legal, because *they* have declared it to be legal. It's called taxation, or surcharges. I'm not justifying one group or another—I'm just calling it as the "little guy" sees it, and I am definitely not condoning crime—whether organized or in the White House. I'm merely pointing out the difference between a mobster and a politician—there is none. The large number of politicians being arrested or indicted these days is astounding, prompting many to ask, who really is the good guy or the bad guy? Or is there a significant difference between a gangster and a government? These days you can't put the evening news on without hearing about a senator, governor, or even a president caught up in some illicit scandal: prostitution, bid rigging, extortion, or bookmaking. There is no difference between these two groups, mobsters or government—one group has organized crime stamped boldly after their names, while the other has the same crime phrased much more eloquently.

ALONG WITH JOHN, on that Christmas Eve, four others were to be inducted. One of the others was Michael Di-Leonardo, a man John had met in the life and had become very close to.

This induction was an entrance into a new world. It was a commencement exercise, and on that Christmas Eve, my brother was as proud as he had ever been. According to him, he was joining the world of our father, a brotherhood more than a century old.

John believed that the other men involved were not hypocrites like the politicians who accepted money, favors, and influence from organized crime throughout history, yet publicly denounced the mob as enemies of the public. It is a historical fact that organized crime helped John F. Kennedy get elected president. Only afterward did his brother Bobby, as attorney general, became a crusader against the mob.

John also believed members of the life were not hypocrites like those in law enforcement who lied, stole, and even murdered while wearing a badge. A glance through old newspapers or the Internet will confirm this. I firmly believe this, too.

And they were not hypocrites like those few men of the cloth who spoke against sin while molesting little boys.

243

According to my brother, they in the Family were criminals, yes. But he believed they were also men of honor. They were men who lived by their own code. Notice my brother's use of the past tense here.

John went on to tell me, "I am not speaking of all of us, unfortunately, and we have had our share of hypocrites, also some of them hypocrites in the extreme. But in time, all institutions decay, all principles become covered with dirt and dust. Yet there are those who shine through time, dirt, and dust, and remain true to their origins."

My father was such a man.

"He might have been flashy when Mafia tradition dictated otherwise, but it was not his style to lay low. He might have gambled to excess, but there are many instances of his financial generosity to the poor and to strangers. He was a man born out of his time, the last of his kind. The last of the old-time Mafiosi," John told me.

MY FATHER WAS not in attendance at my brother John's induction, to avoid an overtone of nepotism to the proceedings and to avoid possible bad luck. The underboss of the Family at the time, Salvatore Gravano, presided over the ceremony. John later told me he had been proposed for induction by the Family Consigliere, Frank "Frankie Loc" Locascio. Others who were present were James "Jimmy Brown" Failla, Joseph Arcuri, "Frankie Dap" Dapalito, and Joseph "Joe Butch" Corrao. These names resound in mob history.

John was the youngest member at the time to be inducted, and with that, of course, would come the jealousy of his peers and back-door unfavorable commentary. Already the plotting would begin. But on that particular day he enjoyed the elation of his formal entry into La Famigila, the Family—the life.

This was one of the most important days in his life, a moment bigger than he could have imagined.

But it wasn't the first time he had been asked if he wanted to be "made." One year earlier, in 1987, John was approached by our uncles to be inducted. It was shortly after my father's acquittal on racketeering and murder charges.

They walked down 101st Avenue in Ozone Park, and my uncle told my brother that my father had intentions that he join, that he get "straightened out," and asked John how he felt about this.

Back then, he was stunned. As far as he was concerned, the men in the life were larger than life. Was he even worthy to be one of them? So he answered my uncle honestly. "I don't know," he said. "Let me think about it."

It wasn't the answer my uncle was looking for. "You want me to let you think about it?" my uncle asked incredulously, then he walked away.

Several months later, another uncle approached him, again with the offer to become inducted. He carried a similar message as before: "If you want this life now, it's time. You won't be asked again."

This time John's answer was different. He nodded his head yes. "I'm ready." That was all he said.

DURING THE INITIATION, my brother told me he was reminded that he entered this world on his feet but he could only leave in a coffin. He was told, "This is your new family; we come first before your blood family. If we call you, you come in when we call you. Even if you have to kill your own brother, this is what it is."

That was part of the ritual line. But rituals are not always correct, despite their being part of an accepted tradition. Vows are broken, traditions upturned. Friendships are betrayed.

BUT JOHN WAS blissfully ignorant of the future on that Christmas Eve of 1988. Instead, John A. Gotti was the happiest man alive. He left the apartment after the ceremony took place and walked the short distance to the Ravenite Social Club in Little Italy.

It was the place where my father held court, and after my brother was instructed to walk directly into the back room, he embraced the man who on that day was the proudest father on the planet. He had given him life, and then brought him into the life. What kind of father would bring his son into this life? What son would want it? Perhaps a father who sensed yet another trial, his third in as many years, coming up again—and the fear of Gotti Senior losing control of a family, a position he'd put before his own life in those days.

"I've shared hundreds of meals with John Junior. We might have even had a martini or two together on occasion." So said Adam Mandelbaum, one of my brother John's attorneys, continuing, "When talk of his father comes up, he admits freely that he idolized his father. 'To me,' John said, 'he wasn't a father, he was a god, back then.'"

Further, he said, "John would wax eloquent about his father's ramrod straight posture, his immaculate appearance, his swagger, his charisma, and his toughness. Hell, the media ate it up by the shovelful, why wouldn't the eldest son?" Mandelbaum and John had this conversation the day John was released from jail.

Also, who wouldn't want the good part of the life? The money, the freedom from nine to five, the food, the broads—and the power?

Of course, there is that other part. Stuff about jail and getting killed. Losing all of your assets to government forfeitures. Things like that could ruin your appetite after an induction ceremony.

But on Christmas Eve, 1988, John Angelo Gotti, son of John Joseph Gotti, who was the head of the Gambino Crime Family, wasn't thinking of anything but his having achieved being a made man. He sat at a huge round table with about ten other men of honor. John later told me, "I swear, I did think about King Arthur and the Knights of the Round Table. I was that impressed."

The club was packed that night. The Christmas Eve gathering at the Ravenite was a tradition started by Aniello "Neil" Dellacroce, the man who had brought my father into the life. Now my father maintained the tradition.

John greeted the others who were in attendance, now not just as the son of the chief, but also a member of the brotherhood. Later on my father, my uncle, John, and his best friend, Bobby Borriello, drove over to the Bergin Hunt and Fish Club in Ozone Park, where many others were waiting to welcome him into the life as well.

At 9 P.M. John went home to a banquet prepared for

Christmas Eve by my mother, who had created a cornucopia of fish dishes, pasta, and all the other Italian trimmings and treats of a traditional Christmas Eve meal. My father's house was always open on the holidays for those friends who had no place to go. Dad always made sure that any of the men without wives or family were never forced to spend the holidays alone. He had a generous pocket and a big heart. He would invite those who would otherwise spend the holiday by themselves—and he made sure there were gifts under the tree for them as well.

My mother had no idea that my brother had just been granted formal entry into the Family—and neither did I.

CHAPTER TWENTY-NINE

"It's a Family Affair"

In July 1989, I found out I was pregnant again—another boy. Frank Gotti Agnello was born April 12, 1990. I remember the doctor looking up at me just seconds after his birth and saying, "How do you feel about the phrase 'my three sons'?" I was beyond excited! Dad was on hand for the delivery because of a warning from my doctor mid-trimester. The baby was RH-positive and I was RH-negative. To avoid another disaster, Dr. Stern prepared all of us in the event a blood transfusion was necessary. I matched Dad's blood type and therefore, if needed, he could donate his blood to save the baby. Thankfully, it was not necessary. But it was priceless watching Dad pace the floor waiting to learn if he was needed. I remember that he arrived at the hospital smiling ear-to-ear. But as he neared the gurney he staggered a little. I later learned he was so nervous about the birth and the fact that he might have to give the baby a transfusion that he downed three martinis. But all his anxiousness disappeared the moment he first laid eyes on Frank. He was named after my deceased brother and had a head of thick, jet-black hair that was astounding! Dad immediately called him "Cochise."

∘   ∘   ∘

AFTER MY BROTHER John's induction, he rose rapidly, becoming a capo in 1990. His first soldier was Bartholomew "Bobby" Borriello. He was also the best man at John's wedding on April 21, 1990, to Kim Albanese, whom he had known since childhood. Kim was nearly seven months' pregnant at the time. The pair was supposed to get married months earlier, just after Kim found out she was pregnant. But Dad wanted the wedding to be a well-planned and lavish affair.

In honor of the wedding, the Helmsley Palace had draped a twenty-foot Italian flag over the outside of the hotel. It made the papers, and infuriated those who did not wish members in the life well. Not all the photographers who sought to attend my brother's wedding were hired—some were on government payrolls.

But Leona Helmsley was a stand-up woman. The law enforcement types who approached her and asked to infiltrate the wedding were told "no." She was later prosecuted for tax evasion by the government in revenge. An elderly woman went to jail because she refused to allow a Gotti family wedding to be violated by enemies. Helmsley may have been dubbed the "Queen of Mean" by the press, but I can honestly say I have never heard a bad thing about her from those who *really* knew her. All I saw was how generous she was to those in need around her; I also saw the woman do anything she could for anyone she liked—like my father. She is dead now, but my gratitude to her still lives.

We had our own security for the wedding. My father had hired an advance guard, who was staying at the hotel to watch for who belonged and who didn't. The law enforcement agents never got farther than the lobby of the hotel, thanks to the security efforts both amateur and professional. We had the main ballroom at our disposal, and a third-floor room for special guests.

There were hundreds of well-wishers. Each New York crime family had a table. The New Jersey boys were there, too. All were in tuxes. My sister, Angel, and I noticed this right away. Unlike both of our weddings, John's celebration was less intimate. There were considerably fewer guests in attendance than the previous Gotti weddings; 800 guests at Angel's—1,500 at mine. Still, the affair seemed cold and very structured. Looking around the room, seeing many faces neither of us knew or recognized, was fitting. Dad was now in the highest position in the organization and John's wedding definitely reflected this. It was, for lack of a better word, very political.

It was an Italian wedding, so there was *food*. Tons of it! Caviar, lobster, shrimp, steak, you name it. Champagne flowed from the Cristal bottles, and the cognac that was served was Louis XIII. The dinner choices were beef Wellington, lobster, or veal. Despite all the food and drink, everybody behaved themselves. There were no drunks on the ballroom floor that night. Everybody was on his or her best behavior at John's wedding.

Entertainment abounded. Besides the orchestra, Jimmy Roselli and Jay Black and the Americans sang, and for a laugh or two, comedian Lou "Baccala" Cary performed. It was definitely an affair to remember. Kim's father was a carpet layer, and my father had made sure everything at his son's wedding was strictly "red carpet."

My father had rented several suites at the hotel for family and friends, especially those from out of town. My parents were in the Presidential Triplex suite, complete with a baby grand piano, butler's quarters, a library, a terrace with a view of the city, and three fireplaces. My sister and I were to stay in our parents' suite, so Dad could be close to the grandkids. I had just given birth to my third son, Frankie Boy, just two weeks before John's wedding and refused to leave the newborn with a sitter. So I bundled up the kids and the baby and settled them safely at the Helmsley Palace with a trustworthy family member. I would rather have stayed home and gotten ready for the wedding there. But Dad had given all of us orders the night before and he expected each of us to abide by them. Because of the press intrusion, we were all forced to leave our homes early the morning of the wedding and meet up at the hotel. The press and the FBI had nearly every church in Ozone Park staked out in the hopes of getting a bird's-eye view of the ceremony and all the guests in attendance. Reporters and agents also went knocking on doors, to nearly every hotel in Manhattan, hoping to get lucky. But Helmsley had warned each of her staff to stay mum about the festivities—and they did.

But the celebration wasn't without a little chaos. One hour before the event, I'd realized I'd left my dress shoes at home. I was wearing a beautiful white ball gown and a pair of bedroom slippers! I didn't have anything else to wear—and most of the stores in the city were closed for the weekend. It was either the slippers or miss the wedding altogether. I was sure it would be the joke on everyone's lips come Monday morning, but I refused to miss my brother's wedding. Dad found out about my problem and within twenty minutes had a beautiful pair of shoes sent to the suite. Once again, he saved the day.

The next day was an all-day brunch held at a restaurant my father was involved with called Da Noi (By Us), on Seventy-fourth Street and York. We drank and ate into the night, and then the women were sent home. My father and John and some of their closest friends partied till the early morning, with grappa and goodwill flowing.

The partying had attracted city sanitation workers outside, who were peering through the windows. They were invited in despite their garbage-covered uniforms. They sat and drank with Dad, John, and the other men who'd accompanied them to the restaurant after the wedding. They had coffee and cake and one toast because they were on the job.

The wedding gifts totaled several hundred thousand in cash.

John shared many a laugh that day with his best man, Bobby Borriello. One of the guests in attendance at the wedding was a man named Anthony "Gaspipe" Casso, a member of the Lucchese Crime Family. He, too, had come to show his respect. He and Bobby drank together that day.

John was now newly married to his childhood sweetheart and a capo in the mob, with lots of cash. The sky was the limit. Life in *the life* was good.

The life was not without politics, its own set of laws, treaties, and board of directors. It had its own version of government, and when it came to peace treaties and wars, the two were very similar. Different mob families fought over territories and control. Sometimes a war would take place within one family—like the Colombo war in the early 1990s. The head of the Family was Carmine Persico. He'd been arrested and convicted in the late 1980s for a bevy of things, like income tax evasion, RICO, and murder. While Persico was in jail, he turned the reins over to his son, Alphonse "Allie Boy" Persico. Allie Boy ran the Colombo Family until he himself was arrested and sent to jail. With father and son in prison, the elder Persico temporarily put his trusted right hand in charge of the Family. Vic Orena stepped up to the position comfortably . . . so much so that he refused to relinquish the reins when news of the younger Persico's release from prison reached his ears. As a result, the Colombo Family was divided. There were those men who staunchly stood behind Persico and those who welcomed change with Orena as their new boss. Between 1991 and 1993, there was much bloodshed. Twelve mobsters and one innocent man mistaken for another mobster fell victim to the bloody Colombo power struggle.

After the war began, every other week it seemed there was another picture of a body riddled with bullets covering the front page of the newspaper. Predictably, a few days would pass and then there was the expected retaliation. It was an "eye for an eye"—a "man for a man." I saw the disturbing images in the newspapers, but I didn't recognize any of the names—I was relieved that the bloody mob war did not involve the Gambino Family. I believed that no one I knew would be hurt as a result. I was wrong. When news spread of Joe Scopo's death, everyone was shocked. Joe was extremely well liked by all who knew him. There were very few men he didn't get along well with. He and Dad were very close—so close that I considered him a relative, even calling him Uncle Joe. He was shot to death in his car just outside his home. His future son-in-law, also in the car, narrowly escaped the barrage of bullets by crawling out of the passenger side of the Town Car Scopo was driving. His wife and son, Joseph Junior, stood helplessly in the doorway of their Woodhaven, Queens, home.

Whoever was responsible had sent a message—the rules were changing. Before, it was unheard of to kill a man at his home or in front of his wife and kids. But the new breed of gangsters didn't care about the old rules. They only seemed to care about money and power.

While the war continued, there was little other Family heads could do. Sit-downs increased as did Commission meetings. Most of the men begged for peace and order on the streets. It was one mob funeral after another. The elders in the life grew increasingly concerned, and order needed to be restored quickly. My father intervened and called a Commission meeting and demanded that the heads of both sides at war be present. Ten hours later, there was still no resolution. While the Colombo men were busy killing each other, the FBI was busy mounting indictments against them. Forty-two Persico soldiers and over a dozen men from the Orena faction were convicted and sent to prison. Orena, too, was sent to jail for life. After his conviction, his men retreated and the war was over. It was the last mob war of the twentieth century—it was also one of the bloodiest.

While Dad tended to important matters within his professional family, certain emergencies occurred in his own personal family. My oldest son, Carmine, was rushed to the hospital the following winter. Carmine and John had been battling a bad case of strep throat.

John seemed to recuperate within a week, while Carmine only got worse. One night he woke up with a fever of

104 and started to convulse. I called an ambulance. At the hospital, he was diagnosed with septecemia, blood poisoning caused by a severe case of strep that had traveled to his heart. He was only four years old and doctors thought he was going to die. The creator of *Sesame Street*, Jim Henson, had died of the exact same illness. And because of this, most people now knew what septecemia was—even my father. Dad had left earlier in the week for Florida, as he had business to tend to down south. Because he had a dislike of flying, he and a few of his men drove down to Miami. Mom let Dad know about Carmine when he called to check in. He literally turned the car around and raced back to New York. Early the next morning, Dad arrived at the hospital, still dressed in the same suit he'd left New York in. He looked worried and worn out. When he laid eyes on his grandson lying helplessly in a quarantined crib, his heart nearly broke. The doctor told Dad the next twelve hours were critical—and that there was a good chance Carmine would die. He spent the next few hours trying to convince me everything would be okay. But behind my back he was already preparing for the worst. He'd told his driver, Jackie, that he was to "get me out of the hospital immediately" if anything were to happen to my son. He knew I could never withstand such a blow. Thankfully, after twelve hours of tears and prayers, the doctor who was head of infectious diseases declared Carmine "out of the woods."

Meanwhile, the investigation of the Castellano murder continued. There was to be a roundup of men all connected to organized crime any day, so every guy, including my father, was prepared to be arrested. No one knew when or where this would occur. My father's lawyer, Bruce

Cutler, even reached out to the Organized Crime Task Force (OCTF) and offered to have my father turn himself in, in an effort to avoid a media circus. No such luck. The agents and politicians wanted their glory. They wanted their public grandstanding and perp walk of one of the most famous faces in the world. They wanted to walk John Gotti into the station, in front of all the media reporters, with his hands cuffed behind his back.

The raid came in the early hours of a morning in December 1990. My father was involved in a high-stakes card game, and when nearly two hundred agents burst through the door of the social club wearing riot gear, flashing badges, and yielding big guns, no one seemed less surprised than my father. He later laughed recounting how he greeted them: "Hey, guys. How are you? How about a game of cards? An espresso?" He never lost his sense of humor. The men turned down both offers and let the room know exactly which men they wanted. Besides my father, Sammy "the Bull" Gravano and Frank "Frankie Loc" Locascio were arrested as well. All were charged with a number of serious crimes including racketeering, obstruction of justice, extortion, and murder.

CHAPTER THIRTY

"Ain't No Stopping Us Now"

The arrest was all over the news by early the next morning, and it was unlikely that Dad would be released on bail. It was hard enough fighting a major RICO case, but fighting the case while detained and having only limited access to your lawyers is far tougher. Another blow came when Bruce Cutler was disqualified from the case. Dad considered Bruce his "lucky charm" and was really pissed when he was removed. The government argued that Cutler was "house counsel" to the Gambino Crime Family and would in all likelihood be called as a government witness, resulting in a "conflict." This was a lie, of course, and Cutler was never used as a witness. It was another tactic to separate what law enforcement believed was a winning team—Gotti and Cutler.

Cutler paraded in a bevy of prospective lawyers—the best of the best—to fight one of the toughest cases in history. My father interviewed each lawyer brought before him with caution. Every one of them had an obvious agenda—all wanted to be dubbed *the* lawyer of the moment, working on the biggest organized crime case since Al Capone was convicted of income tax evasion.

My father finally chose powerhouse attorney Al Krieger from Florida. He was an older gentleman, well experienced in the field of law—especially in high-profile organized crime cases. He came highly recommended by many other attorneys as well; even Cutler—who was severely distraught and depressed over the ruling that he could not represent my father in this case—approved of Krieger.

Most of the evidence consisted of taped conversations between my father and many men. These were telling conversations about the mob and mob life. These valuable tapes were obtained through bugs placed in an apartment above the Ravenite Social Club in Little Italy. The FBI watched the place so much and for so long that they realized only one person lived above the club, a "little old lady" named Mrs. Cirelli. She did as most lonely old ladies do, shop and run errands and go to bed early. The entire OCTF could not figure out why these men went into the Ravenite for such meetings, yet no conversations were picked up on any bugs. These agents would watch the men go in and come out, but no conversations, telling or otherwise, were recorded. Finally, they figured out there had to be another meeting place somewhere in the two-story structure. While agents often bragged about this coup, most people in the streets laughed their asses off, knowing it took nearly two hundred men—agents with access to the most technologically advanced equipment—ten years to figure out that most important meetings or conversations took place in Mrs. Cirelli's apartment on the second floor of the Ravenite.

◦   ◦   ◦

MY FATHER AND his dream team immediately went to work, even engaging in weekly co-defendant meetings involving other men on the case, such as Sammy Gravano.

Gravano was a short man suffering from a Napoleon complex—when he was a teenager, neighborhood bullies constantly picked on him. He was five foot four, and in an effort to compensate for his small stature, he took daily shots of metabolic steroids and worked out daily at a local gym, earning him the moniker "Sammy the Bull."

His parents came from Sicily and later settled in Downtown Brooklyn. Sammy was an only child. His parents owned real estate and a successful garment business. There was no shortage of money and the Gravanos lived a comfortable, middle-class life. This prompted many mob guys to later wonder why Gravano ever got mixed up in a life of crime, since his family obviously had money. Years later, Sammy admitted the reason he joined the life was for the "thrill."

In his memoir published several years ago, Gravano admitted he was taken in early on by the flashy men who walked the streets of Brooklyn. The first chance he got to impress these men he did. As a teenager he often boasted to others of being a burglar, petty thief, and stick-up man, always using a ski mask. Gravano was once arrested for a robbery and caught a vicious beating from the cops. When he appeared in court, his face bruised and beaten, the case was demoted to a misdemeanor, with Gravano promising to join the army. He did, but not right away. He lied about enlisting, but ironically, less than a year later, Gravano was drafted. While in the service, he managed to occupy himself running card games at night and overseeing betting scams during the day. He made his stay in the army bearable by paying off military police and running barracks card games and becoming a GI loan shark. After his release a few years later, he went right back to a life of crime. He became a self-proclaimed "associate" of the Columbo Crime Family and continued to enlist in petty rackets such as muggings.

Gravano admitted to committing his first murder at twenty-five. He whacked another wannabe for making fun of a made man. Gravano seemed to enjoy the surge of power the killing gave him and later remarked, "Killing came so easy to me."

I COULD HEAR THE uncertainty and concern in my father's voice one night when he called me from prison. He wasn't his usual happy self. Usually he asked about the kids and listened intently as I spoke. But during that call he didn't hear a word I'd said.

Finally, I asked him what was wrong. That's when he told me he believed Sammy Gravano had turned rat. This came as no surprise to me. I never liked the guy. I never trusted him. He always reminded me of a weasel. Whenever he was around my father he was always eyeing him up and down, watching Dad in an envious fashion that was very noticeable to others. But my father wouldn't listen to reason—he wanted to believe that every man he had around him was cut from the same cloth as he. Sadly, this proved false on many occasions. But the most damaging one was Sammy. The day before, Gravano's absence from a pivotal lawyers' meeting was telling—and later on a corrections officer working at the prison in my father's ward came by and gave my father information confirming his suspicions about Sammy. The guard told him that Gravano had been "whisked out of the facility, like a thief in the night." The guard said that usually when an inmate was removed so suddenly and in the middle of the night, it generally meant he was being transferred to a nearby army base to be protected as a federal witness. In Gravano's case, the officer was correct. The next day all the newspapers reported Sammy was a "rat." It stunned the world and shook up the underworld. Men associated with the life ran for cover, wondering if they, too, would fall. Not surprisingly, though, Gravano had made what could only be dubbed by newspaper reporters as the biggest "sweetheart" deal ever made. He would get to keep his ill-gotten gains from mob life as well as the profits from some still-existing rackets—and also Sammy was allowed to pick and choose the men he would take down. His buddies and family members would be spared. He confessed to committing nineteen murders and spent less than two years in jail. All of this in exchange for John Gotti's head.

CHAPTER THIRTY-ONE

"Reflections"

One of the rituals for Dad's crew was Saturday afternoon lunch at the Bergin Hunt and Fish Club, a tradition my father started upon his release from prison in 1977.

All of the guys would get together for a big Italian feast. Pounds of veal cutlets, huge bowls of pasta, and an array of meatballs, sausage, and Italian cold cuts were served. Sometimes the men would grill steaks outside in the back of the building. Wine, of course, was abundant. Cigar smoke filled the air. They ate, drank, and enjoyed the food and company as only Italian men can. The men would talk, laugh, play cards, and watch races on the big television at the club for hours on end.

On April 13, 1991, less than a year after my brother John's wedding, the guys were at the club—shylocks, bookies, numbers runners, and various hangers-on of the life came in to pay their respects, take some action, and mooch some food. It was important, especially now that my father was in jail, that their traditions were kept up. It was a way of paying respect to him, the chief.

One Saturday Bobby Borriello was with my brother

John, cracking him up with his jokes as usual. He was one of the funniest guys John ever met—and one of the toughest, too. He was a "happy-go-lucky" guy and loved to play practical jokes on his friends. Just after Dad's trial, Bobby turned up at the Metropolitan Correctional Center and waited on the sidewalk for hours until Dad and a few of the other prisoners noticed him. He put on a street show, directing traffic into such disarray he nearly caused a six-car pileup! Bobby and John were trading zingers back and forth, discussing a little family business, eating and drinking, and all that male-bonding stuff. Bobby left the club at about 7 P.M., taking a jar of homemade pasta sauce to bring back to his family. Little Jackie, a regular at the social club, made it special every Saturday. John didn't know, as Bobby drove away in his big black Lincoln Continental, that it would be the last time he would see him alive. John was next door at the jeweler's, contemplating an anniversary gift for his wife, when he was told he had a phone call. It was Susan, Bobby's wife, screaming that Bobby had been shot. He was lying in a pool of blood on the driveway of his home, riddled with bullets.

John was told that the hit had been well orchestrated. Cars boxed in the ends of Bobby's block so he couldn't run. A carful of men followed him up to his driveway. Bobby had turned to face them, saying, "What the fuck are you doing here?" They fired a shot, hit him, and he managed to throw the jar of sauce he was carrying at one of his assailants. Nine more shots followed, six more hit him.

His wife and his two-year-old child witnessed the killing from the house. Bobby was a big man, six foot one and 270 pounds. Bobby had a big heart, too. But seven bullets proved bigger than him that night.

John later told me, "He was pronounced dead at the scene. A wife widowed, his two children fatherless, and Bobby, at the prime of his life at age forty-seven, dead. My best man, my dear friend, dead." We were all devastated to hear the tragic details.

Like my brother, I received a call from Bobby's widow, Susan. We were longtime friends and all I could hear was her hysterical sobs. She cried over and over, "Bobby's dead! Bobby's dead!" It sent chills up my spine. I had just seen Bobby the day before. He stopped by to wish my son Frankie a happy birthday. He brought a magnificent, custom-made cake, designed to look like Big Bird from *Sesame Street*. The cake cost a fortune and had to be picked up in Manhattan. But that was Bobby, always generous. Always eager to please. Later, my brother accompanied his old friend to the funeral home and helped prepare his body for the wake. Mortician's wax took care of the holes in his body, but they didn't have anything to plug the hole in John's heart. It was the first awakening John had concerning this life that he had chosen and the ugliness surrounding it. Murder and death are ugly. There is no grace or honor in being sprawled out on the pavement, drenched in your own blood in front of your wife and kids. None whatsoever.

THE CASKET WAS open so we could say good-bye face-to-face. It was a mob funeral, the way you'd imagine it. Lots of limousines, flower cars, gaudy arrangements, hundreds of guys in suits paying their respects at Rucuglia's Funeral Home on Court Street.

After some time, it came to light that Anthony

"Gaspipe" Casso, who had been at John's wedding with Bobby and toasted his good fortune with him, had ordered the hit. Gaspipe, onetime underboss of the Lucchese Family, may have thought Bobby was behind an attempted hit on him, one that unfortunately failed. Or maybe he had Bobby killed to try to weaken the Family, maybe as a prelude to killing my brother John. All I know is that my brother saw the life in a whole new light that day. John told me then— even as far back as 1991—that he "wanted out." He said he didn't have the treachery it took to survive or the stomach to withstand the ugliness of "the betrayal" that went with it. It was definitely the beginning of the end for John as far as the mob was concerned.

Casso, who has admitted to thirty-six killings, including the car-bombing of Frank DiCicco, turned into a federal rat in 1994, until they threw him out of the program. While in a special prison unit for informants, Casso was caught bribing guards, assaulting prisoners, being in possession of contraband, and lying to the Feds, especially at my father's trial. I still don't understand why or how any member of a jury can believe what these witnesses have to say. Law enforcement has often addressed this as well and said, "These men are not exactly altar boys—but they are all we have." Knowing a man is trading useful information in exchange for freedom, sometimes life, would make me wonder just how much they say is the truth. Casso revealed that Gravano had lied on the stand, as well.

Another shocking detail about Bobby's death was the revelation that two cops were involved as well. They were on Gaspipe's payroll, had been for years, and were responsible for murdering more than eleven men. Lou Eppolito and

Frank Caracappa, two veteran detectives, had previously visited Bobby's house, knocked on the door, and confirmed that Bobby lived there. They then brought the information back to Gaspipe. They were the advance men, sealing Bobby's fate. According to law enforcement sources, the Feds knew that Caracappa and Eppolito were "dirty" as far back as 1990—a year before Bobby Boriello was killed. Yet they were not arrested and charged until the mid-2000s. They were dubbed "the Mafia Cops" by the media. Eppolito and Caracappa were convicted and sentenced to life in prison for their roles in these murders.

CHAPTER THIRTY-TWO

"Running on Empty"

One condition of Gravano's deal was that he had to tell the absolute truth about his involvement in the life. Every murder, every crime had to be documented. This was done to protect the government's pending case so that no information could come back to damage a witness's credibility. Gravano admitted to many crimes, besides the nineteen murders, most of which were a result of his greed.

My father once concluded in a phone conversation with another associate that Gravano "always managed to convince the powers that be—the Commission—that every man he went into business with was a rat or had wronged him in some way." My father went on to add, "Notice how each time Sammy gets rid of someone he stands to collect all the business interests?" And he was right, as Gravano later admitted in his testimony. The nineteen murders to which Sammy confessed were carried out himself and some for no other reason than money or a small slight. Even Gravano's own brother-in-law wasn't safe from his dangerous jealousy and insecurity. Sammy lured the unsuspecting guy to his garage in Staten Island and killed him, disposing of his remains by cutting the body up in pieces and burying them in his own backyard. Imagine his wife Debra's shock when the family dog came home after a run out in the yard with her brother's hand in its mouth. In the end, Sammy admitted to that murder as well. He was jealous of his brother-in-law's relationship with his wife. Debra claimed she was distraught over the death of her brother, and she even spoke to reporters about what a "despicable human being" Sammy was. Imagine everyone's shock then when Debra decided to join her husband in the WPP (Witness Protection Program) less than a year after he'd gone in. Now, that's amore!

Gravano's testimony—along with the fact that my father was denied counsel of his choice, a judge-ordered sequestered jury, constant government leaks to the press that were damaging to my father, even the then-president of the United States, George H. W. Bush, demanding the FBI "get Gotti, at any cost"—made it utterly impossible for my father to win the case. There were also rumors that the government had "stacked the jury"—a term used when a member of law enforcement is placed in the jury pool. No one would have known during Dad's trial, as each jury member was sequestered at an undisclosed hotel and their names remained anonymous. Also my father's own words, played out in conversations with associates and leaked to the press for public consumption, made the case even more difficult. Sentences like, "You tell him that John Gotti will sever his motherfucking head off the next time he doesn't come in when he's called." If you knew John Gotti at all, you would know his angry side was not particularly flattering, especially when he was dealing with dissension or disrespect in his ranks. My father had a violent temper when provoked. At times he would say things he never meant, letting his anger get the best of him. I remember speaking to my father about being spied on and taped. He'd said to me, "It's the worst feeling in the world to have your personal conversations and thoughts played back for you in court or in newspapers and on television."

THE SAMMY "THE BULL" Gravano show continued. He paraded himself in front of the cameras as if he was a hero. The FBI had made Gravano so comfortable he actually believed they were his friends. One agent even went as far as to say, "Gravano is a good guy. I would trust him with my wife and kids." In truth, the guy wouldn't trust Gravano with his pet pit bull. This newfound "friendship" was the result of a trade-off. Sammy gave the FBI John Gotti's head on a silver platter and they would say or do anything to keep him happy. Yet most people, even those in law enforcement, would later admit he was the lowest form of scum on earth. And after a lawsuit was filed against Gravano by members of his victims' families, law enforcement started to slowly distance themselves from him.

THE ENTIRE FAMILY was in complete disarray for the first time ever. With my father in prison, held without bail, and facing the biggest case of his life, the rest of us just sat around numb. When you have the entire FBI and government gunning for you, there is little chance of a victory.

Not Dad. He remained strong and positive. He refused to let anything break his stride—he remained loyal and dedicated to the life he'd signed on for. He had only one gripe during this time: Bruce Cutler made mention one day during a routine telephone call that Dad was "tired of the food that was ordered for lunch every day"; other than that, Cutler said my father was in "good spirits." Cutler also told me Dad had recently passed a comment about what he wouldn't give to "taste a piece of my daughter Vicki's lasagna." So I asked Cutler if I could prepare some and have it delivered to the courthouse every day around lunchtime. Cutler was thrilled at the thought and couldn't wait to surprise my father the next day.

I woke earlier than usual and made two trays of lasagna, two dozen meatballs, and a fresh carrot cake for dessert. Around 11 A.M., one of Dad's friends from the Bergin Hunt and Fish Club dropped by to pick up the food. Later that night, Dad called me to say it was delicious. He thanked me and let me know the other defendants as well as the attorneys had enjoyed the food tremendously. It was the least I could do. For the duration of the trial, I sent a different lunch each day. It helped me keep my sanity in a situation where there was really nothing I could do. With each newspaper headline and article, I began to lose faith Dad would ever come home again.

But we all kept our heads held high and smiled in public no matter what was going on behind closed doors, just as our father had taught us.

And we continued our weekly Sunday dinners—the tradition my father started when we were still in diapers—just for the sake of pleasing him. Even the grandchildren sensed a profound disruption in their daily lives. Once the cameras stopped rolling, the flashbulbs stopped popping, and each

271

of us was locked safely behind the doors and walls of our homes, we needed to let our guard down and embrace the uncertainty. The media frenzy continued, with each trial day being played out later on the evening news and then again in the next day's papers. It seemed the agony was a constant twenty-four hours a day. There was little left that was considered private.

We each dealt with our own fears and grief in our own way. I chose to lock myself in my home most of the time, writing to keep my sanity. I was working on my first novel at the time. My father was an important figure in my life and there seemed to be a giant void without him. From ordinary mundane problems to monumental ones, Dad always had the right answer. He had the solution to make every situation right again. Without him, we all seemed lost. I know I was.

The only happiness I could find was in my children.

Between the boys and my father's legal problems, I was always busy, but to make matters worse, I was also trapped in a bad marriage with a man I had little in common with, just as Dad had predicted years earlier. Things got so bad at home between my husband and me that I found it nearly impossible to hide my disappointment and unhappiness. After Justine's death, I went into a state of depression. It didn't help matters when Carmine constantly reminded me it was my fault. He blamed our daughter's death on me. Often when we argued, he would spit the devastatingly hurtful words at me. Also, I didn't have many close friends; my husband saw to that early on. His jealousy had extended to anyone in my life who really cared about me. This unnatural jealousy even extended to our children. Carmine became obsessed with my close maternal relationship with our sons.

It seemed to bother him that I devoted most of my time to the boys. It also irked him that I was very close to my family, mainly my father.

His resentment became more heightened during my father's trial. Without my father home, my husband became happier overnight, it seemed. Carmine didn't try to hide this from me, either. The day the verdict was expected, I didn't call my husband. I knew he would feign concern and disappointment that was not genuine. Instead, I remained at my parents' house, with my mother and siblings, waiting for the verdict.

"Guilty" on all thirteen counts, read the jury foreman. Again, no surprise. It was Dad against the entire government, and there could only be one winner. We cried out in disbelief as if someone had died—and in a sense, someone had.

The press coverage outside was astounding. Satellite trucks were set up for blocks. We were held hostage by this insane media frenzy and needed to wait before venturing outside to return to our own homes. When the coast was clear, I grabbed my youngest son Frank and headed to my car. My other children were at home with their father and I needed to get back to them. Just before I reached the door of my car, a bevy of reporters jumped out from behind a parked van. They shoved microphones in my face and threw out question after question.

"Victoria, how do you feel about the verdict?" *I was crushed.*

"Do you think your father had a fair trial?" *No, but did it really matter?* The government had gotten their verdict and now the press wanted their headlines.

"Do you think your father will put in for an appeal?" *Why even bother? When the entire government wants you, they get you, right?* I never supported my father's lifestyle—and God knows I would have given anything to have a "regular" father. But I didn't, as life would dictate, and I couldn't love him any less because of it, either. He was my father—plain and simple. Finally, I could take no more. I turned to face the cameras and spewed, "My father is the last of the Mohicans. They don't make men like him anymore." And I meant it.

CHAPTER THIRTY-THREE

"Rumor Has It"

In June 1992 Dad was sent to the federal penitentiary in Marion, Illinois. Sadly, just three days later, Grandpa died after a year-long battle with lung cancer. Dad was not allowed to attend his own father's wake. The FBI would not allow any obstacles to stand in the way of getting my father to jail. The super-maximum prison was geared to rehabilitate and break terrorists, mostly convicted spies and serial killers. John Gotti was considered "public enemy number one" as far as the FBI was concerned. He was kept locked in a tiny underground cell for twenty-three hours a day, seven days a week. These conditions are more commonly called solitary confinement. He was not allowed human contact with any inmate or guard. He was allowed only one shower a day, while caged and shackled. His mail was rerouted to Washington for inspection and approval, and his visits were closely monitored, using video cameras and recording devices. He was allowed one visit a month with immediate family members only. The visits were grueling and took place in small cubicles, through Plexiglas walls and using old black telephones. The inmates were required to wear bright orange jumpsuits so they were easily distinguishable from the visitors.

We were all subjected to the usual indignities of visiting prison—emptying our pockets, the familiar pat-downs and wand scans. The first time I visited Marion, I was so overwhelmed that I cried. Memories floated in my mind. The difficult trip to the prison, the indignities of being searched, the depressing surroundings and the first glimpse of my father in a bright orange prison jumpsuit brought back all the unpleasantness of my childhood. I hated that my own children would be exposed to the harsh realities that came with that life. Dad would come down to cubicle number six wearing a smile that quickly turned to a confident grin the moment he saw us. It was his way of letting us know he was okay. "Nothing can break me. Not even this!" he would say as he gestured around the room at the dreary, depressing surroundings that were now his home.

He would take a seat behind the Plexiglas booth and reach for the telephone receiver hanging on the right wall. True to form, he would always make a comment about one of the guards giving him a "way too big" jumpsuit. He was sensitive about his weight. He didn't want anyone thinking he'd lost even a pound. As an added measure of certainty, Dad would often open the top of the orange jumpsuit just enough to let us see he was still in great shape. His six-pack abs were still as tight and sculpted as ever. He believed he had to try hard to alleviate any fears or apprehensions we might have had about his life sentence. Still, I was worried.

MY MIND WAS always racing with crazy and terrifying thoughts. Would the government go as far as killing him, then make it look like a suicide? Or perhaps a murder?

Would the government try to poison him? Would the FBI enlist another inmate's help and attempt an assassination? I believed these scenarios were not as far-fetched as one might believe. I put nothing past the government, especially having been through so many trials with my father and my family.

We tried to visit monthly. We took turns flying to St. Louis and then driving another two hours to Marion. The only hotel nearby was a run-down Holiday Inn on Main Street in Carbondale, a neighboring town. The prison received few visitors, and mostly all of them stayed at the Holiday Inn. Usually we would arrive late at night, settle in, and get to bed. Everyone would meet in the lobby early the next morning to grab a quick bite to eat. Most of the visits were five hours long and there was no food or beverages allowed. Not even a simple vending machine filled with candy. Getting processed by prison officials took almost an hour, and by the time we got in to see Dad, it was usually about 10 A.M.

The visits ran a predictable course: the first hour was usually spent talking about the kids and the grandkids. The next hour was usually reserved for any pressing news or events that required Dad's advice or intervention. The last hour or two was usually divided up between us, so we could each have a private conversation with Dad. During this time, the rest of us would take turns sitting at a small kids' table in the back of the visiting room, watching CNN or some other news program playing on an overhead television screen in the corner of the room.

Most of the visits were uneventful yet very productive, as Dad was always the person each of us went to in any time of need. We each craved the few minutes alone with him for one reason or another. Some issues were small or mundane, while others were serious problems that needed to be addressed in a timely manner. That day, I was excited. A few days earlier, I'd received a phone call from my literary agent—after six rejections, my first novel, *The Senator's Daughter*, was going to be published. And it was no easy feat, either—every publisher I met with wanted a tell-all or a memoir about the Gottis. Finally, I had the brilliant idea of submitting the manuscript under my married name— Agnello—a name I never used legally. And it worked! I couldn't wait to tell my father. It didn't help matters that our conversations were all recorded and were usually leaked to the press—it was intrusive and unsettling knowing that someone else was listening in. Because of this, it was difficult to really talk to Dad, but we made the best of it.

One such issue was a recent report claiming that my father had been courting a Manhattan party girl, Lisa Gastineau, just before he was arrested. She was the ex-wife of the New York Jets' defensive end Mark Gastineau. The tabloids had a field day with the alleged affair. Published reports claimed Dad had taken an interest in the woman and escorted her to a few late-night dinners. The *New York Post* even stated that Dad had showered Gastineau with trinkets of gold and diamonds. It all supposedly ended with my dad's 1990 arrest. According to the tabloids, my father was scheduled to take Gastineau to a Sinatra concert and then to a lavish dinner. The relationship was never consummated because Dad was arrested—according to the tabloids.

First of all, my father hated Sinatra and wouldn't dare attend a concert of his. In fact, Dad never attended a concert in his life. He disliked them. He said they were "too loud" and "a breeding ground for trouble." Also, the way my father was being watched in those days by the FBI and the media would have made a public rendezvous with another woman virtually impossible. One report even suggested the two were set to have their first tryst at the Barbizon Hotel in Manhattan. Dad would not have been caught dead in the Barbizon Hotel. The Pierre, the Waldorf, or even the Helmsley, maybe. But the Barbizon? Never! It wasn't his style.

My mother was livid. Not because she believed any of this. She was quite upset because it was the first tabloid report suggesting Dad was cheating on her. She let my father know it in a letter. She demanded his lawyers "fix this lie" and restore her dignity and respect.

ANOTHER ESPECIALLY MEMORABLE visit to Marion had to do with my son John. My father had a bevy of pet peeves, and, ironically, celebrity worship was one of them. Dad believed all men were equal, be it a doorman or Fortune 500 CEO. Heaven forbid one of us idolize anyone not worth idolizing. Take pro athletes, for example. His attitude was that if an athlete was a dedicated and talented player, and he leads his team to victory time and again, pay him what he deserves.

But just as passionate as he was about a deserving player, he was more so about those players who used recreational drugs and shot steroids. These included the players who had egos the size of their million-dollar paychecks and spent the better part of their days chasing pretty models and driving fast, expensive cars—the players who paid little attention to the game and could care less about their team-mates. These men made Dad see red.

The visit began well, but soon escalated to an argument when Dad asked my son John, "What do you want to be when you grow up, son?"

John replied, "A baseball player or a basketball player."

Dad began to lecture John about what it took to be a successful ballplayer and land a seven-figure contract with a pro team: "You need to be a good liar, a good lowlife. You need to take steroids, and anyone who takes steroids is a garbage pail. You also need to rat out your team the first chance you get."

John was silent. I was tense, sensing my father's mood shift from joy to anger.

Dad always got along very well with all the grandkids—he had his own method of communicating with them.

Usually, it worked, and the kids had a special fondness for Grandpa. But that day was an exception. Sensing there might be a disagreement between my father and my son, I suggested that John go to the washroom and wash his hands. Dad stopped me mid-sentence.

"Leave him—I want to finish speaking to him."

I broke out in a cold sweat.

"What do you *really* want to be when you grow up, son?"

John took a moment to answer and then said, "Well, if I can't be an athlete, then maybe I'll be a cook!"

Dad didn't hear him too well through the scratchy old phones. Dad thought he said "crook." And it didn't help matters that he said it sarcastically, either.

I quickly started to correct my son, but Dad was already steaming. The next thing I knew, my father was yelling at him for being disrespectful. He threatened to give John "a kick in the ass the next time he 'sassed him.' "

Needless to say, after John left the cubicle and put some space between him and Dad, the situation was defused. Dad's soft side surfaced just like with us when we were kids. That's not to say John didn't deserve to be scolded. He did. But Dad had made his point and John had learned his lesson. It was the first and last time he would ever challenge his grandfather.

Unfortunately, the incident was far from over. A tape of this entire situation somehow managed to get leaked to the media. Here was this super-maximum prison facility, where visitors are thoroughly searched entering and exiting—and partake in "non-contact" visits with inmates—and somehow, a tape of one of these visits is leaked. It was definitely deliberate. Especially when the headlines read, "DAPPER DON LOSES HIS COOL IN PRISON."

The tape found its way to the Smoking Gun website and the TV show *20/20*: John Miller was the reporter on the segment. The tape became the basis of an hour-long special on a family visit between my dad, my son, me, and my uncle. It was an intimate prison visit among family. At one time, reporters were never allowed to exploit or expose children, but that rule doesn't exist if your last name is Gotti. The leaking of these tapes during the visits with my father hurt us all. What little time we had with him was on display for the whole world to watch and ridicule.

Another memorable visit took place with my brother John and me. Once again we took our assigned seats behind cubicle number six and waited for Dad to come down. This time there was no smile or confident grin. The visit was not an arranged one. Rather, it was impromptu and had to do with a recent newspaper headline and rumors about a possible hit put out on my brother by rival mobsters. The rumors that were circulating suggested that mobsters from a different Family were envious of Junior's newly acquired leadership position and didn't take too kindly to answering to someone young enough to be their son. We were terrified, despite John and Dad's assurances that the rumors were nothing but lies. Dad insisted that the FBI had instigated the rumors and deliberately leaked them. He believed it was an attempt to "stir him up," especially seeing as he was in Marion and his hands were tied. The FBI knew he was pretty much cut off from the outside world, except for once-a-month meetings with his attorneys or immediate family members. The FBI even leaked the name of the man who supposedly wanted my brother dead, Danny Marino. He was a high-ranking captain from the Genovese Crime Family. People speculated that Marino was still seeking revenge for Paul Castellano's death and resented having to answer to "a kid." Despite Dad's denials and the fact that I knew Marino—he was a businessman from Brooklyn who had always shown Dad the utmost respect from as far back as I could remember—I believed Dad was right, that the FBI initiated the rumors and played them up to a much more serious level. Still, in the life at this point you always had to question one's loyalty. Any man in a position of power in the mob needed to closely watch his right hand. That's why I was always leery of Gravano. Unfortunately, my fears were accurate when it came to Sammy.

Mom was beyond upset when the rumors about John surfaced. She, too, believed there was no longer any honesty or loyalty in the life. The new regime was a bunch of young cowboys with no regard for the old rules and regulations. They did as they pleased and didn't care about mob politics or the Commission, especially during a power play or mob war. Many mob watchers, including the FBI, predicted a war when Dad went to jail. They believed there would be a power struggle to gain control of the Family. But because Dad had so many supporters, men who really respected him, mostly the old-timers, there wasn't. The streets remained quiet. In a matter of months my brother John was put in position of "Acting Boss" by Dad and with the support of the elders on the Commission—the elders wanted my father, John Gotti, to hold on to the reins of the Family.

After we heard the chilling threats against my brother, Mom wrote Dad another missive filled with hate and anger. She let my father know that if "anything happened to John, she would never forgive him." She wrote of the pain of losing Frankie Boy and the "hole in her heart" that will never mend. She reminded Dad of his earlier promises to her to always keep John safe and protected—and she let Dad know if he didn't release my brother from the life, she intended to turn her back on him forever. As for John, none of this came as a surprise. We spoke about the rumors and he said he did not believe them, that they were not true. Once again, he let me know the life had little left that he found appealing. He told me that night that he'd made "a big mistake" when he chose to be a part of our father's world. Without Dad out on the streets, John believed the usually loyal, dedicated, and regimented men had been replaced by "a bunch of Indians running amuck—a bunch of Indians all vying to be the chief."

Meanwhile, the OCTF was expected to arrest my brother any day for acting in a supervisory role in the Gambino Crime Family. Honestly, Mom seemed almost glad when she learned of this. I believe she thought it was the lesser of two evils. Having her son arrested was far better than seeing him killed. She was always unhappy with John's choice of lifestyle when Dad was home, on the streets—and now that he wasn't, Mom was terrified something bad would happen to him.

Dad was *not* happy. He yelled and ranted about what he called "bogus charges." "Where does it end?" he asked John and me. He believed that now that he was put away, the authorities would just move on to the next in line in his family, and continue on until we were all gone.

My father had been chased by the FBI and was the subject of seven years of intense scrutiny by the OCTF, NYPD, and DEA. Dad remarked about the fight the agencies put up when it came to him. "It took them four trials to get me. Four. They needed to disqualify my lawyers and all the witnesses we intended to call. That's the only way they could get me."

Now it was my brother's turn and I couldn't be more surprised. The two men couldn't be more different. Dad loved fancy suits and was always impeccably groomed. John, on the other hand, usually donned comfortable jeans and a sweatshirt. Dad enjoyed eating at fancy restaurants and stopping to have a drink at popular clubs. John preferred informal dinners at home with his wife and kids and rarely stepped foot in a bar or club. Dad had many friends and enjoyed having lots of people around him. John was considered a loner. Dad was driven around in an $80,000 Mercedes. John drove a minivan. But John was a Gotti—and prosecuting a marquee name led to promotions, especially during an election year.

It was the mid-nineties and the FBI had bugs planted in all of my brother's phones: his house, office, and any hangout he frequented. He was also being followed daily by at least three shifts of agents. The press had done what law enforcement hoped they would. They portrayed John as a knuckle-dragging Neanderthal and even dubbed him "Dumbfella," despite the fact that John was extremely well spoken, well educated, and very well mannered. He had spent four years at a military academy after all. But the public believed he was a stupid, ruthless thug, and that's all that mattered to law enforcement.

My father left the visiting cubicle with one word of advice for my brother: *"Fight!"*

CHAPTER THIRTY-FOUR

"Money, Money, Money"

Adjusting to life with Dad away at prison was very difficult, to say the least. My brother John tried hard to fill our father's shoes—and not just in the street. Looking after all of us, including the grandkids and Mom, and working diligently on my father's legal issues, weighed heavy on his shoulders. John was left with many burdens, and not by choice, either. Certain obligations and responsibilities fell on him as the oldest son. John tried his hardest to keep all the balls in the air, but sooner or later things started falling through the cracks.

One of John's biggest responsibilities was handling the family finances. I didn't know it at the time, but my brother was left with the responsibility of managing whatever fortune Dad had left behind before he went off to Marion. This amount was reported to be as much as $200 million by the tabloids, which was a complete fabrication. I'm sure there were many millions that Dad's friends and associates helped themselves to—but money for the immediate family was kept separate.

Dad's personal stash was realistically around $12 million. Dad was generous to a fault with his money—every person who came to him with a story and wanted to borrow money received it. Dad also was a heavy gambler—he loved betting on sports and the ponies. Still, his years as a captain and then boss of the Gambino Family allowed him to put away a small fortune. I was working as a columnist at the *New York Post* when the outrageous claims of a huge stash were printed in a rival newspaper. Again, I had a good laugh. I even did a follow-up column about how I should start looking for the money. My first suggestion was to wait for Mom to leave the house one Saturday and then "head to the hardware store, buy a heavy shovel, and start digging up the backyard." Dad instructed my brother to invest the money wisely so that each of us would be taken care of should anything happen to him. Neither my father nor my brother discussed these arrangements with me at the time. John told me years later about his financial responsibilities.

Perhaps it was because I was always too proud to ask my parents for a penny or the fact that I'd always been independent and supported myself, but I honestly never knew anything about my parents' finances. I even refused a car when I turned seventeen. I was "Miss Independent." I never dared ask what was left behind or who was holding what. But this all became a big issue among the family when my brother's legal troubles began.

NEWSPAPER STORIES CLAIMED John's arrest was to happen any day. So his attorney, Richard Rehbock, reached out to one of the heads of the OCTF and requested that his client be allowed to turn himself in. This would spare John's wife and five kids the agony of the predictable early-morning raid the FBI loved to stage. Rehbock's request was denied. The agent told him, "Mr. Gotti is not special and will be arrested in due fashion."

But Rehbock continued, "This will save the taxpayers much money and all of us much grief. Just tell me when and where and my client will be there."

The FBI wanted their glory. Request denied again.

On January 19, 1996, the entire Gotti family gathered at John's house for a formal Sunday dinner. It wasn't a Sunday, but we acted as if it was. Rumor had it John would be arrested the next morning, and we wanted to at least gather one last time for dinner. It was a night of bittersweet memories. All the grandchildren played obliviously in the den with the dozens of action figures and toy soldiers John had bought for them earlier in the day.

John was always a favorite with all his nieces and nephews mostly because he devoted much time and effort to them. He often took the boys out to ball games and the girls to shows, like *The Lion King*. He planned these outings often just because he really enjoyed spending time with the young children. The way John doted on the children in the family was significant, mostly because their grandfather was in prison—and unwillingly could not be involved in their lives as he should have been. John tried hard to fill the void for all the grandchildren—as he himself remembered all too well what it was like growing up without a proper hands-on male role model.

The adults remained mostly in the kitchen and the dining room that night, telling stories and sharing memories. We laughed and even cried when the mention of my brother Frankie's name came up. John remained upbeat and calm that night. He took us into the den, one at a time, to have a private conversation with each of us. When it was my turn, we spent nearly an hour talking mostly about his kids. He made me promise I would help his wife and keep his kids safe. That was his main concern—his kids. He also asked me to hem a pair of jogging pants for him to wear when he was arrested.

At midnight, most of us left to go home. As I was walking out, actor Mickey Rourke was walking in. He'd come by to say good-bye to John. His flight from Los Angeles had gotten in late and he had come straight from the airport. His luggage was still in the backseat of the rental car. Mickey was a loyal friend of John's and wanted to offer his help. The two men retired to John's home office and had a few glasses of brandy in private. I returned at about 2 A.M. with the pants I had altered for John. I left the pants on the kitchen chair and left quietly through the back door. I checked my watch and realized John had just a few hours left before "D-Day." Despite law enforcement's quest for glory, my brother had other plans. And if the plan was going to go smoothly he needed to leave the house no later than 3 A.M.

The next morning, at exactly 5:30, FBI agents swarmed down on my brother's Mill Neck estate on Long Island, wearing blue nylon windbreakers with large, bright yellow letters—FBI—across the front and back, armed with 9mm pistols and rifles. They stormed the front gates and surrounded the sides and back of the house. Camera crews and photographers gathered outside. Dennis Vacco, the New York state attorney general, was up for reelection that year, so it came as no surprise that it was a carefully orchestrated arrest, to be broadcast and televised everywhere later that day. Unfortunately for the FBI, John was one step ahead of them. He was staying in a comfortable room in a nearby hotel in East Norwich on Long Island, some three or four miles from his home. When his wife called him early that morning and told him about the raid, John immediately contacted his attorney and the two headed down to FBI headquarters.

There was to be no grandstanding on the FBI's end, and they were not happy. They refused to allow my brother and his lawyer to drive down to headquarters. Instead, they spent the better part of an hour on the phone with Rehbock discussing John's surrender. Finally, a compromise was made and John and Rehbock drove down to a coffee shop in Yonkers. The FBI met them and took John to another building where other defendants in the case were being held. They were determined to get their perp walk, and they did. When John arrived, the photographers swarmed him. John later told me, "There was more press there than I have ever seen. Obviously the FBI had tipped them off."

The money shot wasn't enough. Later that day, a huge press conference was held. The U.S. Attorney was there as well as the New York attorney general, the director of the FBI, the director of the Secret Service, New York's police commissioner, the IRS, and the Bronx district attorney as well as other powerful figures. More than a dozen news stations were at the scene as well. It was quite an overreaction, considering the charges were extortion and phone-card fraud, not murder or RICO. The entire display of grandstanding was downright embarrassing for the government and the FBI.

CHAPTER THIRTY-FIVE

"The Green, Green Grass of Home"

After the arrest, John was held without bail. The prosecutors deemed my brother a threat to the community and argued that he should be denied bail and kept in solitary confinement until the trial was over. Also, the rumors suggesting that John's life was in danger still loomed. These rumors were leaked deliberately by law enforcement sources hoping to incite something—possibly John's death. Back then, my brother had his guard up, just in case. One night before his arrest, John was summoned to a meeting with a few of the other capos—two men John suspected were extremely jealous of him and my father. The capos claimed they were involved in a beef with a few guys from another Family and needed the matter resolved as soon as possible. The sit-down was to take place in an apartment in Brooklyn. John and one of his close associates, Mike DiLeonardo, were to arrive at 8 P.M. sharp. Usually, John ran late. But that night he was nearly a half hour early. When he and Mike arrived, the apartment was dark and unusually quiet. There was some movement around the back, the sound of a few men whispering and shifting some boxes back and forth. Perhaps it was pure paranoia or sharp intuition, but John decided to change the plans that night. He held two fingers up to his lips and gestured for Mike to follow him back to the car. When they were on the Belt Parkway and heading back to Queens, John had Mike call the other capos and apologize, saying something came up and they would not be able to make the meeting. Years later John told me he had the strangest feeling of doom that night, "like something bad was about to happen." Later, at one of John's trials, a rat testified that John and Mike were walking into a trap, a well-orchestrated hit. Even DiLeonardo admitted under oath that he also believed that he and John would have been killed that night if John hadn't changed his mind about the meeting.

In the end, after numerous bail hearings, John was granted house arrest and was released from Valhalla County Jail in Westchester—but only after I was forced to post my Long Island mansion as collateral toward a $7 million bail package. This prompted the prosecutor to order what's called a Nebbia hearing. The prosecutor suggested that my home was bought with ill-gotten gains. Bruce Cutler accompanied me to this hearing. I was forced to produce all financial records showing how I paid for my house. This included any invoices and documents showing what was spent on the house and the land. Since my husband and I had purchased the property a few years after we were married and later built a house, I had to call each and every company, from the bricklayers to the pool installers, and get copies of any invoices I could. It took nearly two weeks to gather all the information. The prosecutor was amazed that everything was in order. I believe she was prepared to find fault with anything she possibly could, anything to keep the bail package from being approved and John released. Besides the $7 million bail, there was an additional cost of nearly ten thousand dollars a week for security. The only way the prosecutors would give up the opposing arguments denying John bail was if my brother agreed to home confinement with extra security other than just an ankle bracelet. The added security consisted of two guards per shift, three shifts daily. John had no choice. If he was to fight the case properly, he needed to do so from home with access to his lawyers. And to keep his sanity, he needed access to his family.

His "freedom" came at a hefty price. Besides the enormous financial burden it placed on John, there were other issues to contend with. His wife and kids could not come and go as they pleased, either. Everyone had to be identified at the front gate, sign a logbook, and dispose of any cell phones or computers. No electronic devices were allowed on the premises beyond the entrance checkpoint. Also, there was an approved list of guests allowed to visit and those who were not. Even the children's tutors needed to be approved by the government before stepping foot on the premises.

After a few months, John was beyond his breaking point. This was exactly as the FBI had hoped. Soon talks began about a plea deal. The prosecutors offered ten years at first, but John refused. They came back a few weeks later with an offer of seven years. John still refused. In his words, "If I am going to jail and sacrificing years of my life, it better be for something I am guilty of, not these bogus charges."

The alleged "phony" telephone scam was in fact an error on the part of the company that had distributed the cards. This came out shortly after John's arrest. The company had issued the cards in bulk to various vendors, one of whom was my brother. The middle-man companies purchased phone time in bulk and then sold the time to various vendors in the form of prepaid phone cards. Initially, John believed this was a great business venture.

"I can't tell you how great this venture was. We were even written up in a *Village Voice* survey as the number three or four best phone-card company in the business. But the FBI was intent on scrutinizing everything I did. They went looking for a needle in a haystack," John later told me.

The offices were located in a small Queens neighborhood and the phone cards had the Statue of Liberty logo across the front. It was as American as apple pie—even the name of the company, Nic-O-Dan. John's first daughter is Nicolette. His business partner's daughter is Danielle.

"When they came in and raided the offices, some of the agents introduced themselves as Secret Service. I was stunned," John said. "I stopped dead in my tracks. I couldn't imagine what they were doing there. Was I about to be charged with plotting to kill the president? They tore the place apart. They took pictures off the walls. They took Dad's gold watch and some of his jewelry I had in the top drawer of my desk. How was that evidence? They took legal pads with notes to Dad's lawyers and transcripts of his trial, all relevant to Dad's appeal. How was that evidence? Those notes had to do with legal strategy and were privileged, but they took them."

John told me the agents also took all the phone-card records and those cards not yet sold. The business was shut down the moment the cards were confiscated. This distribution company took in many vendors and these vendors paid a hefty price. Most just lost hundreds of thousands of dollars and had to replace the cards they had sold to customers. In John's case, he was arrested. The government wanted their pound of flesh from John Gotti's son.

Another charge involved the strip club Scores, and a man allegedly extorting money from one of the owners. Michael Blutrich was not only an owner of the club, he was also a former lawyer. He'd worked in a firm alongside former Governor Cuomo's son Andrew. He was the FBI's star witness in the Scores charge. Blutrich was arrested earlier concerning a multimillion-dollar fraud case, and in exchange for no jail time, he agreed to hand over John Gotti Jr. What Blutrich didn't tell the FBI was that he had made a deal with some mobsters from the Gambino Crime Family. Blutrich wanted protection from other strip club owners, and the reputation of being "connected." This way, the club would be much more appealing to customers and make them think twice about ever starting a fight in the club. In exchange, Blutrich agreed to hand over any proceeds from the coatroom concession. John never saw a dollar of this money. Even Blutrich agreed he'd never seen John Gotti Jr. at the club or heard his name mentioned when it came to the money. It didn't matter. Because law enforcement had reason to believe John was "acting in a supervisory position" in Dad's absence, John was charged with the crime. Shortly after the case began, Blutrich was busted for downloading kiddie porn on the Internet. Blutrich was forced to admit he was a child molester and the government's case got weaker.

One defendant on the case was a well-known New York radio personality from WHTZ-100, John "Goombah Johnny" Saliano, who was also charged with extorting money from the coat check room at Scores. Those charges were later reduced and Saliano accepted a plea deal that offered him less than a year in jail. He is now back to work at the radio station.

Yet another charge involved a list FBI agents found at one of John's offices in Queens. The list had names on it with dollar amounts next to them. The FBI claimed it was a list of Gambino associates and soldiers and was quite telling as to who was who within the Family. They deemed the list "the Holy Grail" of organized crime. In fact, the list was merely all the names of wedding guests and how much they gave as a present at John's wedding. It wasn't strange to those who knew John best that he would keep this list long after his wedding. He was a pack rat; he saved everything. We often teased him that he still had the first dollar he'd made from his Communion. The FBI even found nearly $300,000, which they claimed was "mob money from ill-gotten gains." Once again, it was wedding money, hidden in a wall safe in John's office.

The last and probably most laughable charge was that John was extorting his own cousin. There was a taped phone conversation where John is complaining to John Ruggiero (Uncle Angelo's son) about unpaid rents. Ruggiero ran an auto parts store that he leased from John. During this conversation John says to Ruggiero, "I'm looking at my books—it says sixteen weeks in rent, Neptune Auto Glass?" To which Ruggiero replies, "Sixteen weeks?" John repeats, "Yes, sixteen—one, six." Ruggiero says, "That's impossible." John then summons his secretary to get the books out and asks her (while still on the phone with Ruggiero), "When did the last check come in from Neptune Auto Glass?"

The secretary responds, "10/16." John then says, "That was the last check you sent." John argues with Ruggiero and tells him he needs to come down to his office later that day. He instructs him to bring his books. At the end of the taped conversation, John says to Ruggiero, "This has to be straightened out by today. No one rents for free. At the end of today, it's either going to be John Ruggiero's business—or it will be John Gotti's."

The FBI claimed John was extorting his cousin. It didn't matter that the two men were as close as brothers, as close as their fathers were at the very same age. Even when Ruggiero told the prosecutors that there was no extortion attempt, that it was merely a landlord trying to collect rents from his tenant, they refused to drop the charge. Instead, the prosecutors kept "sweetening" the possible plea deal. John's lawyers went back and forth. Finally, a deal was offered that my brother believed he could live with. It would put an end to all the unwanted negative publicity and the enormous security bills due each week.

To a man with five young children whom he loves and adores, the stress and uncertainty of a trial can be maddening. John felt that way, even telling me, "I want to guarantee my daughter Nicolette I will dance with her at her Sweet Sixteen and her wedding. I can't risk a jury finding me guilty and sending me away from my kids for twenty years for shit I didn't do."

I understood. My father did not.

So the plea that had taken months of negotiation between John's lawyers and the prosecutors had unraveled. John would never do anything without Dad's approval.

The prosecutors still wanted to make a deal. It wasn't a

highly bankable case from their perspective. Witnesses began to change their stories, and many were caught in serious lies. The DA's office was enveloped in negative press. One of the prosecutors was even reprimanded by Judge Barrington Parker for leaking case-related information to the press. Vincent Heintz, a prosecutor who ran the four-year probe into John's case, was dismissed when the judge learned he was responsible for the leaks to the press. It was a circus. The prosecutors came back with another offer: five years and complete closure.

It wasn't the shorter time in jail that attracted John. It was the "closure" clause. John wanted to put his legal troubles and his position in the life behind him. It was a decision he'd made years earlier but dared not tell anyone. He wanted out, plain and simple—and he saw going to jail as an escape from his obligations in the life. Once, John even said to me: "I almost hope I'm found guilty—so I'll get thrown in jail and get away from the life." Yet he was afraid Dad would disapprove. Especially since he was away in jail and there was no one left he'd considered "trustworthy" to take care of the Family. But my brother stood firm. After many months of laboring back and forth, weighing the pros and cons, he'd decided his family, his children, were much more important than anything else in the world—even money and honor. I understood. Others did not. Higher-ups in the life refused to accept John's resignation. They tried hard to convince him to remain one of them. Even my brother's "Goombah," John Ruggiero, couldn't persuade him. During a routine prison visit a few months later, Ruggiero was heard telling my brother he was recently asked to "join up." In other words, he was a candidate to become a made man. Ruggiero always followed my brother's lead ever since they were kids and therefore he always valued John's opinion. John was livid! He went into a tirade, spewing insults at Ruggiero like "Have you not learned anything from watching me? Look where I am—you think I want to be here? You think that life is worth this? Is it worth losing your wife and kids?" A bug had been planted under a chair in the visiting room of Ray Brook Federal Prison. Some of the recording was inaudible, but my brother John's words are loud and clear: "Run, John. Run like hell. Don't let these people get their hooks in you." My brother ended the conversation by saying, "If you accept and embrace that life—you and me are finished. I made a decision, Johnny Boy, and I intend to stick to it. I can't let you or anyone else pull me back in."

In the end, Ruggiero didn't take my brother's advice—he was too jaded by the bells and whistles that went along with being a made man—and a thirty-year relationship was destroyed. It was the first of many life-altering changes John suffered as a result of his decision to leave the life. At one point he even wondered if he might be killed because of it. Still my brother stuck to his guns. He later told me, "This decision was not born out of anger or fear . . . that life leaves little to be desired, where I'm standing. It's not for me. It's not what I want any longer. I have my kids to think about. Their lives, their opinions of me, mean much more than anything that life could ever offer me." John ended our conversation with "Vicki, I'm not Daddy. He's the last of his kind. He lived for that life, that world. It was his mission in life, to honor and support his men. It's not who I am." I don't think I have ever been prouder of my brother than at that moment. I was so relieved John was getting out; I had waited for this moment since I learned he was made. I never wanted to see my little brother live that life, and I knew his heart wasn't really in it, either. It was all about impressing our father.

Before accepting the plea package, John requested a visit with Dad. John's lawyers went back to the prosecutors and told them John needed to get his father's blessing. The prosecutors objected at first. But in the end they gave in and arranged a visit between father and son.

Two weeks later, John took a flight to Marion, Illinois. He went through the usual process of being searched and scanned. John was considered a regular visitor that day. The only difference between earlier visits to Marion and the visit that day was it would be a "contact" visit. John was looking forward to hugging Dad after nearly ten years of incarceration.

The visit was an emotional one. John would tell me later that Dad understood his decision, but he did not agree with it. He kept telling John the government was lying. He tried to impress upon my brother that there would be no closure in the end. Dad tried his best to convince John the plea deal "reeked." He swore once they got their hands on John and put him in jail, they would never let him out. John believed Dad was being paranoid. Dad also let John know that taking pleas in the life was "not acceptable." Men were expected to stand tall. They were expected to be stand-up guys from the moment they were inducted into the life. Taking a plea was seen as a sign of weakness, and Dad did his best to dissuade John from accepting the plea deal. He told John, "Listen to me, son, you will never get out of prison if you accept this deal. The FBI will never leave you alone. The *only* way to beat these motherfuckers is to fight them. Do you understand me?"

The visit ended with Dad telling John, "Do whatever you want to do. I would never tell you what to do, how to live your life. But I will give you advice and tell you this deal is wrong."

What John remembers most was the hug at the end of the visit. He remembers fondly the way our father felt: "It was the best hug in the world for me. Yet I knew it meant so much more to him. After not having any human contact for ten years with anyone, it must have felt exhilarating."

John returned home with a heavy heart. He had a major decision to make. He wanted to take the deal. He also knew if he did, Dad would be greatly disappointed.

The night before John made his final decision, he said this to me: "I like children. I love mine. I want to be free to raise them while they are still young. Most of all, I don't want them following in my misguided footsteps—ever." John and I went over the predictable scenarios that accompany kids with fathers in prison. They rebel. They get into trouble. Some even end up in jail themselves. John did not want this for his kids. I was proud of my brother—for many reasons. He was man enough to take his own medicine and man enough to walk away from the temptations the life offered. He was also man enough to stand up to our father. He wanted to serve his time and start a new life. I believe his decision was both smart and brave.

In the end, John took the plea deal. A few weeks later, I went to see my father. He was agitated during that visit. All he did was rehash his conversation with John, and then rant some more about how "real men don't accept plea deals—they fight, fight, fight!" I tried telling Dad most men were not like him. Most men were only human and usually followed their hearts. In the end, Dad still disagreed with me and took John's plea deal as a direct sign of disrespect. It was the beginning of a two-year feud between John and our father.

Judge Barrington Parker sentenced John to seventy-seven months. But John paid little attention to the jail time—it was the judge's words that affected my brother the most: "You grew up in circumstances where your father was incarcerated, so you knew the kind of toll that takes on family—particularly children. The pattern, for reasons I am unable to fathom, is duplicated." John took in Parker's words and responded, "I'm a man. I am here to take my medicine."

CHAPTER THIRTY-SIX

"Baby, I Need Your Lovin'"

It was a beautiful spring day in 1998. I found a comfortable shaded spot under a blooming cherry blossom tree in a local park in Old Westbury, Long Island, where my family now lived. That day my sons Carmine and John were excited beyond the imagination. Both were Little League members and their team had made it to the "World Series." I packed a picnic of sandwiches, snacks, and cold drinks. The baby, Frank, was not yet old enough to play on the team, so I brought along some board games and toys to keep him busy. I spread a checkered tablecloth out under the tree and emptied the picnic basket. The kids grabbed at the treats, eyes wide, smiles stretched across their faces; they stuffed themselves silly. Then the coach yelled out and they went running.

The players took their assigned positions: Carmine covered first base, John was the catcher. It took four batters to strike the opposing team out. Carmine was first up at bat. After two tries he hit a double. The next batter got up and struck out, but not before Carmine managed to steal a base, rounding the corner of third. He was fast on his feet. John was the third batter. After two pitches he had two strikes. The pitcher threw the ball and the bat cracked loudly. John hit a home run! Meanwhile, Carmine was heading toward home plate, bringing in the first run of the game. I jumped up and threw my arms in the air, pumping my fists with pride. My children were the reason the crowd of friendly neighbors were on their feet, cheering as loud as they could. The last thing I remembered was my son Carmine searching the crowd for my approving eyes—then everything went black.

I WOKE UP IN St. Francis Hospital Heart Center in Manhasset. My mother was standing at the foot of the bed with a worried look in her eyes. I scanned the room, searching for my husband and children. As if Mom could read my thoughts, she said, "Carmine took the boys downstairs to get something to eat." I looked away from her and stared out the window. "When were you going to tell me you're pregnant?" she asked.

I'D KNOWN ABOUT the pregnancy for three weeks; I'd already been to the doctor for a checkup and confirmation. The news wasn't good. The doctor thought the pregnancy was coming at a bad time. I had just started taking a few new medications for my heart condition and some of those meds were not yet proven safe for pregnancy. Dr. Stern was concerned. She sent me to a specialist. He let me know the pregnancy was going to be risky, but he also offered words of encouragement. I was convinced I would have a normal and uneventful pregnancy. The only person I'd told was my husband. I didn't want to tell anyone else until I got through the first trimester. The day of the ball game, I was nearly ten weeks' pregnant.

Many doctors surrounded the bed; each of them suggested an abortion. I wanted to be left alone. I asked Mom to leave. As I lay in bed, crying, all I could think about was Justine, the daughter I had buried, and my three beautiful sons. It's not a position any woman or mother ever wants to be in. I kept the lights off and tried to sleep. I prayed over and over for God to make the decision for me. If I miscarried, it would have to be God's will. But to abort the baby willingly was not something I wanted to think about. The doctors came back in around dinnertime. They had some test results back from the lab. The results were not good. The pregnancy was putting a tremendous strain on my already weakened heart. A decision would have to be made quickly. More serious, though, was evidence of severe, life-threatening arrhythmias on the EKG. My cardiologist told me I would need a defibrillator to prevent my heart from going into sudden cardiac arrest. I wanted the baby so much, I was hoping for a miracle. At the time, my marriage was unraveling more and more by the day. Carmine and I were fighting over every little thing. Lately, nothing I could do was right. Stupid issues became full-blown arguments. Even my health troubles became fodder for fights. He was spending less and less time at home and more time at the office. I was pretty much left to raise the kids on my own. Even on his days off he found excuses not to spend the day with the kids. In the past he'd take them to breakfast at the local IHOP and then to a park or even the racetrack, but lately he didn't even seem to have time for them. I really did believe a new baby would bring us together again as a family.

My brother John was still home, but under house arrest, and getting ready to go off to jail.

I remember him coming into the dark room and shaking my foot, tucked neatly under the wool blankets. Once I was awake, he put the light on and pulled up a nearby chair. He spoke softly at first, telling me how sorry he was about everything and asking if there was anything he could do. Then, when I started crying, his expression turned dark. He scolded me and let me know getting pregnant was a "stupid thing to do in my condition." I agreed. But it was unexpected and accidental. Then John said, "My heart goes out to the innocent, unborn baby inside you right now—as much as it does for you."

He lowered his head and said, "Right now, I'm also thinking about my three nephews, whom I love like my own kids. They *need* a mother, Vicki. You can't be selfish here. You must put their needs before yours or anyone else's." John left the room nearly in tears.

The phone on the night table rang a few minutes later. It was my father. I was stunned to hear his voice. Immediately I started crying uncontrollably. This upset Dad terribly. He told me Bruce Cutler was able to get him a special call.

I hardly spoke, just listened. Dad told me how sorry he was about the situation. He also reminded me about how much I loved being a mom, and how previously doctors had said I would never have a child. He reminded me of the three beautiful sons I did have and let me know each one was "nothing short of a miracle." He ended the call with, "You need to do what's necessary to save your life—for you and for your children."

I signed the authorization paper and was transferred to

Long Island Jewish Medical Center a few miles away. St. Francis was a Catholic hospital and did not permit abortions. The procedure took about three hours and I was back at St. Francis before ten that evening. It took less than an hour to get me settled in. Mom was with me every step of the way along with Carmine and my brother John.

I insisted everyone go home around eleven. Mom looked exhausted and stressed out. John and Carmine were tired as well. Everyone needed a good night's sleep. In the morning we would discuss the upcoming cardiac surgery.

I fell asleep just before midnight. I slept peacefully for forty-five minutes. Then I woke up in excruciating pain. I pressed the call button clipped to the sheets and waited for the nurse. The nurse appeared and saw that I was hemorrhaging—the sheets were nearly covered with blood. She ran to call the doctor. Meanwhile, the pain was getting worse by the second. At one point it was so bad, I wrapped my hand around chunks of my hair, pulling clumps out as hard as I could in an effort to transfer the pain from my abdomen. They couldn't find the doctor for almost an hour, and when they finally did, she took one look at me and knew right away what was wrong. But there was one major problem: because the procedure was done elsewhere and because of the strict religious ban on abortions, doctors at St. Francis could do little to help me. Politically, their hands were tied. And there was no time to airlift me back to Long Island Jewish Medical Center. The situation was getting more critical and a split-second decision had to be made.

I was shuttled down to the emergency room, where a screen was put up. The doctor needed to perform an emergency D&C. The abortion had been incomplete and was

307

causing internal bleeding. Because of the legalities there was no anesthesiologist allowed. I felt every scrape of the scalpel.

AFTER THE PROCEDURE was over, there was a team of doctors and nurses around me. It was over and I was alive. I was transferred back to my room and slept for two days straight. Three days later I was released. I was not strong enough to have the heart surgery yet. Instead, I was sent home with an external defibrillator. It was a box, the size of a clothing gift box, with two paddles attached. A registered nurse accompanied me home and spent nearly two hours teaching me, my husband, and even the kids how to operate the machine in case of an emergency. It took me nearly three weeks to get out of bed. Four weeks from the day of the emergency surgery, Dad called to see if I was okay. He kept repeating things like, "I can't tell you how awful I feel, how helpless, because I'm here and I can't do anything to help you." He felt so guilty. There was little I could say to change his feelings. He ended the call with, "I lay awake nights realizing just how lucky I am to have a daughter like you." The following week I received a beautiful card in the mail. On the cover was a picture of a unicorn, a beautiful, white unicorn. Inside Dad wrote the words, "Beauty belongs with beauty." I still have that card, framed and hanging in my home office.

CHAPTER THIRTY-SEVEN

"You Don't Have to Say You Love Me"

Six weeks after the abortion, doctors deemed me well enough to undergo the necessary cardiac surgery. The decision was a godsend, as I was not allowed to leave the house without the bulky machine or someone knowledgeable enough to use it in case of an emergency. After the implantation of the defibrillator, I remained in the hospital for a week for observation. It took another six weeks to heal and then I was back to my normal routine. Within two months, doctors allowed me to travel.

As soon as I could, I went to see my father. He needed to see me—to make sure I was okay. We talked about the abortion and about the defibrillator. When we finished discussing my health, the conversation shifted immediately to John. My brother was due to begin his sentence the following week and Dad was still upset about the plea. He said to me, "Do you know why I'm here? It took them $80 million and three lying cases and seven rats that killed a hundred people in the Witness Protection Program to finally frame me. You understand?"

I tried everything I could to calm him, but nothing worked. It was as though my brother had failed him and there was nothing I nor anyone could say to change this. What was also bothering him was the distance now placed between him and John—and the rift between him and Mom. Mom was still angry about John. For years she had argued with Dad about John and the life. It devastated her. She made Dad promise her John would never be in danger. She wrote Dad another letter. Once again, it was nasty and filled with hatred. She reminded him of the son they had lost and deemed John's lifestyle and Dad's encouragement of it as another "death" of one of their sons. This made my father crazy, and on the visit we discussed it.

With John accepting the plea, he'd also made it clear to Dad he wanted out of the life. Surprisingly, Dad was fine with his decision to leave the mob. Usually, there was only one way out: death. Because Dad was the boss, John was given a pass. In fact, before I'd left the visit, my father gave me a message to give Mom. "Tell your mother, your brother is out. He's released from his obligations."

It was music to my mother's ears and to John's. When I returned home, I went to see my brother. We talked about my visit with Dad—and Dad's reaction to John's decision. John was relieved. He'd told me he'd wanted out since 1990. It was the birth of his first son that made him decide he wanted a better life. John talked about the possibility of moving his family away from New York, once he came out of prison. He talked about buying a small farm and living a "simpler life." He wanted his own son away from the streets. He wanted better for his own kids than we had growing up. The one thing we both agreed on was that we didn't want our children to grow up as we had, with a father constantly in and out of jail.

The night before John went to jail, each of us stopped by to wish him well. This time, he did not want a formal good-bye dinner. He wanted a quiet night, alone with his wife and kids and immediate family. I stopped by just before ten that night. I found my brother sitting in the den, looking solemn and distant. He was concerned about his family, and I promised I would help his wife with the kids. I would do my best to make sure they were okay. We also discussed our father—John was still upset and felt guilty about letting him down. I supported John in his decision making as far as the plea deal went and as far as leaving the life. In the end, John agreed it was the right choice for him. He kept saying things like, "Vicki, I am not Daddy. He's a man like no other. Daddy is a warrior and dedicated to the life—a cause he puts before all else. I do not."

We also discussed the government's vendetta. John believed by taking the plea it was the only way to escape the constant scrutiny and harassment. I agreed with him, but Dad's words still haunted me. I really hoped he was wrong about the FBI never letting John out of jail if he took the plea.

That night, John kissed me good-bye at the door, then he walked me to my car. Outside, he hugged me, tighter than usual. He did not feel afraid. He felt liberated. Tomorrow was to be the first day of the rest of his life. I missed him already for my own selfish reasons. I couldn't hold back the tears. "Don't cry," he told me. "This is a good thing. A great thing, trust me, sis. When I get out, we'll all start a new life." What I didn't know then was that John had also decided to relinquish any money Dad had given him to hold, money that was to secure each of our futures if something should happen to our father.

The subject had never come up before, mostly because women were thought of as "weak" and "feeble" as far as men in the life were concerned. I didn't know then that Dad had asked Mom just before he was arrested if she wanted the responsibility of overseeing the financial matters and she said no. She told me, "I didn't want the responsibility. What if it was stolen or lost? I didn't want the scrutiny. I was afraid law enforcement might one day storm the door and confiscate the money." In the end, John had asked one of the attorneys to see to it that Lewis Kasman would properly manage whatever money Dad had left. Lewis was one of only a few people left Dad could trust.

CHAPTER THIRTY-EIGHT

"It's My Party and I'll Cry If I Want To"

The party started at eight sharp. My husband was still getting dressed. The kids were waiting impatiently downstairs, dressed in their Sunday finest. The occasion? Another surprise birthday party thrown by my husband at an elegant wedding hall, the Westbury Manor on Long Island. To keep the element of surprise, he made me believe we were going to a charity event. The last party took place on a yacht. Two hundred guests sailed around Manhattan, dancing to the tunes of the Temptations, the Drifters, and the O'Jays. My husband and I were big Motown fans. It was black-tie only.

The year before, Carmine had thrown another huge and expensive bash; each time, he tried to outdo the one before. Then, he secretly purchased a beautiful, fully-loaded black Lincoln Navigator, wrapped it in a huge red bow, and parked it on the dance floor of Carlton on the Park, the most exclusive event hall on Long Island. The only way to get the truck into the hall and onto the dance floor was to have the back wall removed the day before the party and then replaced the day after.

We were just about to walk out the door when the phone

rang. I thought about just letting it ring. But something told me otherwise—something made me answer it. It was my father. It wasn't a regularly scheduled call. He asked about the kids, twice, and immediately I sensed something was wrong. Then he dropped the bomb.

"I have cancer, Vicki."

I couldn't speak, couldn't even move. The few seconds of silence seemed like an hour. Then I cleared my throat and said, "What are you talking about, Daddy?"

My father went on to explain. He'd had a sore throat for months. In fact, on the last two visits he had sounded more hoarse than before. Then he told me the prison doctors said he had a persistent case of strep throat. They kept prescribing antibiotics. A week later, when Dad told the doctor he "felt like there was a lump in his throat," the doctor suggested it might be E. coli. He prescribed another antibiotic, something stronger. A few weeks after that, when Dad told him he could no longer swallow his food, the prison doctor finally ordered an endoscopy, a procedure to look inside the throat. It took nearly a month for the doctor to schedule the test and another three weeks to get the results. The entire process took six months from the onset of the sore throat before Dad got a diagnosis. He'd waited until the results were back before telling anyone. He also wanted me to know he did not want to tell me, especially on my birthday.

But because he only got the phone once a month, and he was afraid we would learn he had cancer by reading it in the newspaper, he broke the bad news. I sat down on the hall steps and asked him, "What do the doctors think, Daddy?" But I already knew the answer. It wasn't good. By now, my husband knew something was wrong and shut the car off and came back inside the house. I was trying hard not to cry. Dad remained strong and convincing. "I'll be fine, trust me, Vicki. I just wanted to tell you before you heard it any other way. Now, you go and enjoy your birthday and write me all about the party tomorrow." As if I could even think about my birthday and the party.

It took a while to compose myself and get into the car. I didn't say a word to my husband or the kids. In fact, I waited until the next day before I told the rest of the family as well. My youngest brother, Peter, and I shared the same birthday and always celebrated the day together. I didn't want to ruin everyone's night.

We were all in a panic. We believed the worst, and we were right. I made arrangements to go see my father the following week. When I arrived at Marion I went through the usual, grueling routine, being searched once, twice, three times, and being led through not one but four steel doors into the visiting room, to booth number six. I spoke to my father and tried to assure him that everything would be fine. He didn't seem to care about the cancer; he was more concerned about how the family had taken the news, especially the grandkids.

THE VISIT WAS taxing. We spent the better part of five hours talking about new chemo treatments and cancer procedures. We also discussed the radical surgery Dad needed. His head, neck, and face would be split down the middle and the surgeon would remove any mass or suspicious area and hopefully all of the cancer would be removed. He would be left with moveable flaps covering the area on the side of his face and neck; the flaps would be made from skin taken from his pectoral muscles. Then he would need approximately four rounds of chemotherapy. I was terrified. But Dad remained calm. The prison wouldn't tell Dad when the surgery would be scheduled "for security reasons." Maybe they assumed we would try to break him out of the hospital?

Mom was beside herself. She felt so guilty because she had not spoken to Dad for over a year. As soon as she found out about the cancer, she feared the worst and demanded to see Dad right away. I made the necessary arrangements. The visit was great. They laughed and they cried. But, most important, they'd made their peace. It was especially good to see a smile on Dad's face again.

Three weeks later, we found out Dad had the surgery by reading about it in the newspapers. We also learned he was still in ICU. So Mom, Angel, and I boarded a plane and headed to the prison hospital. Because Marion was not equipped to handle a sick inmate, Dad was transferred to a nearby prison hospital, Springfield Medical Facility in Springfield, Missouri. The institution was a far cry from the depressing sight of Marion. Inmates seemed to roam freely about the halls, manuevering wheelchairs or with the aid of a prison nurse. Outside, on the sprawling green lawn, inmates played sports such as football and soccer. Even the cells were more like hospital rooms than jail cells. The sight of my father post-op was startling! No wonder he didn't want any of us to see him. His orders from the start were "no visits for at least a month after surgery."

He looked distorted and disfigured. He'd lost a lot of weight and looked gaunt. He wasn't able to eat anything by mouth, just a diet of pure liquids through a feeding tube. He looked heavily medicated, but tried his best to convince all of us he was fine. He even tried to get out of the wheelchair and into a nearby seat without the help of the prison nurse. It proved too difficult, so he remained in the wheelchair. It was a large room with a large table and twelve chairs. There were no booths or walls made out of Plexiglas and no scratchy old phones. Still, we were told it was to be a "non-contact" visit. The only reason we were allowed to visit Dad in that room was because there were no other "non-contact" booths available that day. I remember most how hard it was sitting so close to him and not being able to touch him, especially since he was so sick.

Dad was in good spirits, despite his frail appearance. He did his best to sit through the visit, but we could all tell he was in pain. At one point the nurse appeared and gave him some pain medication and a can of Ensure, a nutritional supplement that tasted like a milk shake and was loaded with calories. We suggested he go back upstairs and rest. We could always come back in the morning, as was the plan. He refused. He even joked about how hungry he was. He said he would even welcome the normally inedible food the prison dished out, if only he could eat. Little did we know he would never eat solid food again. He brought up my lasagna, and how he would gladly give his right arm for a scoop of it.

A few weeks later, Dad began chemo. We thought this would be done at the prison hospital and were very surprised to learn it was administered through an IV drip in his cell at Marion. He'd been taken back one week after the surgery. Back at Marion there was no nurse to monitor his vitals, so it came as no surprise that Dad woke one night with terrible chest pain. As he got up from the bed looking for a guard, he passed out, hit the floor, and lay in a puddle of his own blood for hours until the guard came to do rounds early the next day. Later, Dad was transferred back to the prison hospital and it was discovered he'd suffered a massive heart attack. Because of the delay in getting treatment, nearly sixty percent of his heart muscle was destroyed. This time the prison kept him in the hospital for less than a week and he was transferred back to his cell. I'm convinced that the warden at Marion knew damn well that Dad belonged in a prison hospital, but he was intent on making John Gotti's stay a living hell.

Another round of chemo was started the next day. I was stunned when I found out. I was my father's designated "medical advocate," and I had access to all my father's records and some authority over his treatment, especially if he could no longer make decisions for himself. That's how I found out they had started the chemo again so quickly. I called the prison supervisor and requested an update on Dad's condition. When he told me about the second round of chemo, I feared another heart attack. So my mother and I jumped on the next plane to Marion. It took us three days to get in to see Dad. Prison regulations dictated what days visits were allowed and what days they were not. So we waited. The newspapers and media reported he was "near death" and we were terrified. I kept calling the prison, desperate for answers, but nobody seemed to know anything. Ironically, the press had more information on my father than I did.

Luckily, because I was working for the *Post*, I usually

learned of some new development before it was even printed.

It wasn't easy working for a newspaper that writes about you and your family on a daily basis. But I loved writing my column and interviewing celebrities so much that I made it work. Besides, I was no fool. The paper considered me an asset, even giving me a desk between two of the best columnists at the *New York Post*, Andrea Peyser and Steve Dunleavy. I got special treatment because of the inside scoop the paper got in return regarding my father and my family, and I used it to my best advantage. They used me, and I used them. It was as simple as that. Dad and I often talked about my job at the paper and what my column would be about the following week. He enjoyed hearing about the outside world and lived vicariously through others.

Finally, when we saw him on the third day, looking weak and frail but with a huge smile on his face, we were somewhat relieved.

The doctors gave Dad a clean bill of health a few months later and marveled at how strong he was for a man his age. He was just sixty and looked like he wasn't a day over forty. When he was able to, Dad went back to his regular exercise regimen, two hundred push-ups in his cell daily. They said he had the stamina of a twenty-five-year-old and was in remarkable shape given what he'd been through. The doctors also said if Dad made it to one year without a recurrence, he had a fifty percent chance of survival. If he made it to the second year, he would have an eighty percent chance of survival, and so on.

One week before the first anniversary of Dad's surgery, I got a call from my father. The cancer was back. We both knew what that meant. I started crying and he spent the remaining ten minutes of the monthly call trying to calm me down. After I hung up the phone I nearly collapsed in my husband's arms. It was the worst possible news at the worst possible time. I had to tell the rest of the family.

Meanwhile, Lewis Kasman, the self-proclaimed adopted son of John Gotti, continued his efforts to raise awareness of the inhumane treatment Dad was getting. Every television show covered stories about my father's cancer and prognosis. Kasman did interviews on all the major news shows. He kept a worried face during each of the interviews, demanding "humane treatment" for John Gotti and suggesting the FBI was involved in a plot to kill my father. Kasman claimed he loved John Gotti more than he did his own father.

Lewis Kasman had first arrived on the scene out of the blue. One day he just appeared and from then on seemed to always want to be around John Gotti. He looked for any excuse to be seen out in public with my father. He was not well received by Dad's other friends and associates, including my brother John. Everyone believed Kasman's concern for Dad was phony. As a result, I learned early on to limit my conversations with Kasman. I believed he was two-faced—he loved gossiping about everyone and everything.

When my brother John was around, Kasman's catty behavior seemed to intensify. It seemed to enrage him that John and my father were close—closer than he would ever be with John Gotti. Kasman let his jealousy get the best of him and was constantly trying to start trouble between them. In fact, after John accepted the plea, it seemed to amuse Lewis to know that Dad was disappointed and the two were not on speaking terms. He often wrote my father letters and almost always mentioned John and the plea. He knew which buttons to push in order to send my father into a rage. Kasman often mentioned John and the plea deal to me. He always tried to extract information from me, from everyone in the family. He would go from person to person, talking badly about someone—trying very hard to get each of us to say bad things about the other. Kasman seemed adamant about breaking up such an absolutely close-knit clan.

CHAPTER THIRTY-NINE

"Take Another Little Piece of My Heart"

I remember when I first found out my so-called hard-working husband was part of the mob. To say I was stunned would be putting it mildly. Most people won't believe me, but I honestly had no idea he had anything to do with the life. My father knew how I felt about this; we had spoken of it many times. He knew about my intentions to raise my family very differently from the way I was raised, living with constant fear that my father wouldn't walk through the door at night. We dreaded the phone call telling us that he'd been gunned down in the street like most powerful mobsters before him had.

Carmine came home one night and said he had "something important" to speak to me about. Dad was very sick at the time and I dreaded every time the phone rang, thinking it was the prison, telling me Dad had taken another turn for the worse. That night, Carmine told me he was going to be arrested. It was something stupid, he said, and he had no clue when it would happen. But he was sure it would. I was shocked. He was a legitimate businessman who had built an empire—I couldn't imagine what he could possibly be arrested for. Sure, he'd made mistakes when he was a kid—he had stolen a few cars, but that was behind him. That, I was sure of. He explained to me as best he could. There was a rival auto parts owner who had recently moved in across the street from Carmine's new metal plant and shredder facility in the Bronx. The guy was his direct competition, and to piss Carmine off, he had increased his price for metal. So when customers came in to sell thousands of pounds of scrap metal, they would get more money from this guy. Carmine had the same loyal customers for years, so when the competition stole many of these clients, Carmine went ballistic. He'd confronted the guy at first and made a thinly veiled threat. Something like, "If you keep stealing my customers, you'll pay the price in the end." A week later, the man increased his prices yet again. Carmine should have realized then that something was terribly wrong. There was no way the guy was making a decent profit offering those kind of prices; he must have been barely breaking even. A week later, someone firebombed one of the competitor's tow trucks. A few days after that, Carmine received a call from his attorney, Marvin Kornberg, saying he was to be arrested, something about a sting operation. His lawyer told him there was a witness, a former employee of Carmine's who claimed Carmine was responsible for the truck fire. I was devastated and angry. Angry that he let a man push him to the point of no return, and angry that he was stupid enough to risk all that he'd built and let his ego get the better of him. But I was most angry when he told me the competitor was in fact an undercover cop. Law enforcement had built a sting operation, and was intentionally egging him on, and Carmine fell right into the trap.

We lived in a mansion in Old Westbury dubbed Tara. It was Carmine's dream for as long as I could remember. He often bragged about building his "dream house" one day. It was, in his words, "a testament" to his success after years of manual labor and hard work. I was satisfied with something smaller—something more manageable. In the end I had little say—it was *his* dream. Carmine had never had trouble providing since the day we got married. He left the house each morning at six and didn't return until eight at night or sometimes even later, his work clothes spoiled with grease from a hard day's work. That grease helped Carmine build an empire worth an estimated $200 million. Setting aside all my ex-husband's faults, one thing was obvious—he was a hard worker and a good earner.

That night over dinner, he seemed agitated and couldn't sit still. I argued with him over the pending arrest—how stupid it was, how stupid he was to let someone set him up, and how he had to move on and start worrying about cleaning up the mess he'd started. I was most concerned about the kids and what other kids at school would say to them.

He put his fork down—he'd hardly touched his dinner. He left the dining room table and settled in the den on one of the sofas. The boys started jumping all over him, wanting some small amount of time with their busy and preoccupied father, but he ignored them. I took the hint and put the kids to bed earlier than usual that night. Afterward, I ran his customary bath in the master suite. While he was in the bath, we talked about his pending arrest. I asked him questions like, "Why you? Why would you be a target for law enforcement?" I reminded him of the fact that he was a scrap metal magnate and not John Gotti. I couldn't understand why law enforcement was so eager to take him down.

Carmine just shrugged. He didn't answer, but there was

a guilty look in his eyes. He knew more—he just wasn't telling me.

I went downstairs and called my mother. She, too, was getting ready for bed. I told her everything I knew about the likely arrest and made a comment like, "I just don't understand why law enforcement is so interested in Carmine. It's not like he's somebody." Meaning somebody involved in the life. My mother's silence was chilling. I went on to say that I hoped the newspapers wouldn't start labeling my husband a mobster, for the sake of the kids. I didn't want the stigma—I didn't want them to be raised like I was; the whispers, the name-calling, and all the stupid things classmates do.

I also said, "If one reporter prints that Carmine is a mobster, I'm going to sue." That's when my mother said, "Vicki, don't get involved in something you know nothing about. You'll only look foolish when the truth comes out." That was when I realized Carmine was in fact part of the life—and my mother had known. I was crushed.

Usually I played the role of the dutiful wife and hands-on mother: I took care of the kids, always making sure they were clean, fed, and did their studies every evening before tucking them into bed.

I had a career, but I always made sure my family and household duties came first. Writing my novels and my column allowed me to work from home, so I could tend to my house and raise my kids myself. Having someone else raise my children was never an option. Besides, I thoroughly enjoyed every moment I spent with my kids, even the colicky, crying fits or late-night feedings. I always took the good with the bad, and the good always outweighed the bad. I was taught to take care of my husband, much the same way my own mother had taken care of my father. It was instilled in me to have a hot meal waiting on the dinner table every night when my husband came through the door—no matter what time it was. In the end, I really enjoyed the life we had built as a family.

After the phone call with Mom, I was numb. Listening to her speak nearly shattered everything I'd built in my life. I was crushed and appalled. How could he be so stupid? How could I?

It infuriated me. Obviously my father knew this—in fact, he'd allowed it. I couldn't understand why, especially since he knew my feelings about the life. I wanted better for myself, my children—didn't he? I didn't know who to talk to. I didn't know who knew about this, and even after he lied and deceived me, I did not want to betray my husband. So I kept it bottled up inside of me, and when we finally spoke and I asked Carmine about it, he denied any claims that he was in fact involved in the life.

The notion that my marriage and my life were in fact a big lie really took its toll on me. I stopped socializing and threw myself into my work at an even more rigorous pace than before. I went from writing twenty to thirty pages daily to nearly fifty in an effort to get my first novel, *The Senator's Daughter*, finished before the expected deadline. I looked for any distraction rather than having to face what was right in front of my eyes.

Carmine and I never brought up the subject again but we found ourselves fighting over the smallest things. I spent much of the next few months sleeping in the guest room of our five-bedroom house. I'd found it difficult to lie beside the very man I'd married, for whom I had lost a tremendous amount of respect. As I often confided to my mother, I felt as if I had been "sleeping with the enemy."

Only once during the next few weeks did I bring the subject up again—and of course my husband denied *any* involvement in the life. He went as far as to shout things like, "I work twelve-, thirteen-hour days, I come home covered in grease and oil, I'm home by seven or eight P.M. and in bed by ten—do you really think I even have the time for that shit? Do you think I even want that kind of life for myself?"

I tried hard to believe him, probably because I wanted to believe him.

ON HALLOWEEN, I'D suggested we have a small party for the kids and their classmates. We don't live in a densely populated area, so trick-or-treating is not something easily done on foot. Carmine turned the "simple" party I'd suggested into a carnival—literally, with a Ferris wheel, a specially built funhouse, rides, popcorn and cotton candy stands, and a hayride that went on for hours. And of course for the adults, there was an Elvis impersonator, flown in from Las Vegas, who not only looked like the real deal, but sounded like him, too! The party was completely over-the-top to any sane person.

Another strange event happened a few days later. Carmine called me to say he'd bought a new Mercedes sedan and it was ruby red. He hated the color red, so this really surprised me. When he pulled into the driveway later that night, he was not happy. "I hate the color," he said as he got out of the car. "I'm bringing it back tomorrow. I already ordered a black one and even a white one for weekends." This sort of behavior was baffling. Usually, he was extremely conscientious when it came to spending his "hard-earned" money. He was usually not a frivolous spender—and, in fact, often complained about the ever-increasing cost it took to maintain the household. I also found out he'd started gambling—betting roughly twenty thousand dollars a week on horses at the racetrack.

These manic episodes became more and more frequent, as did the depressive ones. Just as over-the-top as the bouts of mania were the bouts of depression. These "dark funks," as my husband called them, occurred without notice and almost always around the holidays. It was difficult for me to deal with my husband being happy one day and then deeply depressed the next. I urged him to see a doctor. I even went as far as to set up consultations with a few well-known specialists.

And Carmine found fault with all of them: one was too old, another too young, another a woman, and so on. Finally, we found one who shared his love of horse racing. Carmine took this as a sign. He believed he and the doctor were meant to be, and he thought this doctor was his savior. The doctor quickly diagnosed Carmine as a manic-depressive and confirmed my suspicions that he was a "rapid-cycler," meaning my husband's mood swings would occur rapidly and without warning. He went from going on ridiculously expensive shopping sprees and bursts of happiness to a three- to four-day depression that often left him bedridden. The doctor prescribed medication for him. I found out later that Carmine wasn't taking his pills on a regular basis and therefore there was little, if any, improvement.

Money became an issue for the first time in our marriage. Carmine came home one night, asking to borrow my entire savings (my "mad money")—money I had saved over the years by investing wisely and writing novels. Over a million dollars' worth. Carmine had tears in his eyes and rambled on about the new metal recycling shredder he was building. He let me know he'd invested all of our savings into the plant. He also let me know he was almost a million dollars short. He said if I didn't lend him the money, we might as well kiss our future good-bye. I did as he asked. This would be something I would greatly regret just a few months later.

Jealousy also became an evil force in our marriage. As far as my husband was concerned, every man who looked at me a "certain way" wanted me, even our closest friends. Carmine accused me of everything imaginable, including an affair with my cardiologist. It was all untrue. We fought over this day and night. Depending on my husband's mood swings, the fights ranged from minuscule to mammoth.

One night while I was serving dinner he said something that greatly disturbed me. I had a friend in those days who Carmine was not too fond of, an attractive, recently single woman who lived in Brooklyn. My husband considered her "too wild" and forbade me from even speaking to her. All because she had divorced her husband, a good friend of Carmine's. So I stopped seeing her but did speak to her on the phone now and then. One night at dinner Carmine mentioned something this friend had said to me earlier that day, something no one else would know about a man she was dating. Carmine even knew the name of the guy and began to question me about it. I found this extremely odd and asked him how he knew about this. He didn't answer, but only shot me a strange and unnerving glare.

That night I found it hard to sleep. I lay awake thinking,

and suddenly things came together. Over the past few weeks he'd mentioned things that I knew I had not told him—not secrets, just things that were of no relevance to him. Yet the fact that he knew these things and would later on question me about them unnerved me.

One such conversation was between my mother and me—we were discussing my husband's illness, and how I was finding it more and more difficult to deal with him. My mother, who always had a soft spot for Carmine, tried to downplay the situation, explaining to me that my husband was like "a sick puppy in need of extra attention and care." A day or so after that conversation, my husband made a comment during dinner, something to the effect of "So your mother thinks I'm a sick puppy, huh?"

I was surprised and I called my mother and asked her if she had mentioned any of the conversation to Carmine. She replied, "Of course not—are you crazy? Do you think I would betray your confidence like that?" I didn't, but things just didn't make sense.

Lying in bed that night, it finally hit me—my husband was listening in on my conversations somehow. I climbed out of bed and searched room by room looking for anything, some sign of a recording device. I used a dim flashlight so as not to wake any of the kids or my husband. After I'd searched the last telephone jack I was ready to give up, and that's when it hit me. The main panel for all the phone wires was located in the basement, in the laundry room. I quietly made my way down the stairs, and that's when I found it—a small tape recorder attached to a set of wires leading to the main panel. I opened the recorder, saw a tape inside, closed it, and pressed play. I was shocked and then stunned to hear every conversation I'd had earlier that day. I ripped the device from the panel and held it tightly in my hands. I dropped the flashlight and started crying.

The next morning after my husband left for work, I called my youngest brother, Peter, and asked him to come over right away. As soon as he arrived I showed him the recorder and told him what Carmine had done. When I pressed the play button and let Peter hear some of my conversations, he was beyond stunned. He paced the kitchen floor for ten minutes before he could even speak. Then he said, "This is bad—very, very bad. Is your husband that crazy? I mean, does he know whose daughter you are?"

I couldn't even answer—I just sat down and cried. Peter turned to me and said, "What else has been going on in this house? I want to know everything." I told him about all the episodes and the fighting and even the threats. Lately, my husband had taken to terrorizing me by threatening my life, telling me he would kill me if I ever thought of leaving him. My first novel, *The Senator's Daughter,* was finished and nearly ready for publication. As my excitement grew, Carmine's diminished. Gone was the support he'd always professed to have when it came to my writing and my having a literary career—and in its place was an ugly, green-eyed monster. He later admitted that he felt threatened that I might become successful and have no need for him or our marriage and would want to move on. I couldn't believe my ears, and even after hours, even days of trying to convince him he was wrong, his jealousy continued. Things between us were reaching the point of no return.

Later that night I went to dinner with some of my closest friends to celebrate the publication of my book. Two women and one man. When Carmine found out, he became so jealous, so enraged, he drove to the restaurant and made a scene outside, yelling and pressing down on the car horn. When I refused to come outside, he did the unthinkable: he drove his Mercedes right through the restaurant storefront! Patrons ran for cover and left behind uneaten dinners as well as unpaid bills. While most of the staff hid safely in the restaurant kitchen, I stayed seated and just cried. It was one thing to be jealous, it was another to be insanely jealous—and insane he was! The man with me and my girlfriends that night was Michael, my openly gay friend of nearly ten years. Carmine knew he was gay. Michael never hid his sexual preference. And Carmine always got along well with Michael and never saw him as a threat. But that night everything changed and I saw a side to my husband that convinced me that he definitely was crazy.

My brother Peter was utterly disgusted by my husband's behavior and for the first time he began to see qualities in my husband that he deemed intolerable. I certainly agreed. I asked my brother to get Carmine to leave the house, at least until I could sort things out. I couldn't stand the sight of him. He checked into the Garden City Hotel later that night. For the next three days Carmine bombarded me with phone calls, flowers, apologies, and visits. He showed up at the house late one night, literally in tears. He stood before me crying, murmuring things like, "I love you" and "You're my whole life" and "Without you and the kids I'm nothing." He ended his begging session with, "I swear, Vic, if you don't take me back, I'll kill myself—I swear I will."

∘   ∘   ∘

THE DAY AFTER I'd discovered the bugging device, I left for a regularly scheduled visit to see my father; Peter and the kids came with me. The visit was pretty normal except for my "distant" mood. My father asked me a number of times, "What's wrong?" But all I did was shrug and say nothing. Dad looked first at me, then at Peter. Then he said, "Is Carmine okay? How's his illness? Is he taking his meds?" I just shrugged. Peter stood still, expressionless. Dad grew angry and impatient. "Well, is someone going to tell me what's going on?" I tried to speak, but I couldn't. I found it difficult to talk around the lump in my throat.

"Well, let's have it. Obviously something's wrong. Is Carmine at it again? Is he jumping into the backseat of the car, wondering where the steering wheel went? Is he standing outside the house late at night, howling at the moon? Tell me, what's this moron done now?" It was my brother Peter who finally spoke up. He asked me to take the boys to the vending machine for a few minutes. I knew he was going to tell my father what Carmine had done.

I sat at one of the empty tables, far enough away from the small cubicle where my brother and father were sitting. I was careful to keep the kids far from earshot. I did not want them to hear anything negative about their father, nor did I want them to suspect anything was wrong with our marriage. They had enough to deal with as it was, given the fact that their grandfather was all over the newspapers and serving life in prison. Finally, Peter walked over and said, "Daddy wants to speak to you. I'll stay here and watch the kids." I nearly died.

Surprisingly, he didn't say "I told you so." Instead, with a sympathetic look in his eyes, he said, "I wasn't aware that things were that hard for you at home, Vicki." I stared back at him and after a few seconds found the courage to say, "Well, things are not exactly easy, Daddy—Carmine certainly has his moments." By now I was fighting the urge to cry so hard it nearly hurt my eyes.

My father then said, "I have to figure out how best to handle this. This is not some silly act of jealousy, Vicki, this is *really* serious. Does your husband understand he behaved no better than an FBI agent? Does your husband realize that invading someone's privacy is a serious issue? How would he feel if someone did that to him? How would he feel if someone listened in on his most personal conversations and then played them back for the world to hear?"

My father cleared his throat and continued, "I can tell you firsthand it's a sick feeling—a sick, sick feeling. We all say things in fits of anger that we don't mean. But we never do so thinking the world is listening." I was sure Dad was also thinking of himself at that moment—finding out, just after he was arrested, that the FBI had taped all of his private conversations and had played them in court, even leaked them to the press, for everyone to hear. "What if you were having a private conversation, something of a very personal nature, with your mother?" I knew exactly what he meant and where he was going. One thing my father staunchly believed in was loyalty. Betrayal was not a word in his vocabulary—and what my husband had done was considered a betrayal of a serious kind. He asked me what my plans were. Was I going to stay with my husband or divorce him? Divorce? I hadn't even thought about it—the word wasn't in *my* vocabulary. I looked over at my three sons. They were innocent little boys and I had to take that into consideration. I had to put their welfare before mine. It was at that moment I decided to go home and give my marriage another try. This seemed to please my father. Because, even though he had no love for Carmine and really believed we were an ill-fitting match, he, too, put the welfare of his grandchildren first. My father gave my brother his "marching orders." Peter was to go home and have a serious talk with my husband. He was to let Carmine know that sort of behavior would not be tolerated—not one bit.

Putting the tape recorder incident behind me wasn't easy, but I did make a great effort. Trying to put the pieces of my marriage back together was extremely hard.

Carmine and I still fought, even on our anniversary, which happened to fall on a weeknight that year. We hardly ever went out during the week because I had to get up with the kids in the morning for school, and Carmine had to get up for work. But, seeing as it was our anniversary, my father had gone out of his way to arrange a special dinner at a swanky Manhattan restaurant on the Upper East Side. He had one of his lawyers make the reservation. Dad also had one of his associates order a huge bouquet of "Black Magic" roses, my favorite flower, to be delivered to the restaurant once we'd arrived. But out of spitefulness mostly, my husband decided he was "too tired" to go out that night. I pleaded with him and begged Carmine not to embarrass me in front of my father—as he surely would have taken this as a personal slight. If we didn't show up at the restaurant, word would surely get back to my father. So we continued arguing right up until two hours before the car (my father had sent a limo as well) was due to arrive.

We yelled at each other over the phone and my

husband got annoyed and hung up on me the moment I brought up my father. Carmine was always very jealous of my father—and any time Dad did something nice for me, my husband would look for a way to ruin it. I called back in such a rage and while we were arguing I heard his secretary's voice in the background saying, "Oh, just give in and take her out already." There was a certain familiarity in her tone, enough so alarm bells went off in my head. I became enraged and shouted, "Does the whole office need to know our business? Is there a reason why this stranger is involved in our argument?" Carmine didn't answer and a silent pause took the place of words. He knew better than to anger me further—he also knew I was right and shouted something to the secretary like, "Mind your fuckin' business." But the exchange was a bit too familiar—too comfortable.

Carmine came home after work and we went out for our anniversary. We fought the entire night over the secretary's remarks.

Many more incidents involving "the secretary" took place over the next few months—leading up to me giving Carmine an ultimatum: either she goes or I do. This was not open for discussion. Call it "woman's intuition," but I just knew something wasn't right. It was obvious to everyone it seemed that she had a crush on Carmine. All he would say about the subject was, "Are you kidding me? Do you see what she looks like? She looks like a man, for Christ's sake!" He was right. She was a heavyset woman, around thirty-five years old. She had mousey-brown hair that always appeared to be dirty. And she was always dressed in ripped leggings, an old, grease-stained T-shirt, and a pair of worn men's work boots. I remember the first time I ever laid eyes on her. The one thing that stood out most was the dirt around both her ankles. Any woman with half a brain couldn't possibly be jealous of her—still, there was something I couldn't put my finger on. Something that just wasn't right.

She was fired a short time later.

A few months passed and I came across a recent bank check signed in the secretary's handwriting. It was dated a week before I found it.

I confronted Carmine while he was in the bath, screaming and yelling. I was already packing in the bedroom, when he came running after me with some ridiculous story. I wasn't listening. I couldn't take one more lie. All I said to him was, "If having this secretary around means more than losing your wife and kids, so be it!"

In the end, he finally admitted that she was in fact still working for him. He told me that he'd kept her on because "she really knew the business like no one else did in the office" and he couldn't find anyone to replace her. He said he was sorry a million times and begged, literally on his hands and knees, for me to "please stay." Also, he presented me with a flawless, five-carat, emerald-cut diamond ring. He said he bought it for our anniversary but never gave it to me because he had to wait until the setting was done. That should have been the most telling of all. The next day he came home from work with two first-class tickets to Italy. He wanted us to spend our sixteenth wedding anniversary in Rome. Neither of us had ever been to Italy and we often talked about going. But I refused to go into the next room with him, let alone across the world. Instead, he took our youngest son, Frank, and I stayed at home with Carmine

337

and John. We needed space—time away from each other—and the trip couldn't have come at a better time.

We spoke every night while Carmine was in Italy—mostly we argued. I told him I wanted a separation and he begged me not to leave. He kept bringing up the kids—and what a separation would do to them—and then he would start crying and tell me over and over how sorry he was.

Why I took him back still remains a mystery to me. By now nearly everyone in my family, not to mention everyone at the office, knew about the secretary situation. My husband had my entire family, including my own mother, believing that I was "crazy." He would tell them over and over that he couldn't understand why I was so jealous. My family took one look at her and believed him. But Dad did not. During a visit to Marion, my father told my brother Peter to "look into this matter very closely." My father was afraid this situation was something that would bring much "embarrassment and heartache" in the end.

A FEW MONTHS LATER, my second novel, *I'll Be Watching You*, was published. The publisher threw an elaborate book party at Il Cantinori in Manhattan, with hoards of press in attendance. My husband was noticeably absent. When I arrived home later that night, I found him asleep. He'd sent the babysitter home as soon as he got in around seven-thirty. I wanted to slap him, I was that angry. Instead, I undressed, took a hot bath, and went to sleep in the guest room. He had deliberately ruined my night.

He woke up about an hour after I got home. He came downstairs and put the television on in the room next to mine, and turned the volume up. A few minutes later he was standing in the doorway, holding a VHS tape in his hand. "Do you want to watch a movie?" he asked. I pretended I was asleep. He really was crazy. "I got a great copy of *Good-Fellas*," he said. "Sure you don't want to watch it?" Still, I ignored him. I was too tired to fight with him and too tired even to answer him.

At 3 A.M., I woke with a start. There was a heavy weight on my chest, crushing me with a viselike grip. I opened my eyes and Carmine was straddling me and pointing a gun—my shotgun—at my face, just inches from my mouth. I couldn't speak. I was too terrified to scream. Besides, who would hear me? I prayed the kids wouldn't wake up. I was frozen. Carmine only laughed and said, "So you think you're going to leave me? I don't think so." His eyes were empty of all reason. Empty and dark, with dilated pupils. I was really scared.

"Say something," Carmine said. "If I shoot you in the face you won't be beautiful anymore." Earlier that day, the *New York Post*'s columnist Liz Smith wrote an item in her daily column about the publication of my second novel. She'd referred to me as "the rich man's Pam Anderson." This angered Carmine. Anyone unlucky enough to comment on the article at the office was badly berated or reprimanded. It was one of the reasons he'd decided to boycott my book party.

"What's the matter, cat got your tongue?" The tears were streaming down my face, and my body was as still as a corpse. In the distance, my son's voice was coming from the top of the stairs. Frankie cried out for me, as he often did whenever he woke up from a bad dream.

339

Then, just as quickly as the terrifying incident began, it ended. Carmine started laughing and quickly climbed off of me. He threw the shotgun under the bed and said, "Are you scared? Come on, don't tell me you really believed I'd shoot you."

I didn't speak. My body was shaking. I climbed out of bed and headed upstairs to my son Frankie. I hugged him with all my might, carried him to my bed, and laid him down on the pillow. Once he closed his eyes, I retrieved the shotgun and hid it where it belonged, in the wall safe—a safe that Carmine did not have the combination or key to. I'd bought the shotgun a year earlier for safety when Carmine was not home. It was a legal shotgun that was always kept unloaded. The gun was kept on a high shelf in the closet, while the bullets were hidden in a safe, in a different closet, for safety reasons.

I stripped down in the bathroom and took another bath. In the tub, I sobbed uncontrollably in silence. I got dressed in clean pajamas and went downstairs to check on Carmine. He was fast asleep in the guest room. I grabbed the children from a deep sleep and piled them in my Mercedes, just outside the front door. I started the car and hit the gas full force. I arrived at my mother's house at 4:45 A.M. I didn't tell her about the gun, just that Carmine and I had a fight. I stayed with Mom for nearly a week—agreeing to go home only after Carmine checked himself into the hospital.

Coincidentally, while Carmine was in South Oaks getting evaluated, I woke one morning with excruciating pain in my left arm and shoulder. It was just before Christmas and I had baked six dozen cupcakes for the boys' holiday party at school. En route to the school, I suffered a bout of dizziness that nearly caused me to pass out. So I pulled the car over and called the police.

I was taken by ambulance to St. Francis Hospital, where it was discovered that I'd developed a blood clot caused by the defibrillator. The doctor told my mother that the clot was sitting just one millimeter away from my heart. I was put on high doses of the blood thinner Heparin and placed in ICU for observation.

In truth, the doctor believed I was going to die. And so did the media, apparently. Front-page stories ran in all the major newspapers, saying I was "near death." Magazine news shows did one tribute after another. But once again, I defied the odds. Ten days after I was admitted to the hospital, I was released. I was put on the oral blood thinner Coumadin—and told I would have to take the dangerous medication for the rest of my life.

A FEW WEEKS LATER, on New Year's Eve 2000, I invited some friends as well as the usual family members to our house for a celebration in honor of the millennium. Everyone congregated in the kitchen while I was busy at the stove. We were all waiting for my father to call. He had written a week or so earlier that he would save his monthly call for New Year's Eve rather than Christmas. I really couldn't wait to speak to him that night. Dad was always the backbone of the family, the "voice of reason." He had all the answers and each of us followed his advice precisely. I really needed to speak to him that night; I needed to hear his voice.

I set up the speakerphone right next to the stove. When it rang at exactly ten, I immediately dropped everything and answered it on speaker so everyone could hear. There was silence in the room as everyone stopped talking in anticipation of it being my father.

It wasn't. It was a man who asked if so-and-so was in. I let out a sigh of disappointment and quickly told him he had the wrong number. The man let out a small chuckle and said, "Yes, there is. She's your husband Carmine's girlfriend." I froze, even though I had my back to the rest of the guests in the kitchen, I could only imagine the dropped mouths. I quickly hung up and turned to face everyone, and what I saw broke my heart: my oldest son, Carmine, nearly twelve at the time, sat at the head of the table with his head bowed in embarrassment. I was crushed. My husband was upstairs taking a bath.

I took the stairs two at a time and when I reached the master bathroom I pushed open the door with such force I nearly broke the handle. That's when I did something stupid. Earlier in the day I'd treated myself to a new pair of Manolo Blahniks. I removed my right shoe and tossed it at him, hitting him on the left side of his face before it dropped into the water. He wasn't worth the cost of the shoes.

After the phone call, he flooded me with excuses, from "It's the government. They're doing this to fuck with me" to "It's just some jealous asshole trying to make trouble for us." I couldn't even stand there and listen to him; I couldn't bear to be in the same room with him. So I went out into the hall and sat at the top of the stairs and cried, too embarrassed to rejoin our guests. I'd had enough. Nothing else mattered but getting away from Carmine Agnello.

CHAPTER FORTY

"I Will Survive"

Two days later, Carmine was arrested for suspected arson in the firebombing incident at the undercover competitor's scrap metal business. It happened just after he left the house at 6 A.M. and was heading to work. Two unmarked cars at the corner of our street stopped him. The officers had the decency not to arrest him in front of his family, especially his kids. They took him away in one of the police cars and impounded his black Mercedes. The undercover operatives running the phony business never expected that Carmine would land right in their laps and do something so stupid. They had him on tape arranging to pay two thousand dollars to a guy who agreed to throw bottles full of gasoline onto the other business's property. The undercover investigation was initially intended to uncover crimes in the stolen auto parts market. Carmine walked right into their trap. He threatened them, and when they didn't back down, he ordered the firebombing.

Later that day, Carmine was let out on bail. A few days later, newspaper reports suggested that the recent arrest of Gotti's son-in-law would be taken over by the feds. There was the predictable amount of jealousy over the state having

gotten to Carmine first. Because of who Carmine was—
John Gotti's relative—the Feds wanted the glory. All the
FBI had to do was prove Carmine had an affiliation with
organized crime members—and just like that the case went
from state to federal. The fact that the Feds wanted the
case was also a telling sign my suspicions about Carmine
being involved in the life were true. Immediately, Carmine
contacted his attorneys, who tried to arrange a peaceful
surrender now that the case was going to be federal, but the
FBI refused. Once again, they wanted to do what they do
best—grandstand.

THE NEXT MORNING, at approximately 6 A.M., the telephone rang. I answered and was surprised to hear an FBI
agent on the other end asking for Carmine. He told me there
were more than a hundred agents surrounding our house.
He requested that Carmine come out quietly. I was stunned.
I jumped from the bed and ran to the window. Outside, men
wearing navy blue windbreakers with bright yellow letters
showing FBI surrounded the house. The agents were armed
with large rifles and handguns. I even spotted a small group
of men wearing jackets that said SWAT. It was surreal, a far
cry from the state arrest a week earlier. Unlike the state,
the FBI wanted press coverage. It didn't matter that there
were young children in the house. They couldn't give a shit.
Carmine was accused of throwing a Molotov cocktail at a
competitor's truck, but given the show the FBI put on, you
would think he was accused of being a terrorist!

I raced out to the hall and before I could get to the
kids' rooms, they were already up and aware of what was

happening. I will never forget the look in their eyes as they watched their father being cuffed and dragged away. Carmine was denied bail. At the hearing it was disclosed he'd admitted to bribing a member of the jury during my uncle Genie's trial. The trial had started in 1989, and Carmine was approached by a middle-aged black man. The man showed up at his scrap metal business one afternoon and told my husband he was on the Gotti jury. He made some remarks suggesting he could be bought for the right price. At first Carmine said he thought he was being set up. So, he checked the guy out and found he was for real. Carmine agreed to pay the man for a not-guilty verdict. My husband actually believed he was doing something good, too! As a result, he didn't tell my uncle or my father—or anyone, for that matter—about the bribe. He just sat back and watched the trial unfold. Years later Carmine got a grand jury subpoena concerning the jury tampering incident. He conferred with his lawyer and was advised to tell the grand jury everything. Because his lawyer had arranged what's called "immunity," Carmine could not be prosecuted. All he had to do was tell the jury *all* the details surrounding the matter—and he was released. Apparently, the key issue then had been the fact that the juror had approached Carmine and not the other way around. According to the law, this could be looked at as some sort of entrapment.

But Carmine did not get off scot-free in the end. His earlier mistake had great impact on his later arrest. In federal court the judge believed Carmine might try to influence witnesses or members of the jury and remanded him without bail.

And the bad news continued. Mom called a few hours

later, crying. She had received a call a few minutes earlier from her half-brother, John. Their father was dying. He had been battling bone cancer for nearly two years and was on his deathbed. Mom was torn about whether she should go to Florida or not. In the end, she decided to go and say good-bye to the father she had never really known.

We spent two days in Fort Lauderdale and Mom had two emotional visits with her father. On the third day we flew home and landed at LaGuardia Airport around midnight. After I put Mom in a cab headed to Howard Beach, I hailed one for myself. Just as I was climbing into the backseat, a *New York Post* delivery truck pulled up and tossed a pile of newspapers to the curb. There, on the front page, was a picture of me and Carmine and an inset photo of the secretary, with the headline "DIVORCE FOR AUTHOR, GOTTI."

CHAPTER FORTY-ONE

"Didn't I Blow Your Mind This Time?"

The hardest part of divorce is deciding whether or not to actually do it. Anyone who has ever been married knows how hard it is to finally say good-bye, especially when there are children involved. I went into a temporary state of denial. But it was now or never. With Carmine locked away in jail, it was the perfect opportunity. I didn't want to believe Carmine was having an affair. I also couldn't believe I'd allowed him to clean out my savings account—or that I had let him get away with half of the shit he pulled in recent months, like putting a gun to my head, joke or no joke, sick or not. Most of all, I couldn't believe I was about to become a single mom with three sons to raise. The most important man in my life was dying thousands of miles away and there was little I could do. I felt alone and helpless.

The first thing I did was visit Dad. He told me what I already knew. There was no other option but to divorce Carmine. Dad was against divorce; he was too old-fashioned to accept it. But given the ugly publicity attached to the scandal, he realized there was no other way for me to hold on to my self-respect.

"I only hope you are able to weather the storm, and bounce back from all the ugliness," he said.

The nights that followed were long and difficult. I walked the floors, thinking, unable to sleep. During the day, I wandered the gardens and yard aimlessly, unable to eat or do anything productive.

Carmine called often and most of the time I didn't accept the collect calls. When I did, all he would do was beg and cry. He even went as far as to offer me money and diamonds if I stayed married to him.

"I'll pay you five thousand dollars a week, tax-free. I'll also order you the most magnificent, ten-carat diamond in the world. Just tell me you won't leave me!"

I wasn't even tempted. My self-respect was worth a hell of a lot more than that. Besides, his offer of money was insulting. My mind was made up. I contacted a local lawyer, Stephen Gassman, with a great reputation. Lewis Kasman was summoned to escort me, given the fact that my brother John was in jail. I went for the initial consultation and listened to Gassman as he went through the process of divorce. All of it was surreal. I don't believe I heard a word he said that day. All I knew was Carmine would be served in jail.

He called me later that night. I wouldn't accept the call. He redialed and spoke to the children. He begged them to make "Mommy stop hurting Daddy."

When they came crying to me, I was crushed. Carmine had made me out to be a monster. I was the bad guy. I was now the reason why our family was breaking up. It took me months to make the children understand what had happened. It didn't help that reporters continued writing articles about the ordeal almost daily. One article claimed that the secretary had a tattoo on her lower back, with Carmine's face on the body of a bulldog, and his name in script across the bottom of the tattoo. Because the criminal case was work-related, some of my husband's employees were arrested as well. The secretary was one of them—and I can't say I didn't get a dose of happiness and a dash of revenge when that happened. After she was arrested and strip searched, news of the tattoo surfaced.

I later learned Carmine had bought the woman a small home in New Hyde Park and would often stop there after work at night. The secretary made numerous threats to him to tell me about the affair if Carmine didn't put her up in a lifestyle that was at least "comfortable." The house was only a few minutes away from our home in Old Westbury. How convenient for Carmine. I even learned she was driving a brand-new, candy-apple red Camaro that was purchased by my husband's company.

Besides being taunted by the press with daily articles of my failed marriage, law enforcement was also determined to see to it that Carmine and I broke up, for good. Two FBI agents came to my house with a picture of the secretary and Carmine standing in front of the recycling plant, looking as if they were arguing. The agent went on and on about their relationship and said he was sorry I had to go through such "an embarrassing ordeal." The other agent chimed in and asked, "How does John Senior feel about this? He can't be too happy." That's when I slammed the door.

Even after going to such great lengths to make sure I

found out about the affair, law enforcement then had the nerve to later accuse me of staging a "fake divorce" to try to save assets they were trying to confiscate from Carmine as part of the criminal proceedings. I realized then that members of law enforcement would stop at nothing to win a case, even if it meant destroying lives.

CHAPTER FORTY-TWO

"On the Road Again"

I threw myself into my work, writing my weekly column for the *Post* and working on a new novel. I needed the money now more than ever. I had three children in private school and Carmine refused to pay child support. My lawyer went to the judge and requested "emergency relief." The judge, Ira Raab, granted the request and ordered Carmine to pay child support plus all "arrears monies" that were owed. This included money for the children's school. I was awarded $12,500 a month for alimony and $12,500 for child support. Carmine was also ordered to pay all school costs as well as health insurance, life insurance, and maintenance on the marital home. The monthly payments were to come out of rents Carmine was collecting from nearly thirty commercial pieces of property we both owned. He paid nothing. My attorney went back into court. This time the judge was losing patience with Carmine, but what could he do? Throw him in jail? Carmine was already in jail.

The newspapers got wind of the judge's order and printed the motion in its entirety. Dad was livid.

On the next visit, he and I had an argument. He scolded me and said, "You are not to take one dime from that piece of shit. Do you understand? Any money you need, I will provide. Let Carmine keep his money and choke on it." Dad was most upset by the revelation that Carmine had turned over all the commercial properties we owned to the government in exchange for a nine-year prison sentence on the racketeering charge and a $10 million fine. How generous. Especially since half of the assets were mine! All of these properties were supposed to be in both of our names and in trust for the children. They were not. This shocked me. Did he really believe his own children would steal from him?

Dad was also angry about the money Carmine had "stolen" from me, which he claimed he needed for the shredder he was building. I later learned the FBI had confiscated three bank accounts when he was arrested, one of which was an account in a St. Louis bank that had nearly $2 million in it. He never needed my money—he just didn't want me to have it. Dad said Carmine wanted to "subjugate" me, and he ordered my uncle Pete (Dad's older brother) to get "back what was rightfully mine." On the visit, he turned to Uncle Pete and said, "He can keep his money and choke on it. But what's hers is hers! She earned that money without his help. Get it back!"

A month or so later, I was on a plane heading to Marion to visit Dad again. Uncle Pete turned to me and said, "Vicki, there is no reason to tell your father I haven't been able to get your money back from Carmine yet."

I just stared back at him. He continued, "It's just that Carmine is in jail and it's very hard to get to him. I'll take care of the situation, but let your father think it's already been taken care of."

I told my uncle I wouldn't lie. Uncle Pete was not happy

with my answer. I would never lie to my father—for anyone. I also wondered if getting to Carmine would be so hard if the money were my uncle's? Probably not.

My uncle Pete and I discussed some pressing news— Sammy "the Bull" Gravano was being investigated again, this time for drug trafficking. Apparently, Gravano had managed to build one of the biggest Ecstasy rings in the West, using his wife, son, daughter, and his daughter's boyfriend to push the pills to college kids in some town in Arizona. How ironic, since Sammy was the one who questioned my father's decision allowing John to be inducted into the life. Gravano, much to law enforcement's dismay, went on to write a book, do television interviews, and launch his own publicity campaign in an effort to create some level of celebrity status for himself. Gravano wrote in his memoirs that he could never understand how any father could ever allow his son to be a part of that world. Yet Gravano did even worse. He'd built a drug business and allowed not only his son, Gerard, to get involved, but even his wife *and* pregnant daughter. See what I mean about these witnesses? Gravano also managed to put together his own crew and was suspected of hiding an entire arsenal of weapons in a bunker in his backyard. Another investigation concerning Gravano had to do with a detective he was suspected of murdering—a murder he did not reveal when he had agreed to become a federal witness. Before the government can accept a witness into the program, he or she must come clean about every criminal act they'd ever committed—mostly because the prosecutors never want to be caught with their pants down during a trial when the witness is cross-examined by a defense attorney. The cop killing was never disclosed by Sammy, making his government application to become a rat null and void. Gravano and his entire family was later arrested and charged. No surprise. The aftermath caused many future witnesses to deem Sammy's testimony against John Gotti nothing but lies. The ironic results also embarrassed a lot of law enforcement types—like former prosecutor John Gleeson. According to news reports, the two became quite chummy during and after Dad's trial. Gleeson and Gravano reportedly stayed in close touch with each other for years after the trial. Today, Gleeson is a judge. He was handed the promotion after Dad was convicted. I wonder how Gleeson and many, many others feel about the ironic outcome of their "star witness"—the guy the FBI swore was reformed and had turned into a pillar of the community?

Uncle Pete and I discussed how we would present the news about Gravano to Dad. Both of us wondered if he'd be angry or happy. But knowing that all the members of law enforcement finally discovered that Gravano was a liar and a fraud pleased Dad. The FBI may have believed Sammy, as did the prosecutors and the jury, but who knew better than Dad what a cowardly liar Gravano was?

DAD DID ASK me about the money on that visit—and I didn't answer. I walked to the bathroom and left the two men alone. When I returned, Dad did not look happy. He said something to Uncle Pete about making "sure he handled the situation the exact way he was told to." Then he changed the subject.

I could tell Dad was upset with the intrusive press and media coverage surrounding the divorce as well. So I called the lawyers the minute I returned home. The next day my attorney went before the judge and requested the divorce be "sealed." Normally, it's very difficult to get an order to seal a divorce. It's supposed to be of public record. In my case, the judge made an exception. The seal would mean there would be no more "leaks" about intimate and embarrassing details of our marriage.

A month later, I visited Dad again. This time, he seemed calmer when the subject of my divorce came up. But he asked why it was taking so long. It was as if he'd wanted me severed from Carmine as quickly as possible. Dad even asked about my social life, and why I wasn't dating yet. I was surprised, given how old-fashioned he was. He let me know it was "time to move on, time to get on with my life." He suggested I get my "party dress out of the closet and go dancing. You'll never meet anyone sitting on the couch," he said. I started going out, attending premieres and parties. The gossip columns had a field day. The reporters couldn't wait to link me with someone.

There was an article saying I was dating baseball player Mike Piazza, and actors Vin Diesel and Jack Scalia. If I was seen talking to a man, it was assumed we were "dating." These articles reached Carmine and he blew up. It came as no surprise one day when I received a call from Bruce Cutler. He said a DA in Chicago had contacted him. The DA passed along some news. A man recently convicted of robbery and manslaughter had called his office looking to make a deal. The man claimed Carmine had asked him to put a "contract out on my life." The man claimed my soon-to-be-ex had offered to pay him fifty thousand dollars, and said he would testify against Carmine if it would get him out of jail. The DA refused the offer, but as a matter of law he contacted Cutler.

I received the call from Cutler toward the end of the day as I was getting ready to leave my office at the *Post*. Bruce tried to sound calm. He even downplayed the incident by saying, "Young Victoria, I don't believe the man. Obviously he's desperate and looking to get out of jail. I don't believe Carmine would go that far."

I was not so sure.

There was a doctor, a female psychologist, who was working with Carmine just before he went to jail. She called and asked me to meet her. I dropped by her office the next day.

"Look," she said, "my visits with my patients are confidential. But if they tell me something that indicates they could harm themselves or someone else, I am obligated by law to report it." I continued to listen.

"It's none of my business what goes on between you and your husband. However, when a man tells me he has 'thoughts of killing his wife,' I have to take them seriously." She went on to tell me she knew who my father was. She asked me why I hadn't gone to Dad with this problem? I told her the truth. My father was sick with cancer, and besides, if I jumped the gun and something happened to Carmine as a result, I would have to live with that for the rest of my life. How could I face my kids? Carmine had never hit me during our marriage. Mostly because he knew I would never tolerate it, and also, because he was afraid of my father—no matter how much he pretended he wasn't. I believed the recent threats were related to his mental illness. The doctor's observations, combined with the phone call from Cutler, made me wonder whether Carmine was capable of making good on his threats.

In the end I never did tell my father. But I did speak to my mother. She was shocked, to say the least, but observed, "He's always had a dark side to him. And when it came to you, I knew he'd never let you leave willingly." Cutler also felt it was best not to bring this news to my father. We both knew it would only destroy him. All that mattered to us was his well-being. We didn't know how much longer Dad had left.

CHAPTER FORTY-THREE

"Smile, Though Your Heart Is Breaking"

I spent many nights wondering if I'd made the right decision, especially when I noticed the changes in the children. They went from happy, healthy, obedient, and well-disciplined to quiet, depressed, and at times rebellious. Nothing I could do seemed to help the situation. I worked longer hours at the *Post* to try to keep up with the bills. Carmine still refused to pay any support; he wouldn't even pay half of their tuition. When my attorney called his attorney, he was told, "My client doesn't feel it's necessary to keep them in private school." I was stunned. This from a man worth nearly $200 million! This from a man who had stolen almost $2 million from me! This from a man who had lied, cheated, and broken nearly all of his wedding vows. This from a man who was married to John Gotti's daughter.

I blamed myself. In time, I, too, became withdrawn and more depressed. The breakup of my marriage couldn't have come at a worse time. Dad's health was failing by the day, and I couldn't face the fact that I was going to lose him. My family became very concerned and staged what they called "a necessary life intervention." My brother Peter came over one night around ten o'clock when the kids were already asleep. He literally dragged me in front of a mirror in my bedroom and said, "I used to be so proud of you. You were always beautiful and so smart. Look at yourself." He held my head with both hands and forced me to take a good hard look. "You would let a man do this to you?" Peter was right. It was bad enough I allowed Carmine to do all the terrible things to me while we were married, but to continue to let him ruin my life was ridiculous.

Then he pulled out the big guns.

"Daddy would be so disappointed if he saw you like this." He was right again. I was wasting away to nothing. I needed to get ahold of myself. My family needed me and I couldn't allow my physical and emotional deterioration to go on any longer. With a father dying in jail, a brother also incarcerated, an estranged husband behind bars, and various health problems, it was easy to slip into a dark place, but I had to snap out of it. I needed to channel all my energy into my father and his battle with cancer.

MEANWHILE, MY BROTHER John was serving his sentence at the Federal Correctional Institution, Ray Brook in Upstate New York. It was near Lake Placid and bitterly cold in winter. The visits there were taxing, especially on the kids. Thankfully, his five-year sentence was coming to an end and he would soon be home. He would once again take back the reins of the Gotti family, and I could be free of responsibility and worry. I was nearing my breaking point. And then more bad news: newspaper articles surfaced that John was to be indicted again. This time, the Feds were going to charge him with being in a supervisory position of the Gambino Crime

Family. Dad had been right. John had foolishly believed the language in the plea agreement. He believed taking the official plea would bring him closure—how wrong he was.

Dad's health was getting worse and worse by the day it seemed. I had filed a request with the BOP (Bureau of Prisons) seeking permission to have Dad treated by private physicians. This would alleviate the federal government of any monetary responsibility and give us peace of mind and hope. It was not an unusual request and had been granted to other inmates before, including organized crime members. I believed there was a chance our request would be granted, since even some prison doctors admitted to us that the cancer would not have spread as quickly as it had if it had been treated properly in the early stages. I also believed the government and BOP thought we might sue. The answer came nearly a month after application. It was denied.

The family continued our regularly scheduled visits, but the prison wouldn't allow any extra time, even though Dad was dying. On one visit, Mom looked tired and pale. She complained of a stomach upset that had started a few days earlier. Dad seemed concerned. When she got up to go to the bathroom he handed me a note. He could no longer speak and his only means of communicating was by writing down brief sentences on a legal pad. "Take Mom to the hospital when you get home. I don't like the way she looks."

I didn't even wait to go home; we went to St. Francis Hospital Heart Center directly from the airport. Dad was right. One of her main arteries appeared to be eighty-five percent blocked, but the doctors needed to do an angiogram to be sure. Afterward, she would probably only need a stent, the doctors said. I was relieved; I couldn't handle having another parent seriously ill.

The angiogram should have only taken a few minutes. After twenty-five minutes, and no word from the doctor, I went into a panic. Finally, he came out. He told me, "Victoria, during the procedure your mom's artery ruptured. It's a one in a million occurrence. We need to operate immediately." The rest of the family was down in the waiting room. I sent the orderly down to get them. The doctor allowed me to see Mom for "only a minute." Normally, she would have been whisked to the OR, but seeing as the doctor was a friend and seeing as I might never get a chance to say goodbye, he allowed me to go in.

I remember trying to stay calm. All I wanted to do was scream, cry, and panic, but I spoke to Mom clearly and calmly. I told her there was a small problem and the doctors would fix it. She looked so scared. I kissed her on the forehead and said, "I love you." Then they wheeled her away.

The surgery took hours. Doctors had to stop the internal bleeding first before they could attempt to replace the damaged artery with one from her leg. The cardiac care nurses wheeled her out of the OR, and I remember she looked very, very gray. Honestly, I thought she was dead. She was hooked up to monitors and machines and she had tubes coming out of the side of her neck. I cried.

The next day, Mom was conscious and moved from the ICU to recovery. Three days after that, she was moved to a private room. When she was released after ten days, she came to live with me for a while. I couldn't sleep without her there.

Dad, meanwhile, was furious that he couldn't speak to

us. He was allowed to call only twice that month. One call was a regular scheduled call and the other was considered a "special call" due to a family emergency. It was so hard to understand what he was saying. His words came out like a bunch of groans and grunts. But rather than draw attention to it—as I knew he'd be terribly embarrassed—I just rambled on about how well Mom was doing. I assured him Mom would be fine. I didn't need him worrying. John was also distraught. He felt helpless because he could not be with us or with Mom. It was the first real emergency without a man to hold down the fort, as Peter wasn't even thirty years old, and I don't know how I managed.

Financially, I was out of money, but I dared not tell anyone. It was my responsibility to provide for my children and I was too proud to ask for help. Carmine had promised to "strangle me financially" if I moved forward with the divorce and he made good on his promise.

After three months, Mom was well enough to go home. I was so used to having her stay with me and was deeply saddened to see her leave. So I asked her to move in permanently. She thanked me for the offer, but she was too independent and politely refused. Luckily, my younger brother Peter had a better plan. He and his wife and four kids decided it best to move in with Mom. They lived a few blocks from her anyway, so it wasn't a difficult move.

A few weeks later I received a call from my divorce lawyer. The judge had awarded me the marital home despite Carmine's claim to half of it. That was good news and I was relieved. At least it was one less thing to worry about, even though the divorce battle with Carmine and the government over the remaining assets continued. The bad news was finding out the son of a bitch had taken out a million-dollar mortgage against the house without my permission. The monthly mortgage payment was a whopping thirteen thousand dollars! I was in more financial trouble. While Carmine fought for a fifty percent share of the house, he was ordered to pay all of the maintenance as well. But the moment the judge awarded me sole custody of the marital residence, Carmine stopped paying even that. When I arrived home from work one night, I found the electricity had been shut off. The kids and I sat in the dark for nearly three days until I could raise nearly four thousand dollars to turn the power back on. As a result of the divorce and Carmine's legal troubles, I was financially bankrupt.

I was too embarrassed to tell my father—instead, I borrowed the money from Lewis Kasman.

But that was nothing compared to the blow I received next.

CHAPTER FORTY-FOUR

"Time to Say Good-bye"

June 10, 2002

can remember what I was doing when I learned my father was dead.

Where I was standing.

What I was wearing.

I was at my desk in my home office. I was trying to keep myself busy, working on extra stories for the *Post*. The television was on; someone at CNN was talking about yet another politician caught up in a scandal. There was a moment of silence, then the newscaster announced there was "breaking news." For a second I couldn't catch my breath—my heart started pounding. The anchor said, "This just in: Mob boss John Gotti has died of throat cancer. Gotti, often dubbed 'the Dapper Don' for his flamboyant fashion sense, was serving a life sentence for murder and racketeering in Marion, Illinois. He was sixty-one years old." Next came the news crawl at the bottom of the screen: "MOB BOSS JOHN GOTTI DEAD AT 61."

It felt like time stopped and everything was still around me. Then the calm passed and I started screaming, beating the wall with my fists. At that moment my children came in from school and learned the news.

My oldest son, Carmine, walked with his head down to his room, locked the door, turned the lights out, slipped into bed, and got lost in one of his deep black holes. The man who had served as both father and grandfather his whole life was gone, and the impact was enormous.

Frank, the youngest, broke down in the hall, looking to me for comfort. But I couldn't go to him—I was still caught up in my own shock and grief. I imagine the scene must have terrified him.

John, my middle son, reacted like the strong, in-control little man his grandfather always bragged he was. He rushed to my side and hugged me with all his might and whispered, "Everything's going to be okay, Mommy. Don't worry, I'll take care of you."

Less than an hour later, we were in the car heading to my mother's house.

We were the last family members to arrive. My mother was lying on the couch, crying, with a bunch of old photos of Dad scattered on the coffee table in front of her. My brother Peter had called earlier asking for a nice picture of my father for the funeral mass cards. My sister, Angel, was in the den, sitting in Dad's favorite chair, an old, comfortable recliner covered in rich burgundy velvet with black piping on the seams. She was staring into space, her eyes watery and red.

Through a window in the den, I could see groups of reporters, photographers, and curious neighbors gathering outside. Minute by minute, the crowd seemed to grow, and within an hour there were so many people outside the house the local police arrived. The group was mostly friends and neighborhood men and women who had come to show their support. Some were crying and one man held a sign saying, "We'll always love you, John."

I drew the curtains for privacy, but also I didn't want my mother to see the commotion that was going on outside. It was a taste of things to come.

IT TOOK TWO days to get my father's body released. The amount of red tape was astounding. The warden had to "sign off" on all the paperwork before we could remove Dad from the prison. The media surrounding the Springfield medical facility was similar to the waiting press circus in New York. My brother Peter had a difficult time. He had been witness to my father's rapid transformation from robust and buff to frail and emaciated. Peter had sat constant vigil, at least on designated visiting days, at Dad's bedside for the last six months of his life. Maybe he was hoping for a miracle like the rest of us. In our eyes John Gotti was the toughest man on Earth. Nothing could rattle him; nothing except cancer.

The emotional toll caused by watching our father die was noticeable. With John in jail, Peter had to step up as the man in the family, and much of the responsibility fell on his shoulders. It was clear that trying to care for Dad and navigate all the prison policies and bureaucracy was wearing on him.

My last visit with Dad was a month before his death. It was so emotional I was sick in bed for two days afterward. Both he and I knew that the end was near and it would probably be our last visit. Since he could no longer speak, he wrote everything on a small blackboard he kept on the bed.

We were talking about Andrea Bocelli and his new CD. The last thing Dad wrote was how much he loved the song "Time to Say Good-bye." He wrote the word "ironic."

Amid my grief, I was mad, angrier than I'd ever been, ever since I'd found out that the prison had performed an autopsy despite strict orders from my father and protests from me. Since I was Dad's "designated next of kin," anything pertaining to his medical care had to be approved by me. The moment my kid brother found out about the autopsy, he called me from the prison. We had already made arrangements for a local funeral home to pick up my father's body. These plans were made even before Dad died, just in case the warden tried to pull something. Dad and I had signed affidavits, notarized and reviewed by lawyers, stating that there would be no autopsy. You didn't have to be a rocket scientist to know what my father had died from; he had been treated for throat cancer for the past four years.

I felt somewhat responsible about the autopsy for not seeing to it that my father's last wishes were carried out. My emotions danced between guilt and grief. My family and I imagined the prison officials doing the procedure and tossing Dad's organs around the room, laughing at the warden's behest. Believe me, it's not as far-fetched as it seems. Months after my father's death, we learned that a man had somehow gotten hold of Dad's prison jumpsuit by bribing one of the guards. This same man wrote a book and offered a small swatch of the jumpsuit (he'd cut it to pieces) with the purchase of each book as a means of generating sales.

PETER REMAINED IN Springfield until my father's body was released. Lewis Kasman arrived within hours of Dad's death, with Leona Helmsley's private jet, to take him home. Kasman later told me Helmsley had called him the moment she'd learned of Dad's death and offered her services, whether it was her private plane or anything else she could do to help out. The prison released my father's body in a body bag, no coffin or even a wood box. Peter boarded the plane and couldn't bear the notion of my father lying in the back of the aircraft like cargo, so he took the first two seats and laid our father's body across him, resting our father's head in his lap. He later told me he'd even unzipped the top of the bag, exposing Dad's face and head. He said he couldn't bear the thought of our father zipped up in a vinyl bag—not even for a second.

BACK IN NEW York, the media's temperature was just about at the boiling point. Helicopters swirled around the darkening sky, shining bright lights down on their target—a black hearse cruising down the Long Island Expressway at moderate speed. The oversized, black vinyl body bag was unloaded from the jet amid hundreds of reporters from as far away as Rome, all hoping to catch the money shot that would no doubt grace the covers of all the morning newspapers.

I was lying in bed when the live coverage splashed across the television. I tried in vain to erase the disturbing images of the hearse driving along the LIE, but it was on all the channels. I remained still, under the warm goose-down blanket, watching through watery eyes. The coverage bounced back and forth between split-screen aerial views and still shots taken earlier just outside the prison. "Talking heads" described blow-by-blow accounts of my father's "last journey home." The helicopters above kept in constant stride with the black hearse, while dozens of reporters on the ground gave chase in cars. On the screen the commentator gave an exact location each time the vehicle passed an exit. It gave me the chills.

I got out from under the blankets—I could no longer bear the intrusion into my family's private hell. I made my way outside onto the balcony. I needed air. The cool June summer breeze whipped past me and actually calmed my nerves a little. Now I just felt plain worn out. I had always relished the peace and quiet of this balcony overlooking my manicured lawns. It had been my haven for the past fifteen years.

I sat on the ledge and lit a cigarette, a habit I'd given up twenty years earlier and now only indulged in whenever I was stressed beyond my limit. Then I heard the commotion, and in the far distance, over the evergreens and beyond the back of my property, even beyond the service road of the expressway, I saw the caravan of vehicles—hundreds of cars surrounding the hearse that carried my father's body. Above, the now-deafening roar of the helicopters indicated they were continuing their pursuit. I realized at that moment, from an obscure angle of my house, that I could see the faint trace of the Long Island Expressway and the passing cars without even squinting. Next, what can only be described as an "electrical jolt" coursed through my body. The hair on my arms stood up. It was as if I could actually feel my father passing ahead of me—and I started to cry again.

*   *   *

MOST OF THE funeral preparations were arranged by Lewis Kasman—the funeral home, the casket, limos, security, and the service. He even decided he would give the eulogy. He would also read a two-page tribute I had written for my father weeks before his death. I was too broken up to read it myself.

In the chapel, at St. John's Cemetery, Kasman stood before the packed room and rambled on and on about how much he loved my father. He kept repeating the words "the long journey home," and openly cried. He told the audience he was grieving the loss of not a friend but a father. Later, he told my mother and me that he had been so upset he had to take a tranquilizer.

After learning there was to be a street gathering along 101st Avenue in Ozone Park, Queens, Kasman instructed the funeral procession to make a detour there before heading to the cemetery. Earlier that morning, masses of people had lined the streets of Howard Beach, the neighborhood John Gotti had lived in for nearly thirty years. They held signs and wept; some even tied large banners to trees and streetlamps.

The never-ending line of cars snaked down 101st Avenue, stopping in front of the Bergin Hunt and Fish Club. Neighbors, store owners, and friends filled the streets. The turnout was astounding. Above the train trestle, a twenty-foot-by-twenty-foot likeness of Dad swayed gently in the wind like a flag. Men, women, and children stood at the curb, holding signs with fond messages for Dad. Some of those signs had the Italian flag on them, others were simple, with just the words "We'll always love you, John."

One man, with a face I recognized, tapped on the window. He was known for playing both sides of the fence. He was a former member of law enforcement, but he had many friends in the life. I cracked the window slightly—I was in no mood to talk to anyone. All he said was, "I loved your father. I'm only telling you this because I also respected him. Kasman's a *rat*. He's been working for the government for years."

I closed my eyes and laid my head against the backseat. I couldn't absorb the man's words. Often in the past, others had been wrongfully labeled. Yet this accusation was not one that should be taken lightly. Kasman? The self-proclaimed adopted son? The man parading himself all over television in support of Dad, begging for humane treatment of John Gotti?

Leaning down against the slightly opened window, the man continued, "All the while he was fighting the BOP to have John Gotti moved out of Marion, he was secretly telling the FBI that John Gotti is *still* the boss and *still* running the Gambino Family. Kasman is the reason your father was kept in that hellhole for ten years." The man stepped away from the car, waved good-bye, and receded into the crowd of onlookers. I closed the window and took one last look at the Bergin Hunt and Fish Club. A last look—as I knew I'd never again have reason to see it, not with Dad gone. I thought about Kasman, about him being a rat, and it made sense to me. The FBI seemed to always be one step ahead of my father—they seemed to always know intimate and private details about my family, unimportant things like silly gossip and family business. Someone was filling them in. I didn't want to believe it was Kasman. I couldn't. The mere notion would have destroyed my father. Unlike how it was with Sammy, Lewis and Dad had a more personal relationship. It had little to do with the life and everything to do with love, trust, and family. Dad never *really* knew Sammy—but he *did* know Lewis (or so he thought, anyway) and he trusted him.

But I couldn't think about Kasman then—my father was dead and I tried so hard to concentrate on him. The camera in my mind flashed to familiar images. Memories that took me back in time, back to Brooklyn: Angel and I were playing jacks on the front steps of the old, dilapidated apartment building. John and I raced up and down Eighth Street looking for cardboard boxes to make a clubhouse. John and John Ruggiero holding hands while crossing Knickerbocker Avenue; Frankie with his beautiful, thick curls and innocent, dazzling smile, giggling gleefully from the old, handed-down pram as Mom wheeled him up and down Eighth Street. I saw visions of Mom and Dad in war and in love. Memories of Dad and Uncle Angelo, young and handsome, standing in front of the social club in Brooklyn.

We never had enough money and poverty was all we knew as young kids. Maybe it was the age, perhaps the innocence, but despite the depressing surroundings, I remember being happy. Having Dad safe and at home was the only time I wanted to remember. As the years passed and the money came and our living conditions improved, there was never the same amount of happiness or enthusiasm. Dad went off to jail, many times. Mom walked around unhappy and depressed. It seemed with the more material things we acquired, the less we enjoyed. When we had nothing, life was much easier. We had each other and that was enough.

The years when our family was whole, with Frankie Boy and Dad at home, seemed like a complete closed circle. Now that circle was open and exposed. I missed my brother. I ached for my father. I was terrified of what the future could hold. I opened my eyes and looked over at each of my sons, three fine young men.

I see a new generation, a new lineage. I see promise and hope where there was once poverty and abuse. With Carmine, my oldest son, I see promise of creativity. An artist? Maybe even a musician. With John, a scholar, perhaps a successful career in law? With Frankie, my youngest, I see ambition and effort—an accomplished businessman? Most of all, I see hope. Hope for a changed world for the new generation of Gotti men. I see a new code of ethics, morals, and integrity. This is the *real* legacy John Gotti left in his wake: "In the end, family is all anyone really has." To have his sons and grandsons pay for the "sins of the father" was never his intention. He *really* believed that his sins, his ambitions, and his way of life would die with him. Instead, they were passed on to his children. Let's hope it dies here, and the new legacy of Gotti men will produce promise. I mourn the loss of a man, but not the loss of *the life*. I fight many demons trying to distinguish my father from his choice of lifestyle. I loved him. But I loathed the lifestyle he chose. And God knows, I have tried to understand—tried to make sense of it all. Then I remember my father's own words:

"My life dictated that I take each course I took. I didn't have any multiple choices. Listen to me carefully. You'll never see another guy like me if you live to be five thousand."

Like it or not, he was right.

EPILOGUE

Sunday Dinners

After the divorce, my first instinct was to put the house up for sale, as there were only bad memories left. But I thought of the kids and decided that another disruption in their lives would wreak more havoc on them. At the time, I could hardly afford to keep them in private school, let alone the ridiculous monthly house maintenance. After my job at the *Post* ended, I took a much more lucrative one at *Star* magazine. The increase in salary bought me some time, enough to figure out what I wanted to do and where I wanted to go.

Judith Regan and Bill Stanton approached me. They had a crazy idea about doing a show—a show revolving around me and my daily life as a celebrity journalist, author, socialite, and mother. I thought it was a joke and blew both of them off. After many meetings, though, the pair managed to convince me to do it. I didn't expect anything to come of the show except perhaps low ratings once it premiered. Imagine my surprise—no, shock—when *Growing Up Gotti* debuted to record-breaking audiences across the country! The *New York Times* called the show one of the Top 10 of 2004.

With the praise came the insults. There were those who believed I did the show to exploit the family name and myself. In truth, I did it to show the world I was anything but a "Mafia Princess." I was a single mother with three kids to raise on my own. I also did it for the money, for their college funds. Regrets? Yes, I have a few, as the song goes. Radio and television pundits talked about the premiere episode for days. Of course, the main topic was the high ratings, while others poked fun at my three sons—at how badly behaved they were. And that was exactly what the network had hoped for. It was their own private publicity tool to generate buzz. The scene in which the boys seemed rambunctious was used in five more episodes in one season alone. But it was steady, high-paying employment, especially since my other job at *Star* had come to an end. I resigned after I became ill—more trouble with my breasts. I kept this very quiet, and I didn't tell my kids. They'd lost their father to prison and always feared they would lose me to heart disease.

During the third season of *Growing Up Gotti,* we went to Italy for a family vacation. The trip was put together by the network and used as a premise for the season premiere. Before we left, I made the mistake of confiding in someone about my recent medical troubles. I told the husband of someone familiar with the disease, a man whose wife had a history of cancer. He and his wife were members of the press. He asked me about rumors he had heard about me being very sick. We got to talking and one thing led to another. By the end of the night, he asked if he could print what I had discussed with him. I said, "No!" I let him know I wanted my medical stuff kept separate from everything else in my life that always managed to find its way into the press. I also let him know that my family, my own children, did not know.

I was in Italy for three weeks when I got the message. It was my friend's wife, the news reporter. She called to tell me my "secret was out." She went on to say something about another reporter shopping the story to her editor—and blah, blah, blah. I wasn't listening after that. The initial shock was too much to bear. I managed to call her later that afternoon. She begged me to let her tell the story. I still refused. When we returned home a short time later, I was bombarded with more messages from her. She was doing the story "with or without" my help. I had to tell my family—my mother and my sons, mostly. I spent the entire night convincing them I was now fine. It was the cover story the following morning for the New York *Daily News*. It was the eve of the Season Three premiere of *Growing Up Gotti*—but my illness was all anyone in the media talked about. As with any season premiere, I had a rigorous schedule of television, radio, and print interviews lined up for the entire week. Imagine my shock when I received a call from my press rep, Tammy Brooks, telling me that the *New York Post* had called and deemed my illness a fraud. Someone had called in and told them it was a publicity scam. That *someone* was a disgruntled press rep who had worked on the show and was recently fired by the network. I was livid! He had based his accusation on the fact that he'd watched an interview earlier in the day—an appearance I had made on *The Big Idea with Donny Deutsch*—in which I stated, "I am fine. It was just a scare." The disgruntled press rep took this as a denial from me and set the press blitz in motion. Some press outlets claimed I never had the illness and others claimed I did but it was not a serious condition. They said I had overdramatized the not-so-serious condition for the purpose of added publicity for my show. It took enormous amounts of damage control to get the situation in hand. Network heads worked day and night. Finally, I was forced to do the unthinkable—bare my breasts and the horrific scars (left over from nearly a hundred stitches and numerous reconstructive surgeries) to a reporter. I also proffered my medical records, under the condition the names of the hospitals and doctors not be printed. Some of the press outlets started to backpedal. Especially when the American Cancer Society came out with a statement that the disease intraductular carcinoma in situ (IDCS) was in fact cancerous and serious and afflicted millions of women each year.

No matter, I was destroyed inside, as were my children. They didn't know what to believe: Was I well? Was I dying? On a less serious note, ratings for the show dropped drastically as a result of the negative publicity. The show was on a downward spiral, and was cancelled a short time later.

One of the last episodes was a Christmas show, which rehashed previous seasons with clips of memorable scenes of the boys and me. The holiday special ended with us sitting around the dining room table during one of our Sunday dinners: the boys, as well as my sister, Angel, and my brother Peter and me. We talked about growing up, about being poor and living in Brooklyn. We laughed. We cried. Mostly, we missed Frankie Boy. An empty chair at the far end of the table was a constant reminder of his absence. Above the empty chair was his likeness painted just months after his death—a constant reminder of how handsome and happy he was. A beautiful boy, a beautiful life cut short. The chair at the head of the table was also empty. It was

Dad's designated seat. He was always with us in thought, especially after his death. At the opposite end, across from Dad's chair, was my brother John's regular place. He was now the man of the family. All burdens and responsibilities fell on him. After he was indicted the second time, a jury failed to reach a verdict. A second trial also ended in a hung jury. Even a third trial could not produce a decision. Three different juries of men and women could not agree on a verdict. Finally, the government gave up. The lead prosecutor announced to a packed courtroom that they would not seek a fourth trial. I was so relieved, I was emotional for nearly a week. But the trials were not without casualties.

A few weeks later Mom was raced to the hospital. She'd suffered a massive stroke and the doctors didn't think she would survive. Watching her son stand trial three times had finally taken its toll on her. I was terrified. Losing one parent is hard—losing both is unimaginable. I camped out in the hospital for days and nights—and when I nearly passed out from exhaustion, my sister and brothers took turns staying with Mom. After two cerebral angiograms and a delicate and risky brain operation, she was released. The doctors deemed her recovery nothing short of a miracle.

Mom moved in with me again. She needed constant, round-the-clock care. Twice she needed to be rushed to the emergency room because her blood pressure had spiked really high. The second time, she suffered a grand mal seizure.

Lewis Kasman came to visit Mom. He showed up at my house unexpectedly one evening. Mom could barely sit up. She was taking high doses of pain medications and tranquilizers to keep her comfortable. Kasman carried on a lengthy conversation with her, anyway. I didn't hear much, as I was mostly in the next room preparing dinner. Ever since I'd heard the rumors that Kasman was a rat, I tried to keep my distance. I wouldn't leave him alone with Mom, either—so I remained within earshot. I do remember hearing Kasman mention money a few times. I wondered what relevance it had at the time. I remember there was something strange in Lewis's demeanor. He seemed anxious and nervous and he kept going to the bathroom.

A few months later, newspaper reports began to surface about yet another possible indictment against my brother John. It was more than Mom could take. Her condition remained critical and heavily guarded. I was worried about her, and I was anxious over John. Just after my brother was indicted for the third time, it was revealed that Kasman was in fact an informer. This time there was proof, and the daily newspapers had a field day. It also came out that Kasman wore a wire while he visited Mom at my house that day— and the reason he kept going to the bathroom was to turn the recorder on and off. He also wore a wire to a relative's wake and taped a conversation with me. He cornered me in the parking lot. He spoke fast, shooting off topic after topic, and everything seemed to revert to money—money Dad had left in his care that was no longer there. Lewis blamed John for the deficit. He told each family member, including me, that John had pilfered any money Dad had left for us. He was very convincing—especially when he repeated remarks that he claimed came from Dad. Kasman said Dad had written these things in letters addressed to him—letters no one ever saw. Kasman tried to turn each of us on the other with his tall tales. And he was quite convincing. For a short time, I actually did believe that John had cheated us all out of any savings left to us by Dad. But once all the facts came out, especially that Lewis was a rat, we all knew that he was a liar as well. It was clear then that John did not take the money. Kasman did. Kasman also bragged to people that he paid for Dad's funeral. He sure did—with the money Dad left in his care.

I believe Lewis really did love and idolize my father. But I have come to believe that Kasman loved money more. He found the temptation too hard to resist. Many people speculate that Kasman spent a large portion of Dad's money—enough to keep his family in a more than comfortable lifestyle for many years. He owned a mansion in Woodbury, Long Island, and many expensive cars. He often took exotic vacations and invested in various restaurants and business ventures. He, like many others before him, got in way too deep. Kasman's only way out was to flip—to betray his self-proclaimed "adopted father"—and every time Kasman screamed for justice for John Gotti, he was shoving the knife even deeper in Dad's back. In the end, it was all about fear. Kasman claimed to law enforcement that the Gottis were greedy and cared only about the money left behind. I believe Kasman was afraid of facing the music about the missing money. He was also afraid of going to jail. He wasn't strong enough to survive on the inside. Actions speak louder than words. In the press, it was revealed that Kasman even robbed the Feds. He was involved in an attempted sting with a known mobster down in Florida. When the mobster angrily asked where his eighty grand went, Kasman shut off the recorder. But the Feds already had him, and in the end, Kasman admitted he took the money from the mobster and hid it from the Feds.

Soon, news of another rat surfaced as well—John Alite, another former friend of my brother's. Apparently the FBI went from prison to prison trying to convince any inmate to testify against my brother John in exchange for a lesser sentence. Alite was one of those inmates. He had been arrested in Brazil on drug charges. Most law enforcement sources said Alite was facing life in prison—some even said the death penalty. At first Alite couldn't offer the Feds any help. He explained he hadn't seen John in many years. But of course it was in his best interest if he could. When it came time to face the seriousness of the crimes he'd committed, Alite had a change of heart—or a change in memory. My brother is facing life for crimes Alite committed—and Alite, having already admitted to dealing drugs and committing many murders, is hoping for a deal even sweeter than Sam Gravano's. Those are his own words—that's what Alite said at another recent trial. In the end, Alite handed the Feds a story—he claimed my brother John was partners with him, and they bought it hook, line, and sinker. No tapes, documents, or secret recordings—just the word of another lying coward. John was charged with the same drug offenses as Alite. During his testimony at the same trial, one of Alite's allegations was that he had an affair with me soon after I married Carmine. Alite claimed that this affair caused him and my brother to end their friendship. I was sick with anger and frustration. The newspapers had a ball once again. I thought mostly of my kids, now three young men, faced with whispers and lies about their mother. I denied the allegations. I even went as far as taking a lie detector test. The man who performed the test was an expert who had worked for the Queens DA at one time. I knew that whoever I went to would be scrutinized beyond belief, so his credentials needed to be solid. I passed with flying colors. Alite is a despicable coward who would stoop to any level to save his own ass, like Kasman and Sammy before him.

Another witness is Kevin McMahon, a familiar name from the past. He was the boy who lent my brother Frankie the minibike. Although he vehemently denies this, I remember it well. Interestingly, these three witnesses have three totally different accounts of people, places, events, and dates.

My brother John was charged with a bevy of criminal activity, from drugs to murder. Any crime committed by any member of the Gambino Crime Family was attached to him. The Feds claimed John was/is still in a supervisory position and therefore these acts were committed with his blessing. The indictment also includes what's called the withdrawal clause. Once again a jury will have to decide whether he is guilty or innocent of each charge—and then decide if John did or did not leave the mob within the time period under the statue of limitations. I can tell you he did. In fact, I would stake my life on it.

At a recent Sunday dinner, the Gotti clan gathered again. The dinners were becoming few and far between. Dad had been right. The family was beginning to splinter, but only physically. Emotionally we are all still very much together. The topic of conversation that day was mostly the effects of a recent newspaper article. It stated that after a nearly six-year court battle, my house was being foreclosed on—the same house Dad loved and always praised. I say it's only a house. It's a home that matters most. Still, I told the Gotti clan that day, "This, too, shall pass."

A few weeks after the foreclosure article surfaced, I

received word from my attorney that we had reached a settlement with the government and my ex-husband. A ten-year court battle was now over. Marital assets, including the home I had worked so hard for and had set aside for my children, would be spared. Still, I intend to sell the house, and start fresh.

What will become of the Gottis? I only pray for peace, mostly for my mother's sake. While we lie in wait for the outcome of John's trial, we pray that this next jury is able to put aside any bias and judge him with their hearts and heads fairly.

As for my father, there are those who stop me and remind me of the love they have for him, while others only stare and whisper of their contempt. Love or hate? Robin Hood or common thug? Some nights I go to bed so angry at him I could cry, while other nights leave me crying for just one more day with him.

One thing was for sure: John Gotti was a mystery wrapped up in an enigma the world wanted to know more about. If I could have one last conversation with him, I know exactly what I would ask: Was it all worth it? The destruction? The aftermath? The end result: the fact that he'd died like a dog, alone in his cell. All of this because he refused to let anyone break him—or strip him of his dignity. This brotherhood called the life had ravaged his body and mind far worse than the cancer had. Knowing him as well as I did, his answer would most likely be: "My body is in prison—but my spirit will always be free."

Too bad I can't wrap my arms around his spirit.

AFTERWORD

USA vs. John Angelo Gotti

September 14, 2009

The prosecution questioned witnesses for days, and my brother's life was laid out in horrific detail. Scene after scene had John Gotti Jr. portrayed like a common street thug—exactly what the government had hoped would happen.

The first offensive tactic was to ignite a smear campaign against the defendant. There was a childhood fight in a bar between two men (neither of them my brother). A witness for the prosecution took the stand and told the packed courtroom what he remembered about that night. He told only half the story—there was a fight between many men. He couldn't see who hit whom. All he remembered was John Gotti Jr. exiting the bar and then coming back to do a Porky Pig imitation before fleeing in a car. The witness claimed he was merely an innocent spectator with a vague recollection of the most pertinent facts. Under cross-examination, it was apparent the witness had left out much of what he *really* remembered about that night, and the truth began to trickle out.

It was revealed that the bar fight actually started over a girl (as always). The girl in question was the witness's wife.

AFTERWORD

It was also revealed the witness had an argument with John Gotti Jr.'s best friend, Anthony Amoroso, because he was dating his wife. Amoroso and the scorned husband had words that night in the bar. And words led to a shove here and there.

Amoroso was no fool. He knew he was far away from his home turf and was clearly outnumbered. He left the bar and made a phone call. Within minutes, a group of his childhood friends arrived—one of them was John Angelo Gotti.

Inside the bar, both sides traded offensive remarks. It's not clear who threw the first punch, but within seconds a melee ensued and bodies were thrown all about the seedy Ozone Park bar. There were multiple one-on-one fights. Most of the teenagers managed to walk away with no more than a few cuts and scrapes. All except one—Danny Silva, who was fatally stabbed.

According to two witnesses during the trial, John Gotti had been involved in fisticuffs with a man called "Elf," yet the prosecution was determined to convince the jury that John might have been the one who killed Silva. He was not. Early police reports stated a man named "Fat Mark" was positively identified by three women in the bar that night as being the man who fought one-on-one with Silva—the women gave statements that Fat Mark was in fact the man who stabbed Danny Silva. Predictably, a few days after the statements were made, all three of the women suffered from a case of amnesia—and Fat Mark was no longer questioned. It remained a "cold case" until John Gotti's trial some twenty years later. But, ironically, John Gotti was not charged with Silva's murder. There wasn't enough evidence. Members of the jury were confused—and asked why, then, were they being told about this murder, all these years later?

The judge declined comment and instructed the jury to remain open-minded until the trial was over and deliberations began. And so the smear campaign continued with the next witness.

John Alite entered the federal courtroom on Worth Street in lower Manhattan. His appearance was subdued—dressed in gray sweats and a white turtleneck to conceal a tattoo on his neck. The ink, now somewhat faded, was a row of stars—a recognizable symbol of gang affiliation. Alite had testified the previous year at another mob trial against Charles Carneglia. Alite made quite a spectacle of himself then—he was cocky, brash, and way too confident for the likes of the reporters sitting in the courtroom. News stories surfaced about the trial, and about Alite. He was painted in a very dark light. He cursed during his testimony, even admitted he was a pathological liar. It was during *that* trial that he lied about having an affair with me. Alite claimed this happened while I was married. None of this was true, of course, and the government had egg on their faces when I took a polygraph test with a well-known former employee of the Queens DA's office.

Now during my brother's trial, Alite's demeanor was most startling; he was quiet, unassuming, and quite apologetic. He was unnervingly polite, too, greeting the jury with remarks like "good morning" and "excuse me" and "thank you." Later, under cross-examination, it was revealed that the FBI had groomed Alite for the trial. Thousands of hours, rehearsing dozens of scenarios and the manner in which he was to present them to the jury. He spoke directly to the jurors, making eye contact with each one. All of the coaching, polishing, and rehearsing for his big performance made Alite almost believable, but those who knew him *when* knew better.

With the prosecution having launched a successful plan of attack, Alite found it simple to continue the charade. He spoke clearly and precisely, telling the jurors about his sordid, criminal past. He listed a shocking résumé involving burglaries, drug dealing, even murders he had committed. And all of his crimes were blamed on John Gotti.

Alite claimed he and John had been friends for a few years. He tried to convince the jury that he was super-close to my family. He spoke of different holidays and weddings, and even mentioned he had taken me to a bridal gown fitting. He was right about this—John was supposed to drive me, but couldn't, so he asked Alite to do him the favor. I went with my then best friend, Diane, and I hardly spoke a word to Alite that day. But Alite was trying to convince the jury that he was like one of the family—he was not.

Not surprisingly, Alite backpedaled when it came to the alleged affair between him and me. All he said was that we had developed "special feelings" for each other over the years, one of the many lies he told while under oath. One criminal act in particular involved Alite burning down a private gym on John's orders, claiming John had a "beef" with the gym owner, Keith Pellegrino. My brother sat silent and still as he watched Alite weave his tale, too slient and still for my liking.

Upon cross-examination, Charles Carnesi questioned Alite. He asked him about the gym—about *his* relationship with Pellegrino. It was revealed that John Gotti and Pellegrino did not know each other, but Alite and Pellegrino did. Carnesi produced a copy of an old letter addressed to

John. The letter was written in Alite's own hand. It was a sappy apology attempt after John had chased him, some twenty-three years ago. In the letter, Alite begs John "not to listen" to his other friends, who are "jealous." The letter was clear—Alite had burned down the gym for his own gain. As a result, John Gotti was pissed beyond belief. So pissed, he chased Alite away for good. It was the last time the two would be friends.

When Carnesi presented the actual letter for Alite to read, the color drained from his face. He was no longer relaxed and confident. He grew fidgety and nervous—stuttering for words. When Carnesi asked him if he remembered writing the letter, Alite said, "No." Then he changed his mind and replied, "Yes . . . uhh, yes, now I remember." Alite tried to regroup, saying something silly like, "I wrote it [the letter] in code." Even the prosecution found this hard to swallow. One prosecutor shook his head and sank lower in his chair. You could hear a pin drop when Carnesi read the ending of the letter: "I only hope you read this, John, before throwing it in the garbage."

No one, not the prosecution, not even Carnesi, knew about the letter in advance. John had saved it for nearly thirty years. Reporters called him a "pack rat." I called him brilliant.

CARNESI CHECKED IN with his service the minute court broke for lunch. His secretary had some bad news—an important witness for the defense, Carol Alite, had changed her mind about testifying. Carol was Alite's first wife. Just as he was a shit in the streets, he was a shit for a husband. He constantly cheated and had children out of wedlock with other women. Carol knew about his dalliances and about the growing number of love children he produced as well. Alite was abusive, both verbally and physically, and Carol had told Carnesi she was prepared to tell the world. The most important fact Carol was going to inform the courtroom of was how John Alite had called her and confided in her numerous times about how he was using the government's vendetta against John Gotti Jr. to gain his freedom. There were in fact three witnesses set to testify about the very same thing. Alite told a few select people (his ex-wife, a close friend, and a cell mate from Tampa County jail) about his plan to say anything he could to get out of jail—even if it meant baselessly accusing John Gotti Jr. But Carol got cold feet. Although Alite was in jail and presumably under the FBI's close supervision, he somehow still had access to a cell phone. Alite called his ex-wife repeatedly, Carol told me, and threatened her and told her if she even thought about testifying, he would be out in less than a year and he would kill her. Carol's fear only heightened when she noticed two men lurking around her New Jersey home. Her fiancé had an uncle in the FBI who did a check on the two men. They were FBI agents. Carol believed her ex-husband would have no trouble getting to her with help from the FBI.

Before the trial, Carol had managed to put Alite far behind her. She landed a job as a loan adviser in a mortgage company and began dating the owner of the company. Soon the two were engaged. She didn't care about Alite, but she was still terribly afraid of him. She was sure he would make good on his promise to hurt her.

While I understood Carol's concerns, this was a terrible blow to my brother's case. To fight the entire government, with unlimited resources on their side, a tough battle plan would be needed. So I called Carol at home and arranged a meeting. On a Sunday night, I drove nearly three hours to south Jersey. We met at a restaurant just off the turnpike. Carol was with her fiancé. He was a handsome and well-mannered man who seemingly adored her. We spoke for a few minutes about the usual topics two people discuss when they haven't seen each other in years—the kids, our careers, and our hopeful futures. I was so tired, I cut to the chase within a few minutes. I told Carol her testimony was imperative. I also explained that without it, Alite might very well get out of jail after only one year and for sure he might try and harm her. I believed she had a better chance fighting him than not. Perhaps, if he wasn't successful in convicting John Gotti, the government might not be so generous when it came to setting him free. Her fiancé agreed. He told her Alite would always be a thorn in their sides. He told her she needed to do this for herself. I realized her fiancé also wanted Carol to testify as a means of proving to him that she was in fact really over John Alite. In the end, Carol gave in. She agreed to appear early the next morning. I nearly floated home.

I called Carnesi at 1 A.M.—he was sound asleep, but welcomed the news. I told him the only problem was Carol would be a bit late for court, given the ride was more than three hours. He said he would do all he could to stall the judge.

The next morning, Carnesi addressed the court and explained to Judge Castel that one of his lead witnesses would be late. Carnesi expected the judge to call a recess, to give him time to call an important witness. But instead, Castel said something like, "Counselor, if your witness is here before the train leaves the station, so be it. And if she's not, closing arguments will begin." I was stunned beyond words. The only person more angry than me was Carol Alite after she arrived and was told she could not testify. Sadly, she'd stayed up the entire night, gathering more evidence and paperwork to further expose John Alite as the manipulative criminal he was.

Also not on the witness list was Louis Kasman. The FBI had gone to great lengths to use Kasman against John, even putting a wire on him and sending Louis to speak to certain people. I was one of them. When Carnesi discovered Kasman would not be called as a witness, it came as no surprise to any of us. There had been strong rumors about Kasman being caught in numerous lies by the government and the FBI. "Too many inconsistencies," said one government source. "The prosecution was afraid to use him." It was also revealed that Kasman had stolen large sums of money from the FBI.

But the biggest blunder during the trial came from a former prosecutor, Joon Kim, called by Carnesi as a witness. Kim had worked on a mob case just a few years earlier involving Sonny Franzese, a Long Island mobster. Franzese was picked up on wiretaps telling an informer that he'd heard about John leaving the mob, and suggested he be killed for quitting. At the time, Kim called Carnesi and told him about the threat. Kim also told Carnesi it was a legal requirement to report any threats overheard by the government. That was just three years ago. But during John's trial, under oath, Kim inexplicably forgot these events. He remembered making the call to Carnesi, but couldn't remember why. He claimed he didn't even recognize the name Sonny Franzese. Even Judge Castel seemed surprised by Kim's testimony and ruled Carnesi could enter a transcript of the wiretapped conversation between Franzese and an unidentified informer, into evidence.

I BELIEVE THESE FACTORS helped to create a mountain of reasonable doubt, but I also think it was the letter that had the most impact. The jury deliberated nearly a week, with no requests for any readbacks or evidence. Whatever was going on behind closed doors seemed nearly unanimous—one way or the other. On day six of deliberations, a note was sent up to the judge. The jury was deadlocked. Carnesi expected that the judge would read the Allen charge, and then order the jury to continue deliberations in hopes of reaching a verdict. But Judge Castel shocked the packed courtroom by refusing to give the Allen charge and sent the jurors back to deliberate.

Downstairs, in the courthouse cafeteria, I sat worried and anxious, not knowing what to expect. Reporters approached the table and one after the other asked what I thought about the judge's ruling. I didn't know what to think—I couldn't think—but to me it was obvious that the judge was biased against my brother and hoped for a conviction. I based my opinion not only on his refusing to accept the deadlock, but because it seemed to me that all through the trial, Judge Castel time and again ruled for the prosecution and against my brother. One decision was to throw out valuable evidence that would surely help to clear my brother—especially about whether or not he *really* left the mob. There was a CD of a visit between my father and John. On the visit, Dad and John are overheard discussing John's decision to accept a plea (for an earlier case) and his decision to leave the life. Castel ruled only to allow a sentence here and a sentence there. Once or twice he would throw the defense a bone, I felt, just to shut sympathetic reporters up—but to me his opinion was obvious: he believed John Gotti Jr. was guilty.

Carnesi tried to calm me. He was slightly discouraged by the judge's actions, but not totally beaten. He believed the jury would deliberate for another hour or two and come back with another deadlock. This time the judge would have no choice but to read the Allen charge. It was after 3 P.M., less than two hours left before court was over for the day. Carnesi believed the trial would be over before the day ended.

Carnesi's cell rang and the judge's clerk announced there was another note from the jury. Carnesi was sure it was the last deadlock note. If so, Castel would give the Allen charge and perhaps John would be home before nightfall. I walked into the courtroom calm and quiet. Inside I was dancing, hoping. I just wanted it to be over. I wanted to call my mother and tell her John was coming home. I wanted peace, finally.

But Judge Castel had a different plan. He refused to address the jury's note. He said he would read it—but not address it until Monday. Everyone in the courtroom seemed confused. It was Thursday, and because Friday was a predetermined day off from deliberations, it would be a three-day weekend before deliberations would resume. Then Castel did the unthinkable. He announced he was giving the jury the rest of the day off—for no apparent reason other than saying, "Because I decided to," when Carnesi asked, "Why?"

Castel also read the note, in which members of the jury asked one question: If we don't believe the defendant is guilty of charge "B," do we even need to deliberate charge "C"? Although the turn of events had not been good, the note was an indication that the jury was leaning toward a "not guilty" verdict. The second charge was drug dealing. The third was murders connected to drug dealing.

Once again, the reporters were in an uproar. I couldn't even speak around the lump that had formed in my throat. I could barely move. I managed to gather up my siblings and leave the courthouse amid the flurry of flashbulbs and curious onlookers. Outside it was raining and the sky was unusually dark for 4 P.M. I had a terrible feeling in the pit of my stomach. I realized then that getting past the decision of an entire jury wasn't the issue; it was whether or not the judge would allow the jury to vote fairly—and the thought terrified me. I am not the type of person to believe in conspiracy theories and such, but at that moment I believed the government was capable of doing anything to get a guilty verdict. I returned home and locked myself in my room and cried the entire weekend.

John called me constantly over the next few days. He was anxious, nervous. He wondered about his fate. He was mostly fatalistic about the verdict. I tried to keep him upbeat and positive, even though I wasn't. But he wasn't buying what I was selling. He said crazy things like, "Just promise me you'll help my wife with the kids if things go badly." We talked about different scenarios that might happen. He feared the government would go on a smear campaign again over the weekend, leaking this and that, as they had a million times in the past. The onslaught of mud slinging had a great impact on John. He said to me, "The way the press has portrayed me, with the help of unknown government leaks, is horrible. I don't even like myself—and I *know* it's not true!" He also feared the FBI might approach one of the jurors. Anything and everything went through his head. News programs ran story after story about the trial—different networks ran polls. Most were in favor of John. People on the street were taking bets. It was all anyone could talk about: "Will John Gotti Jr. be sentenced to life, or not?"

I was an automaton the entire weekend. I welcomed the time away from deliberations, when anything could happen at any moment. But, at the same time, I just wanted all of it to be over. I needed to exhale. I needed to breathe again.

That Saturday afternoon, I received an unnerving call from Carnesi. He told me he'd just gotten a call from the judge's clerk, Flo—she had called to tell Carnesi that the judge wanted both the prosecution and defense to put a feasible and agreeable bail package in place should another deadlock note come back. Even though John Gotti had been held for nearly two years without bail, it was unusual to continue to hold a defendant once a jury of his peers has tried him and no verdict was reached. This news from Carnesi should have made me happy, excited. Instead, I remained skeptical. I didn't tell my mother, sister, or brother for fear of raising false hope.

Monday morning the jury resumed deliberations

promptly at 10 A.M. Before noon, another note was sent out. It was a request for evidence—a lot of evidence. It seemed to me and to many that the judge's tactics were working. I assumed there were some jurors now questioning their earlier decision.

But then, in another unexpected turn, on the tenth day of deliberations another note came from the jurors—DEADLOCKED! This time the judge read the Allen charge and the jurors returned with another note—they were still deadlocked. John was released less than an hour later.

After court let out, a bevy of reporters met with most of the jury members in a conference room. Not surprisingly, there were more jurors in John's favor than not. Also not surprising was that none of the jurors (even one who believed John was guilty) had believed John Alite. The government's star witness was an unbelievable dud. Even members of the prosecution team began to distance themselves from the case. And rightfully so, as it reeked of improper tactics and behavior. It seemed as if no one wanted to dirty their hands any further.

Christmas and New Year's were quiet and uneventful. We spent both holidays at my house, as we always had in the past. But this year, having John back at the head of the table was as good as it gets for the Gotti family. Watching John gave me great pleasure. Seeing him laugh and play with the youngest members of the family was delightful. He walked around my house with a glass of red wine, speaking to nearly everyone. He devoted nearly half an hour to each person—trying to catch up on lots of lost time. On New Year's Eve, John filled dozens of glass flutes with champagne and made a short toast before the ball dropped in Times Square. He let the roomful of people know he loved them and thanked them all for their support. There wasn't a dry eye in the house.

Just two weeks after the trial ended, I became sick with a serious tooth infection. Because of my underlying heart condition, the doctors were nervous about the infection spreading to my heart. I was hospitalized at St. Francis Hospital Heart Center. I had a minor surgical procedure that turned major when complications arose. No one could know I would develop a major staph infection while in the hospital.

John was waiting outside the OR when I woke up and visited me every day in the hospital. When I was released just before Christmas, he called every morning to see if I needed anything and dropped by every afternoon.

Two weeks after New Year's, I was still on strict bed rest. John came by one day to keep me company. I didn't like the way he looked. Gone was the constant, easy smile I'd grown used to since he'd come home. In its place was a worried frown. I asked him over and over, "What's wrong?" He only nodded and changed the subject. The next day I spoke to Charles Carnesi. He told me he had had a conversation with my brother just a few days before. He sounded nervous. Then he dropped a bombshell: he believed the government was looking to try John again. All along, even before the trial ended, Carnesi often remarked that he was nearly certain there would not be trial number two. He explained the reasons why. For one, the prosecutors didn't want the case to begin with and were very surprised when the Florida judge shifted the trial from Tampa to New York.

Also, the witnesses were career criminals and not particularly believable to members of the jury. And the fact that most of the evidence (flimsy to begin with) was based purely on hearsay didn't help to build a strong case, either. But because weeks had passed and Carnesi had not heard from the prosecution office, he had to assume there would be a second trial. Much as he hated to burst everyone's balloon, he needed to prepare John. My brother kept the information to himself. He didn't want to upset anyone, most of all Mom.

John sat across from me in the living room of my Old Westbury home. I told him I had spoken to Carnesi and I knew about a probable second trial. I told him I would help him as much as I could. My offer of help did little to change his mood. He told me all about the havoc this last trial had brought him; the mental and emotional stress, not to mention the financial strains. My brother had definitely aged some ten years in the two years he'd spent in jail awaiting trial. Solitary confinement will do that to a man. His biggest concerns were his children and their welfare. He begged me once again to help his wife, should anything happen. I told him I would and let him know I would also help him financially as best I could. We both knew the money needed to try the case again would be exorbitant. Legal woes had nearly drained John over the years. Fighting the entire government, over and over, can drain even the wealthiest of men. In the past, I had helped John as best I could. I knew how much it drained me; I couldn't imagine the impact it had on him and his family. But you do what you can for family, because the trade-off is disastrous.

After hours of brainstorming, John said good-bye. He told me not to worry about him or another trial. He thanked me for my offer to help him financially, but politely declined. He told me I'd done enough for him already and that I should worry about my own situation and the welfare of my kids.

Later that day I tossed and turned in bed. I walked the floors, unable to rest. Despite the fact that I was running a fever and was remarkably weak from the staph infection, I was extremely agitated and anxious. I couldn't get John or the trial out of my mind. The phone rang and I let the machine answer. I was not in any mood for chitchat. At 5 P.M., the phone rang again—this time I noticed John's cell number on the caller ID screen. I answered with a quiet whisper, "Hi."

John didn't say hello back. Instead, he shouted into the receiver, "Vic, it's over! The government just announced they are not seeking a second trial!" For a moment I was silent. I didn't know if I should yell or cry—so I did both. I screamed out to the kids and to no one in particular, "It's over—it's finally over!" Because John had visited with me earlier, I was the first person he'd called after learning the news. We said good-bye, as he had many calls to make, many people to tell. I climbed under the blankets and lay my head down on the pillow. My laptop was already booted up and resting beside me on the bed.

Within minutes, I received nearly seventy-five e-mails, mostly from friends and colleagues just learning of the good news. There were twenty-three e-mails from reporters, all congratulating John and wanting a comment or quote.

Some things never change . . .